NUESTRA

A Latin American
Church History
Sourcebook

ONDINA E. GONZÁLEZ
JUSTO L. GONZÁLEZ

Abingdon Press

Nashville

Library of Congress Cataloging-in-Publication Data

González, Ondina E., 1958–
    Nuestra fe : a latin american church history sourcebook / Ondina E. González and Justo L.
González.
        pages cm
    Includes bibliographical references and index.
    ISBN 978-1-4267-7426-3 (binding: pbk. / trade / adhesive perfect binding : alk. paper)
1. Christianity—Latin America. 2. Latin America—Church history—Sources. I. Title.
    BR600.G675 2014
    278—dc23

                                                                                    2014011178

14 15 16 17 18 19 20 21 22 23—10 9 8 7 6 5 4 3 2 1

MANUFACTURED IN THE UNITED STATES OF AMERICA

To Jorge Luis

CONTENTS

List of Illustrations. ix
List of Primary Sources
  Employed xi
Acknowledgments xv
Introduction 1
1. Foundations 3
  Source One: A God-Given
    Destiny 5
  Source Two: Ancient Beliefs 9
  Source Three: A Surprising
    Market 12
  Source Four: Conversion of
    an Inca 15
  Source Five: A Tragedy in
    Pictures 19
2. Arrival 25
  Source One: A Gift from the
    Pope 27
  Source Two: Justifying the
    Unjustifiable 31
  Source Three: A God
    Compromises 35
  Source Four: The Virgin Speaks
    to Juan Diego 37
  Source Five: A Scholar's View . . . 42
  Source Six: An Entire People
    in Hell? 45
3. Shaping 51
  Source One: A Priest Reports . . . 53

Source Two: On Becoming a
  Saint 56
Source Three: Theology in the
  Kitchen 60
Source Four: The Inquisition
  at Work. 63
Source Five: Magic and Love. . . . 66
4. Reforms 71
  Source One: The Royal Throne
    and the Holy See. 73
  Source Two: Cloak and Dagger. . 76
  Source Three: Who Can Say,
    "I Do"? 78
  Source Four: Correction or
    Abuse?. 82
  Source Five: Travels in Brazil 86
5. Turmoil 91
  Source One: Submit and Be
    Good. 93
  Source Two: *El Supremo*'s
    Temper Tantrum 95
  Source Three: A Slave Code 98
  Source Four: Faith in a
    Healer. 100
  Source Five: An Alternate
    Creed 107
  Source Six: A Last-Ditch
    Effort. 109
6. Protestant Presence 113

CONTENTS

Source One: The President's
Visit 115
Source Two: Unwelcomed
Peddlers. 119
Source Three: Race and
Mission 123
Source Four: A Woman's
View 127
Source Five: A Radical
Perspective 130
Source Six: A Poet's Fear and
Faith 134

7. Protestants and Catholics . . 139
Source One: The Archbishop
Complains. 143
Source Two: A Catholic Woman's
Plan for Action. 147
Source Three: A Call to Change
from a Nobel Laureate 150
Source Four: Justifying a
Presence 154
Source Five: We Are Not All
Catholic 158
Source Six: *La Violencia*. 162

**8. The Catholic Church Faces
New Situations** 169
Source One: The Bishops Look
Forward. 172

Source Two: Liberation and
Change 175
Source Three: An Official
Reprimand 177
Source Four: The Magi 182
Source Five: A *Retablo*. 185
Source Six: Another *Retablo* . . . 187

9. A Complex Reality. 189
Source One: The Holy Spirit in
Chile. 192
Source Two: Quichua
Pentecostals 196
Source Three: A Charismatic
Priest. 203
Source Four: Shangó 206
Source Five: Reyita's Faith 211
Source Six: An Immigrant's
Tale 214
Source Seven: The Catholic
Response. 217
Source Eight: A Protestant
Response. 223
Source Nine: Graffiti
Theology 229

Epilogue. 231
Notes. 233

ILLUSTRATIONS

Figures

1.1 Guaman Poma: A Priest Instructing an Indian Leader. 20

1.2 Guaman Poma: A Priest in a Classroom 21

1.3 Guaman Poma: A Priest Hearing Confession. 22

1.4 Guaman Poma: A Priest Correcting a Worker 23

1.5 Guaman Poma Revisted: The Spitting Llama. 24

2.1 Vilcabamba 34

3.1 Medina's Biography of Martín de Porres 56

3.2 An *Auto de la fe* 69

4.1 A Recumbent Christ 81

5.1 Votive Offerings. 107

8.1 A *Retablo* 186

8.2 Another *Retablo* 188

9.1 Shangó. 210

9.2 A *Graffito* 230

PRIMARY SOURCES EMPLOYED

1. Foundations

One. A God-Given Destiny: *Vida y hechos de los Reyes Católicos*, Lucio Marinero Sículo, 1587.

Two. Ancient Beliefs: *Historia general de las cosas de Nueva España*, Bernardino de Sahagún, 1575–1577.

Three. A Surprising Market: *Historia verdadera de la conquista de Nueva España*, Bernal Díaz del Castillo, 1601.

Four. Conversion of an Inca: *Instrucción del Inca Don Diego de Castro Titu Cusi Yupanqui*, ca. 1570.

Five. A Tragedy in Pictures: *El primer nueva corónica* [sic] *y buen gobierno*, Felipe Guaman Poma de Ayala, 1615.

2. Arrival

One. A Gift from the Pope: *Inter caetera*, Alexander VI, 1493.

Two. Justifying the Unjustifiable: *Requerimiento*, Juan López Palacios Rubios, 1513.

Three. A God Compromises: *De las antiguas gentes,* Bartolomé de Las Casas, 1550.

Four. The Virgin Speaks to Juan Diego: *Virgen de Guadalupe*, Nican Mopohua, 1560.

Five. A Scholar's View: *Relectiones de Indis*, Francisco de Vitoria, 1557.

Six. An Entire People in Hell? *Sermão*, Antônio Vieira, 1653.

3. Shaping

One. A Priest Reports: *Historia natural y moral de las Indias*, José de Acosta, 1590.

Two. On Becoming a Saint: *Proceso de beatificación de fray Martín de Porres*, ca. 1670.

Three. Theology in the Kitchen: *Respuesta a Sor Filotea*, Sor Juana Inés de la Cruz, 1691.

Four. The Inquisition at Work: *Auto de la fe celebrado en Lima*, 1639.

Five. Magic and Love: *Confissão de Guiomar d'Oliveira*, 1591.

4. Reforms

One. The Royal Throne and the Holy See: *Concordato*, 1753.

Two. Cloak and Dagger: *Instrucción . . . para el Estrañamiento . . . de los Jesuitas en estos Reynos de España*, 1767.

Three. Who Can Say, "I Do"?: *Pragmática de Matrimonio*, Charles III, 1776.

Four. Correction or Abuse?: Letter from Fray Junípero Serra, 1769.

Five. Travels in Brazil: *Travels in Brazil*, Henry Koster, 1815.

5. Turmoil

One. Submit and Be Good: *Etsi longissimo terrarum*, Pius VII, 1816.

Two. *El Supremo*'s Temper Tantrum: Letter from Dr. José Gaspar Rodríguez de Francia, 1816.

Three. A Slave Code: *Bando de gobernacion y policia de la Isla de Cuba*, 1842.

Four. Faith in a Healer: various sources about Miguel Perdomo Neira, 1867, 1872.

Five. An Alternate Creed: *Credo de los liberales*, ca. 1910.

Six. A Last-Ditch Effort: *La entrevista de última oportunidad*, 1926.

6. Protestant Presence

One. The President's Visit: Letter from James (Diego) Thomson, 1822.

Two. Unwelcomed Peddlers: Eighty-first Annual Report of the American Bible Society, 1897.

Three. Race and Mission: *South American Problems*, Robert E. Speer, 1912.

Four. A Woman's View: "Women's Work in Missions in Latin-America," 1913.

Five. A Radical Perspective: "Church and Society in Latin America," ISAL, 1966.

Six. A Poet's Fear and Faith: "Temblor," Julia Esquivel, 1986.

7. Protestants and Catholics

One. The Archbishop Complains. Letter from the archbishop of Lima, 1864.

Two. A Catholic Woman's Plan for Action: *Acción pública y privada*, Celia LaPalma de Emery, 1910.

Three. A Call to Change from a Nobel Laureate: "Cristianismo con sentido social," Gabriela Mistral, 1924.

Four. Justifying a Presence: "The Validity of Protestant Missions," John A. Mackay, 1942.

Five. We Are Not All Catholic: *Hacia la renovación religiosa*, Gonzalo Báez Camargo, 1930.

Six. *La Violencia*: "What's Behind the Persecution in Colombia?" James E. Goff, 1961.

8. The Catholic Church Faces New Situations

One. The Bishops Look Forward: *The Church in the Present-day Transformation of Latin America*, CELAM, 1973.

Two. Liberation and Change: *Liberation and Change*, Gustavo Gutiérrez and Richard Shaull, 1977.

Three. An Official Reprimand: "Instructions on Certain Aspects of the 'Theology of Liberation,'" Congregation for the Doctrine of the Faith, 1984.

Four. The Magi: *The Gospel in Solentiname*, Ernesto Cardenal, 2010.

Five. A *Retablo*: New Mexico State University, 1945.

Six. Another *Retablo*: New Mexico State University, n.d.

9. A Complex Reality

One. The Holy Spirit in Chile: *Historia del avivamiento pentecostal en Chile*, Willis C. Hoover, 1948.

Two. Quichua Pentecostals: Interviews by Eloy H. Nolivos, 2006.

Three. A Charismatic Priest: Letter from Emiliano Tardif, 1993.

Four. Shangó: "Afro-Cuban *Orisha* Worship," Miguel "Willie" Ramos, 1996.

Five. Reyita's Faith: *Reyita: The Life of a Black Cuban Woman*, María de los Reyes Castillo Bueno, 2000.

Six. An Immigrant's Tale: "Trinidad Salazar: A Call to Service," Jane Atkins-Vásquez, 1988.

Seven. The Catholic Response: "National Pastoral Plan for Hispanic Ministry," USCCB, 1987.

Eight. A Protestant Response: "Report of the Committee to Develop a National Plan for Hispanic Ministry," General Board of Global Ministries, The United Methodist Church, 1992.

Nine. Graffiti Theology: Photograph, Puerto Rico, 1980.

ACKNOWLEDGMENTS

The authors are most appreciative for the help of: Kathy Armistead, Abingdon Press; Jane Atkins-Vásquez, Programa de Adiestramiento de Liderato Laico, Presbyterian Church (USA); Oscar Báez Hernández, Casa Unida de Pulicaciones, S.A. (Mexico City); Sue Branford, Latin American Bureau (London); Jeffrey M. Burns, Academy of American Franciscan History; Matthew Butler, University of Texas at Austin; Francisco Cañas, General Board of Global Ministries, The United Methodist Church; Allan Deck, Loyola Marymount University; Joan Duffy, Yale University; John Fleury, Comunidad Siervos de Cristo Vivo (Santo Domingo); Doris Goodnough, Orbis Books; Gustavo Gutiérrez, University of Notre Dame; Kristin Hellmann, American Bible Society; David K. Jordan, University of California San Diego (emeritus); Griselda Laerty, Columbia Theological Seminary; Eloy Nolivos, Wesley Seminary, Indiana Wesleyan University; Eliseo Pérez-Alvárez, Seminary Consortium for Urban Pastoral Education; Miguel Ramos, Ilarií Obá, Florida International University; Mary Sperry, United States Conference of Catholic Bishops; David Sowell, Juniata College; Carl A. Talbert, Jr., United States Conference of Catholic Bishops; Stephanie L. Taylor, New Mexico State University Art Gallery; Cherie Velasco White, Seminario Gonzalo Báez Camargo (Mexico City).

Special thanks also go to Carlos Cardoza-Orlandi, Perkins School of Theology, Southern Methodist University, for his invaluable help in locating sources.

INTRODUCTION

It was the last Sunday before Christmas, 1511. On the island Columbus had named Hispaniola (now Haiti and the Dominican Republic), people flocked to church. One can imagine the festive spirit at mass as the Spanish settlers prepared for the celebrations of Christmas.

They were in for a shock. Dominican friar Antonio de Montesinos approached the pulpit, where he was to deliver the sermon. The Gospel passage assigned for the day was the story of John the Baptist, who said of himself, "I am the voice of one crying out in the wilderness, make straight the way of the Lord."

Then Montesinos said:

> I am the voice of one crying in the wilderness. In order to make your sins known to you I have mounted this pulpit . . .
> This voice declares that you are in mortal sin, and live and die therein by reason of the cruelty and tyranny that you practice on these innocent people. Tell me, by what right do you hold these Indians in such cruel and horrible slavery? . . . Be sure that in your present state you can no more be saved than the Moors or Turks.*

Needless to say, his words were not well received. There were protests lodged first with the Dominicans on the island who had approved what Montesinos had to say beforehand and then with authorities in Spain. Although harshly treated by many for the rest of his lifetime, now Montesinos is honored in Santo Domingo by a monumental statue that dominates the landscape for several blocks around—a monument you may see on the cover of this book.

This was far from an isolated event. Indeed, one could say that the confrontation between Montesinos and the other Dominicans on the one hand and the Spanish settlers on the other hand set a pattern that would continue

1

throughout the history of Christianity in Latin America. Montesinos was a Christian. The settlers were Christians. They all belonged to the same church. But they represented two different and contrasting faces of that church.

As you read this book, you will have ample opportunity to see these contrasting faces of Christianity in Latin America. You will see efforts to justify exploitation and to assuage the conscience, and you will see daring calls to radical transformation. You will see attempts to use Christianity to call the oppressed into submission, and you will see resistance and even rebellion, also in the name of Christianity. Look for the various expressions of these contrasting views as they evolved through the centuries, as they responded to African slavery, to the call for independence, to programs of social transformation and revolution. You will note that they manifested themselves not only in the Catholic Church but also among Protestants when they entered the picture.

These two faces of Christianity, however, do not exhaust the wide variety of religious experiences, beliefs, and practices in Latin America. In the pages that follow you will also learn of Native and African religions and how significant elements of those religions survived, often under a veneer of Christianity. You will encounter a woman who tried to regain her husband's love by means of magic. You will learn of a man who was killed under the accusation of being a secret Jew but perhaps really because he was too wealthy and successful. You will see an extraordinarily intelligent woman seeking to retain her freedom to study and to learn in a world dominated by men. You will read the secret orders of the Spanish crown for taking possession of Jesuit properties by surprise. You will witness a heated discussion between the president of Mexico and two bishops representing the Catholic hierarchy. There will be people calling for a reformation of the church, others defending the rights of the church against what they see as an encroachment on the part of government, and still others blaming the church for the ills of their nations. There will be missionaries, saints, poets, theologians, and most certainly sinners! You will read the words of popes and the words of peasants. You will witness the struggles and the dreams of people at the margins of society.

At times, you may find it difficult to reconcile these divergent voices, this hodgepodge of opinions and agendas, of faith and disbelief, of dreams and nightmares. But this is just a reflection of the struggles of life and the complexity of any society. Read then this book as one looking through a window into the chaotic beauty of Latin American life and society.

Open the window. Take in its vistas. Enter into the life and faith of Latin America.

1
FOUNDATIONS

Introduction

As every child knows, "In 1492, Columbus sailed the ocean blue." The morning that the *Niña*, the *Pinta*, and the *Santa María* were filled with hardtack and the sailors weighed anchors, the world was forever changed. But the transformation brought by Columbus's voyage to what would become known as the Americas did not take place in a vacuum. The impact of the voyage and the response to what Columbus found were shaped by the civilizations that encountered one another. Thus, in order to understand what happened *after* 1492, one needs to understand what was happening *before*, both in Spain and in the Americas. One might argue that such is the case particularly when studying the evolution that occurs when different religions meet, clash, and ultimately reconcile, even if one "conquers" the other. One way to grasp the complexity of those civilizations and religions is to listen to the words, look at the art, and read the myths of the people. In the selections that follow, we will do just that.

We will begin with the Spaniards, whose world in 1492 was undergoing rapid changes: The Jews were expelled from the country; the Moors were finally defeated at Granada; and Isabella granted Christopher Columbus the right to sail under her flag.

Columbus and the people who for years followed after him brought with them not only their food and diseases but also their attitudes toward warfare and religion. Source One, "A God-Given Destiny," presents the reader with an avenue to understand the religious fervor and all-encompassing ethos of

3

the *Reconquista*. This centuries-long process, whereby Christians militarily reclaimed the land that had been conquered by the Moors in 711, culminated in 1492, just before Columbus sailed. By that time, the myth had developed that the process of reconquest was conscious and continuous. This recasting of the past served to create an ethos in which Spain identified its own nationalistic endeavors with God's purposes.

Religion also shaped the way that the original Americans responded to the Spanish spiritual and military invasion and conquest. This is evident in our second selection, "Ancient Beliefs," in which we look at the birth myth of the Aztec war god *Huitzilopochtli*. This narrative brings to life Mexican cosmology and the belief that the world was born out of chaos and conflict.

The conquest of Mexico is described in some detail in "A Surprising Market," an excerpt from a chronicle by Bernal Díaz del Castillo. This source allows modern-day readers to enter the world of the conquerors as they moved across Mexico. Of particular interest to us is the inner conflict that Spaniards experienced as they tried to reconcile what they saw with what they believed about the Aztecs. The description of Tatelulco (now known as Tlatelolco), a thriving marketplace in the Aztec capital, presents us with a small slice of that inner conflict.

Efforts to understand the "other" were not limited to the Spaniards, as is made clear by our fourth source, "Conversion of an Inca." In Prince Titu Cusi Yupanqui's account of the mistreatment of his father, Manco Inca, at the hands of the Spaniards, we see an Andean ruler trying to understand just who these invaders were. We also read about Titu Cusi's own conversion to Christianity and glimpse how faith was a tool used by both sides. Felipe Guaman Poma de Ayala also recounted the abuses of the Spaniards in the Andean world. However, in our fifth source, "A Tragedy in Pictures," the selections presented are not written. They are illustrations that graphically represent the conquerors' actions as interpreted by the conquered.

As you read these sources and contemplate the drawings, ask yourself what, if any, were the points of commonality between the pre-European Americas and the pre-American Europe. How would divergent worldviews have affected the Encounter? In what ways did prominent elements evident in these sources contribute to the interpretation of the conquest?

In each of these sources, the writer or artist expresses his—they were all men—perception of the world around him. In seeing the world through the eyes of the actors in the Encounter, the modern reader can begin to understand why the post-1492 European and American worlds, including their Christianities, evolved as they did.

Source One
A God-Given Destiny

Introduction

By 1530, a few years after Columbus set sail on his final voyage to the Americas, both Isabella of Castile and Ferdinand of Aragon were long dead: Ferdinand for almost fifteen years and Isabella for more than twenty-five. Yet it was in that year that Lucio Marineo Sículo published *De rebus Hispaniae memorabilibus Libri XXV* (XXV books on memorable Spanish things). The Sicilian-born chaplain to Ferdinand penned a most impressive history of Spain, in which he included accounts of "the illustrious life and heroic deeds of the Catholic Monarchs," as Ferdinand and Isabella were known. As Marineo gloried in the richness of his adopted country and the reign of these monarchs whose rule marked the beginning of early-modern Spain, he wrote of the area's geography, the culture of its residents, and its military and religious history. A key part of military/religious "history" guiding Isabella's Spain was the myth of the reconquest (*la Reconquista*). This myth held that from the time of the Moorish invasion of Spain (711), Spanish Christians had valiantly struggled to reclaim their country for the glory of God. The notion that God was on the side of the Spaniards and the Spaniards on God's side was deeply entrenched in most aspects of late-fifteenth- and early-sixteenth-century Spain. The excerpts we have chosen focus on Ferdinand and Isabella's efforts at the end of the fifteenth century to unite Spain under one faith, practiced one way. You will read of the Inquisition and heretics—mostly Jews who had converted to Catholicism only to revert to their old religion—of reform efforts against nuns and monks whose lifestyles fell far short of that required by the rule under which they supposedly lived; and of the war against the Moors in Granada. As you read these selections, be sure to reflect upon what religious unity meant for the rulers of Spain and why Marineo would include it in an account of the monarchs' heroic deeds. You might also ponder how the understanding of military success as being a reflection of both God's benevolence and a people's faithfulness to God would ultimately affect the conquest of the Americas. At what points can you discern the myth of the *Reconquista*?

The Text*

Since we have already discussed the customs of the Jews, we shall now tell briefly how they became Christians in Spain. In past years, and almost in our own time, there was a man from the city of Valencia whose name was Fray Vicente Ferrer, of the Order of Preachers, who was a famous theologian and marvelous preacher. . . . Through his preaching and very strong arguments and obvious reasons, he proved to the Jews all the errors and obvious deceptions by which they were blinded. He thus converted many of them to the Catholic faith. These, when they came to know the Christian religion and our faith as most holy and true, by their own will were baptized and received all the sacraments of the church, thus beginning to live as Christians. But later, as time went by, through a diabolic persuasion, or through the contact they had with those Jews who had remained in their love . . . they easily returned to their own sinister and traditional customs. Thus, these new Christians, imagining that Christ was not the one whom God was to send, and whom they awaited, and repenting from their conversion, looked with contempt upon the Christian religion and continued celebrating the Sabbaths and Jewish ceremonies in secret places in their homes, going barefooted at night to their synagogues and keeping their paschal feasts and the memory of their ancestors, as they had done before.

. . . Thus, time itself, or rather the justice of God, made it be known to the Catholic Princes [Isabella and Ferdinand] that there were young men who were sinning in the dark, at night and in unlit places, and no longer allowed such practices to remain unpunished. With the advice of the Cardinal [Ximénez] . . . the Catholic Monarchs brought a remedy to these evils, at first by ordering all priests and religious men that in all the cities and towns they should admonish and instruct all new Christians by means of public preaching as well as privately and individually, that they do this diligently, and [that they] keep and confirm them [new Christians] in all the sacraments of the church and in the holy Catholic faith. And later when they learned that this was achieving little or nothing, they sent ambassadors to Rome before the Holy Father. The latter having listened to the embassy, marveling at the new heresy and mournful of the dishonor and insult which the heretics brought on Christians and on the honor of God, sent his bulls to the Catholic Monarchs, signed with the apostolic seal. Through these bulls he ordered that a diligent inquisition be made and punishment be brought to those who did not have the right attitude towards the Catholic faith, and opposed it, or had deviated in any manner whatsoever. Thus the king and the queen . . . ordered that the inquisitors, who had been chosen from among all the priests in their kingdom, people very correct in their customs and doctrines, that in all the cities of Spain as well as in its towns they should publish their public edicts, by apostolic authority, and declare publicly that those who had committed the crime of heresy, who within a certain time would come forth and confess their errors to the inquisitorial fathers, humbly asking for forgiveness and thus being reconciled to the church, would make a public penance for their errors. Through this judgment, before the term expired, almost 17,000 people appeared before the fathers, counting men and women. To these people, the church, which is a fountain of mercy and a mother of piety, content with their penance, which each did depending on the nature of their error, gave life to many who perhaps did not merit it. Those on whom reliable witnesses informed that they did not wish to obey these commandments and persevered in their heresies were imprisoned and put to the question by torture. Once they had confessed their errors, they were burnt. Among these some lamented their sins and confessed Christ, and others persevered in their errors, calling upon the name of Moses. Thus in a few years almost 2,000 heretics were burned. Some who repented and mourned their errors, even though they had sinned grievously, were put in perpetual prison, where they did penance. Others who were spared both life imprisonment and death were punished by having their names condemned and being declared unworthy of occupying any public offices. They were not allowed to wear any gold or silk, but rather were to wear *sambenitos* [cloaks of shame] with two red crosses, one in front and one behind, over all their apparel, so that everyone could see them and recognize them. They also took measures against those among the dead who were known to have sinned while living. Confiscating their goods and depriving their children of them and of all ranks and offices, they also disinterred their bones from their tombs, which were many, and burnt them. And many other Jews, fearing this justice and knowing their own evils, abandoned their homes with many goods, and also left Spain, fleeing some to Portugal, others to Navarre, many to Italy, and some to France and other regions, where they thought they would be safe. The Catholic Monarchs used the [confiscated] goods, both in real estate and in moveable form, in their wars against Moors, and this was a large amount of money. Thus, in Andalucía alone more than 5,000 houses were left by Jews who had fled with their wives and children. And since, as we have already stated, the contact with Jews on the part of those recently converted to our faith was harmful to them, giving them occasion to sin, the Catholic Monarchs forever expelled all Jews from their kingdoms and dominions. Since the edicts and admonishments of the government ordered that they would not be allowed to sell their houses or to take money with them, some were arrested for carrying such in the saddlebags and in the ears of their donkeys. . . .

We have easily seen how much care and diligence our Catholic Monarchs devoted to the conservation of virtue and honesty, not only in temporal and human things, but even more so in those divine and spiritual things having to do with the honor of God and human salvation. They were always as mindful and zealous about this as they were about the governing of their kingdoms. They, therefore, appeared as priests and holy pontiffs no less than as rulers, constantly ordering very holy laws both for the honor of divine worship and for human matters and the ordering of their kingdoms. Since they saw many among the religious, particularly Friars Minor, Observants, and Preachers, who kept their rules, and at the same time that other cloistered people of various orders lived unworthily, not keeping that to which they were supposedly committed, the monarchs ordered that all monastics should observe their rules and live worthily. They also prohibited the visits of men in nuns' monasteries, where the latter lived dissolutely and in much liberty. These were forced into their religious observances by being cloistered in their monasteries, and forbidding them any freedom, suspicious conversations, or going out of their monasteries.

. . . But now I return to the Moors of Granada. These were in possession of the city . . . as well as of many other places and were constantly trying to push forward. They were involved in many battles and skirmishes, and continually attacking those Christians who lived near them. This resulted in many captives, prisoners, and deaths on both sides. But there was no lack of very Christian rulers of Spain, valiant men of great courage and zealous for our Christian religion, who in open battle, having conquered and demolished the Moors, pursued them to the very gates of the city of Granada, and attacked its walls. . . . One night, very quietly, [the Moors] came to the place called Zahara, which belonged to Christians. They climbed over the walls with ladders and then, with great and frenzied impulse, they broke open the gates. Forgiving neither women nor children, they cruelly killed the Christians who were within the walls, who were sleeping naked, trusting the truces that had been made, and without guards or watches. The cruelty of the Moors against the Christians is incredible. And after these atrocities, they left a garrison in the place they had taken and happily went to repeat their deeds in other Christian places. I believe all of this was allowed by God in order to lead to the war of the kingdom with Granada and for the final destruction and perdition of the Moors. The news of the horrendous death of the Christians and the frightening cruelty of the Moors awakened and provoked the Catholic Monarchs, as well as all the grandees and people of Spain, in a marvelous manner, seeking the destruction of the Moors with ferocious zeal.

On this, once these Catholic Monarchs Don Ferdinand and Doña Isabella . . . were convinced of the evil and deeds of the Moors, they diligently sent letters and messengers to all important people and to all the cities and places in the provinces of Andalucía and Cartagena. They informed them of the Moors' cruelty and admonished them to guard and strengthen their towns and to gather as much cavalry and infantry as they could. The monarchs would take care of all things necessary for the waging of war. They would diligently and with great vigilance see to all the things that would prevent the entry of the Moors. The Monarchs promised that they would soon come to them with an army or would send their captains and many people to their aid and succor. The knights and towns of both provinces, whose responsibility it was to defend themselves and their property from their enemies, although they had willingly and diligently seen to all that was necessary to guard and defend themselves, now, with the news and admonishment of their rulers, and having hope of aid and succor, became more forceful. . . . And since the Moors, through their spies, learned of this, they not only desisted from what they had begun but also began to withdraw fearfully. The Christians, having prepared the necessary arms and other matters, were alert and ready, awaiting the coming of the Catholic Monarchs or their command as to what they should do.

Source Two
Ancient Beliefs

Introduction

Huitzilopochtli, the Mexican god of war, was born out of dishonor, so Aztec informants told Fr. Bernardino de Sahagún. Beginning in the 1540s, less than thirty years after Hernán Cortés's conquest of Mexico, Sahagún, a Franciscan missionary, collected the history of the Aztec world, its culture, and its society by interviewing Nahuatl-speaking elders. The resulting *Florentine Codex* (so called because it is now in Florence), or *Historia general de las cosas de Nueva España* (General history of the things of New Spain) as it is also known, is the compendium of that history recounted to the priest. Sahagún had been commissioned by his order to compile this history as a tool for the conversion and Christian instruction of indigenous Americans. An accomplished linguist, Sahagún also produced a Spanish/Nahuatl dictionary and a grammar. These sources, particularly the ethnographic *Florentine Codex*, are our best window into the Aztec worldview before the arrival of the Spaniards.

Think about what the story of *Huitzilopochtli* tells us about how the Aztecs understood the world. Also consider how that view might have affected the Aztecs' reception of the Spaniards. How might the Spaniards have used it to their advantage? (In considering this last question, you may wish to look at our next source, "A Surprising Market.") As you read the excerpt about *Huitzilopochtli*, consider how a missionary might have used the information in efforts at conversion. At what points might a Christian have "connected" with the story of the war god in order to make Christianity more acceptable and understandable to Indians? How might Sahagún's race and religion have colored what his informants told him? Why would the elders among the natives have participated in Sahagún's project?

The Text[†]

1- About the beginning of that devil called *Huitzilopochtli*, to whom the Mexicans rendered much honor and service, the older natives said and knew that:

2- There is a mountain range called *Coatépec* next to the town of *Tulla*, and there lived a woman by the name of *Coatlicue*, who was mother of some Indians called *Centzonhuitznahua*, who had a sister called *Coyolxauhqui*. They said *Coatlicue* did penance every day by sweeping the mountain range of *Coatépec*. And it happened one day that as she was sweeping a small feather ball descended on her, as if it were the result of spinning. She took it and placed it on her breast next to her stomach, under her petticoats. After she finished sweeping she looked for the little ball and could not find it, and it is said that this impregnated her. When the *Centzonhuitznahua* Indians saw that their mother was pregnant, they were greatly angered saying, "Who impregnated her and thus dishonored and shamed us?"

3- And their sister *Coyolxauhqui* would say, "Brothers let's kill our mother because she has dishonored us by secretly becoming pregnant."

4- When *Coatlicue* learned of this, she was very sorrowful and afraid. But her child spoke to her and gave her consolation saying, "Do not be afraid, for I know what I have to do."

5- After hearing such words, *Coatlicue* was quieted in her heart, and she was no longer sad. But the *Centzonhuitznahua* Indians had already devised the plan to kill their mother, for reason of that dishonor and shame that she had brought upon them. They were very angry, jointly with their sister *Coyolxauhqui*, who prompted them to kill their mother *Coatlicue*. Thus the *Centzonhuitznahua* took up arms and got ready for battle, braiding and tying their hair, as valiant warriors do.

6- One of them was called *Quauitlícac*, and he was a traitor, for when the *Centzonhuitznahua* said something, he would go and directly tell *Huitzilopochtli*, who was still in his mother's womb. He would tell him what was happening, and *Huitzilopochtli* would answer, "Oh, my uncle, see what they do and listen carefully to what they say, for I know what I am to do."

7- After having agreed to kill their mother *Coatlicue*, the *Centzonhuitznahua* went to her. They were led by their sister *Coyolxauhqui* and armed with all sorts of weapons, papers, and bells, as well as arrows. So the said *Quauitlícac* went up to the mountain range to tell *Huitzilopochtli* that the *Centzonhuitznahua* were coming against him in order to kill him. *Huitzilopochtli* answered, "Take care to see where they come." He answered that they were already coming to a place called *Tzompantitlan*. . . .

8- As the *Centzonhuitznahua* Indians were arriving, *Huitzilopochtli* was born, bringing with him a shield that is called *teueuelli*, with an arrow and blue rod, and his face was painted, and glued to his head was a mass of feathers, and his left leg was thin and also covered with feathers, and his two thighs as well as his arms were also painted blue.

9- Then *Huitzilopochtli* told one whose name was *Tochancalqui* to light *xiuhcóatl*, a snake made out of firewood. This he did, and with it *Coyolxauhqui* was wounded, so that she broke into pieces and died, and her head remained in that mountain range which is call *Coatépec*, and her body fell in pieces.

10- So *Huitzilopochtli* arose and armed himself and went out against the *Centzonhuitznahua*, pursuing them and casting them out of that mountain range of *Coatépec* down to the valley, fighting against them and four times going around the range. The *Centzonhuitznahua* were not able to defend themselves and had no recourse against *Huitzilopochtli*. They could do nothing to him and thus were conquered, and many of them died. So the *Centzonhuitznahua* pled and begged *Huitzilopochtli*, asking that he would no longer pursue them and that he would withdraw from the struggle. But *Huitzilopochtli* would not do this nor agree to it until he had killed most of them, and very few had escaped from his hands. They went to a place called *Huitzlampa*, and he despoiled them, taking the weapons that they brought called *anecúhiotl*.

11- . . . and the said Mexicans have held *Huitzilopochtli* in great respect and have served him in many ways, having him for their god of war, for they said that *Huitzilopochtli* favored them greatly in war. And the manners in which the Mexicans served and honored *Huitzilopochtli* were taken from what used to be done in that mountain range in *Coatépec*.

11

Source Three
A Surprising Market

Introduction

A marketplace filled with untold variety of goods and merchandise: Who would have believed that a people as barbarous as the Aztecs could have such sophisticated commerce? After all, Aristotle had declared that advanced commerce was a key marker of civilization, which in turn revealed a people's place within humanity—namely as slave or master, as human or subhuman. And Aristotle was held in the highest regard by many early-modern Europeans. Bernal Díaz del Castillo, a soldier-chronicler who traveled with Hernán Cortés, was one of those who found the juxtaposition of "civilization" with "barbarity"—the latter evidenced by, among other things, human sacrifice—incomprehensible. Yet, here it was in the central Valley of Mexico.

In his *Historia verdadera de la conquista de Nueva España* (The true history of the conquest of New Spain), Díaz del Castillo describes the arduous and destructive campaign across Mexico, the wonderment and the cruelty of the Spaniards, and their entry into Tenochtitlán, the Aztecs' capital city. It was in Tenochtitlán that he saw economic activity that rivaled any in a European capital city.

In the excerpt below, Díaz del Castillo gives a detailed description of the many goods he found in the market. Consider the Spaniard's attitude as expressed in his astonishment. What kind of conflict would the extensive marketplace create for a European trying to understand the place of the Aztecs within humanity? Or perhaps more accurately, trying to judge the very humanity of the Aztecs? At what points do we see "evidence" of the indigenous as subhuman? As human? Consider how religion informed and formed the Aztecs' economic world. Also consider what Díaz's description reveals about the economic structure of the Aztec Empire. You may want to reflect upon how such a system could aid or hinder the conquest, both spiritual and physical, of the Aztecs.

The Text[‡]

Let us leave aside Montezuma, who as I have already said had gone ahead, and return to Cortés and to our captains and soldiers. Since it was our custom to be armed day and night, and Montezuma saw us thus when we visited him, he did not see anything new in our being armed. I say this because our captain and all the others who had forces, and later most of our soldiers, went to

12

Tatelulco. There were also many chiefs whom Montezuma had sent to keep us company, and from the moment we arrived at the great plaza called Tatelulco, having never seen such a thing, we were awed at the multitude of people and merchandise that was there, and the great organization and order that they had in all things. The chiefs who accompanied us were showing us what was there. Each kind of merchandise was in a particular area, and they all had their places clearly determined. Let us begin with the merchants of gold and silver and precious stones and feathers and capes and crafts, as well as of the Indians who were there as merchandise, as slaves, both male and female. I say that they brought as many of them to sell at that plaza as the Portuguese bring blacks from Guinea. They brought them tied to long rods and with rings on their necks, so they could not escape. But others were loose. Then there were other merchants who sold coarser clothes and cotton and things made out of spun linen, and peanut venders who sold cacao, and in this way there were as many kinds of merchandise as exist in all of New Spain. This was organized in the same manner in which it is done in my own homeland, which is Medina del Campo, where they have fairs, so that in each street a particular kind of merchandise is sold. Thus they were organized in this great plaza, those who sold plates and rope made out of hemp fiber, and *cotaras*, which are the shoes that they wear and are made from the same plant. There were also very well cooked sweets and other confections that they draw from the same plant. Everything was in a section of the plaza appointed for it. There were skins of tigers [jaguars], lions [pumas], otters, jackals, deer, and other similar animals, badgers, and wildcats. Those that were cured were in one section and the others in another. And elsewhere there were other sorts of things and merchandise. Let us move ahead and speak of those who sold beans and chia seeds and other legumes and herbs, all in a different section. We then can move on to those who sold chickens, turkeys, rabbits, hares, deer, and mallards, little dogs, and other similar things, also in their own section of the plaza. We can then talk about the women who sold fruit and others who sold cooked food, porridges, and puddings, also in their own section. There were also various pieces of earthenware made in a thousand ways, from big pots to small jars, and they too were in their section. And there were also those who sold honey and molasses candies and other sweets that were like nougat. Then we moved on to those who sold wood, boards, cribs, and bins, and chopped logs and benches, all in their own place. We then moved to those who sold firewood, fat wood, and other such materials. What else can I say but that, as I speak with modesty, there were those who sold canoes filled with human excrement, who had their mats near the plaza, and this was used to cure skins, for they say that without this ingredient the hides are not good. I can well understand that some men will laugh at this, but I say that it is so. And I even say that they had the custom [that] along their roads [were] places made with cane or straw or grass, so that people going by would not see them and where they would go if they felt the need to clear their bowels, so that this filthiness would not be lost. But there is no point in my spending so many words attempting to describe what they sold in that plaza, for it would be a never-ending task to describe all things in detail, such as paper in this land which they call *amal* and some small tubes for perfume with liquid amber, filled with tobacco and other yellow ointments and such things, again all in their own place. And they sold much cochineal under the portals in the great square. There were many herbalists and other sorts of merchants. They also had their buildings in which three judges served, and there were also some people who served as bailiffs who examined the merchandise. I was about to forget the salt and blades made out of flint, and how they were making them from the stone itself. There were also fishermen and others selling little loaves that they make out of a sort of slime that they collect in that great lake, which is then curdled in order to make breads that taste like cheese. And they also sold hatchets of brass, copper, and tin, and bowls and some much decorated vessels, all made out of wood. It would be impossible to say all the things that were being sold there, for there were so many and of so many different qualities that we were not able to see it all or to inquire about all, for while the plaza was filled with people and surrounded by portals, it would take more than two days to see it all. We then went to the great temple, and as we approached its great yards, and before even leaving the same plaza, there were other merchants who, as we were told, were those bringing gold to sell still as nuggets drawn from the mines. These they placed in very thin tubes [of bone] taken from the geese of the area, and they were white so that one could see the gold from outside. On the basis of the length and thickness of the tube, they could know how many capes or large leather sacks of cacao the tube was worth, or how much to pay for slaves or anything else for which they traded them.

So we left the plaza without seeing more and came to the vast yards and fences where the great temple is. Before coming to it, there was a vast circle of courtyards, which I believe were bigger than the plaza in Salamanca, and all surrounded by two fences of mortar and stone, and the yard and the entire place is paved with large stones, like white and very smooth tiles. And where there were no such stones, everything was white-washed and polished, and everything was very clean, so that there was in the entire place neither straw nor dust. And as we approached the great temple before we were able to begin mounting its steps, the great Montezuma sent from above, where he had been celebrating sacrifices, six priests and two important men to accompany our captain. And upon mounting steps, which were one hundred fourteen, they were going to take him by the arms to help him climb, believing that he would be fatigued, as they helped their lord Montezuma. And Cortés did not let them come to him. After we climbed to the top of the great temple, there was a small plaza on top where they had a space made like platforms, and there were great stones where the unfortunate Indians were placed to be sacrificed, and there was a great shape like a dragon and other evil figures. Much blood was spilled that day.

Source Four
Conversion of an Inca

Introduction

Conquering a people is rarely easily accomplished, despite accounts to the contrary, and the conquest of Peru by the Spaniards in the early 1530s was no different. The Spaniards entered the region while it was in the midst of a civil war to determine the new ruler—or Sapa Inca—of the Inca Empire, a war won by Atahualpa. Taking advantage of the situation, the Spaniards killed Atahualpa and eventually installed Manco Inca—Atahualpa's brother—as a puppet ruler. But Manco Inca proved to be less compliant than the Spaniards would have wanted. In 1536, he placed Cuzco, the center of Spanish power, under siege. Ultimately the siege was unsuccessful, and Manco Inca and his followers fled to Vilcabamba, north of Cuzco, where they remained independent of Spanish rule. After Manco Inca's death in 1545, his son Titu Cusi Yupanqui, the self-proclaimed Sapa Inca who usurped power from a half-brother, became ruler of this pocket of Incan resistance. Titu Cusi ruled until his own death in 1571, yet his approach to life with the Spaniards differed significantly from that of his father. He claimed to believe in what might be called "peaceful co-existence"—as evidenced by his efforts at negotiations—while at the same time conducting hostile acts against the Spaniards. Ultimately, Titu Cusi allowed missionaries to enter the Vilcabamba region and eventually professed conversion to Christianity. In 1570, the ruler dictated his version of the conquest and emphasized his rightful claim as the only lord of the Incas. (Spain had installed yet another puppet ruler in Cuzco.) In the excerpts from his account, note how Titu Cusi recounts his father's view of the treachery of the Spaniards. Consider if there was a political reason for this version of events. As you read about Titu Cusi's conversion to Christianity, at which time he assumed the name Don Diego de Castro Titu Cusi, reflect on his reasons for conversion. How might he have used his profession of Christianity to his advantage? What can you discern about the role of the church in pacifying areas of Indian resistance and independence?

The Text[§]

Document that the Manco Inca gave to the Indians, when he wanted to withdraw to the Andes. The manner that they needed to have with the Spaniards.

My beloved children and brethren who are here present and have followed me through all my trials and tribulations, I believe that you do not know why I have ordered that you gather here as one before me. I shall tell you briefly. I beg you not to be disturbed by what I am about to tell you, for you know that need quite often compels people to do what they would rather not do. Thus, since I find myself forced to satisfy those Andes that have been beckoning to me for a visit for a long time, I shall do their bidding and visit them for some time. I beg of you not to be pained by this, for I love you as children, and I do not wish in any way to cause you pain. Therefore, you will cause me great happiness if you do as I am about to tell you. You know that quite often even before now I have told you about the manner in which these bearded people came into my land under guise of claiming to be *viracochas* [gods]. And you as well as I believed this, because their garb and their faces were so different from ours. Thus, on the basis of the advice and evidence given to us by the Tallanas Yungas [a particular tribe] about things that they saw these men do in their lands, as you have seen, I was led to bring them to my lands and my people and treated them as everybody already knows and gave them the things you also know. And you have seen how they responded to my gifts of land and things. And not only they, but also my brothers Pascac and Iguill and Vaypar dispossessed me of my land and tried to kill me, which I avoided thanks to the warning of Antonico, as I told you a few days ago, who was eaten by the Andes [disappeared in the mountains] because he did not know how to manage in the area. And having seen all those things and many others that I will not mention for the sake of brevity, I ordered that you would gather in Cuzco so that we would repay them some of the evil they have done to us. It seems to me that either because their god helped them or because I was not there, you did not succeed, which pains me greatly.

Response of the Indians to the Inca

. . . If they were really sons of Viracochan [God] as they claim, they would not have done what they did, for Viracochan is able to flatten the mountain, to dry waters, and to create hills where there are none. He does not do evil to anyone, and we see that these people have not done this, but rather instead of doing good they have done evil taking from us our property, our women, our sons and daughters, our fields, our food, and many other things that we had in our land. They have done this by force and guile and against our will. People who do such things we can never call children of Viracochan, but rather, as I have told you before, of Supay [devil]. Even worse, for in their deeds they have imitated him and have done such shameful things that I do not even want to mention them.

The most important thing you ought to do is, if by any chance they tell you to worship what they worship, which is nothing but some painted cloth, which they say is Viracochan, and they tell you to worship this as a *huaca* [a spirit-endowed place or thing], which is nothing but a piece of cloth, you do not do this but rather hold to what we do. For you see how the *villcas* [synonymous with huaca] speak with us, and we can see the sun and the moon with our own eyes, and what they [the Spaniards] say we do not see well. I believe that sometimes either by force or by guile they will force you to worship what they do, and when you have no other alternative do so before them, but do not forget our own ceremonies. And if they tell you to destroy our huaca and force you to do this, obey them in as little as you can, and hide the rest, which will cause me great happiness.

Here begins the manner and method by which I, don Diego de Castro Titu Cusi Yupanqui, came to have peace with the Spaniards, of which peace, by the kindness of God, whom before we called Viracochan, I came to be Christian, which is what follows:

. . . Since your Lordship wrote to me repeatedly asking me to become a Christian and telling me that this would serve to ensure peace, I asked Diego Rodríguez and Martín de Pando, who were the most important among the religious people in Cuzco, what religion [monastic order] was most convenient and significant. They told me that the most significant and authoritative and flourishing religion in the entire land was that of St. Augustine and its prior. I mean that from among all the friars in Cuzco, he was the most important. Having heard and understood that this was so, I developed great affection for that order and religion above any other, and I decided to write many letters to the prior asking him to come and baptize me personally, for I would rather be baptized by him than by anybody else, for he was such an important person. And, since he is such an honorable religious man, he did me the favor of taking the trouble to come to my land to baptize me, bringing with him another religious and Gonzalo Pérez de Vivero as well as Tilano de Anaya, who arrived at Rayangalla on the twelfth of August in the year of 1568. I went there from here, Vilcabamba, in order to receive baptism as I understood they had come to give it to me. And there, in that town of Rayangalla the said prior Fray Juan de Vivero and his companions and others spent fourteen days teaching me the matters of faith. At the end of those days, on the day of the glorious doctor Saint Augustine, the said prior baptized me. My godfather was Gonzalo Pérez de Vivero and my godmother was Angelina Siga Ocllo. And after baptizing me the prior remained another eight days directing me in all things on the matters of our holy Catholic faith and teaching me its things and mysteries. At the end of all this, the said prior left with Gonzalo Pérez de Vivero and left in my land a companion by the name of Fray Marco García, so that he could remind me little by little of the things that the friar had taught me so that I would not forget them. He would also be able to teach and preach the word of God to the people in my land. And before he left I told my Indians why I had asked to be baptized and brought those people to my land and the benefits that people drew from being baptized, as well as why this father was remaining in our land. They all responded that they rejoiced in my baptism and in the presence of the father in the land and that they would seek to do the same as I had done soon, for this was the purpose of the father's presence.

For two months after the prior left, the friar remained in Rayangalla, teaching and working on the matters of faith and baptizing some children with their parents' agreement. He decided to go with Martín de Pando to visit the land that is beyond the pass towards Huamanga. There he remained for months doing the same work, setting up crosses and building churches in the towns where he arrived. These towns were eight. In three of them churches were built, and in the others crosses were set up. In total he baptized ninety children. Having done all of this and leaving behind young men who would continue the teaching, he returned to the aforesaid town of Rayangalla where he remained alone seven months baptizing and teaching the Indians of the area. By the month of September, another father came to join him, and together they remained in that land until I brought them to this town of Vilcabamba where we now are. Here they have not baptized anybody because the people in this land are still too new in the matters that they are to know and understand having to do with the law and commandments of God. I will work so that little by little they come to know all of this.

Source Five
A Tragedy in Pictures

Introduction

How does one capture the attention of Philip III, king of Spain from 1598 to 1621? Felipe Guaman Poma de Ayala decided the best way was to write a massive history of the Incan Empire both before and after the arrival of Europeans and to include line drawings to illustrate his points. Guaman Poma was an indigenous nobleman from what is now southern Peru. He was petitioning the king for a reinstatement of lands he believed were his birthright and complaining about the mistreatment of the Indian population at the hands of the Spaniards, religious and non-religious alike. It is doubtful that the almost 1,200-page *El primer nueva corónica* [sic] *y buen gobierno* (New chronicle and good government), written in the early 1600s, ever reached the king, although there is some evidence that it did arrive in Spain. Nevertheless, it is a rich source for those seeking to understand the history of the pre-contact Andean world—at least from the eyes of a displaced and displeased seventeenth-century Indian noble—and the initial contact between European and American.

The following illustrations deal primarily with the abuses and excesses of the early priests and friars. Think about why Guaman Poma would portray the Spaniards in such a negative light. How would this further his cause with the king? As a reader of the past, what cautions must one apply in interpreting these drawings? What information do they provide about the Andean world?

Additionally, taken as a group, what do these drawings tell you about gender roles in Andean society? What do they reveal about Guaman Poma's expectation of the Spanish priests? What can we learn about the intersection between these two groups?

(A word on the captions: Some of Guaman Poma's drawings have two captions. The first is a translation of the text that appears on the drawing itself. The second, in parentheses, is an explanation of the drawing provided by the authors of the Guaman Poma website. The page numbers on the drawings also need a word of clarification. Guaman Poma himself numbered the pages in two different manners, and in our citation for each drawing, both numbers are given. When looking for the drawing on the Guaman Poma website, search by the number in the brackets.)

The Images*

First Drawing (Drawing 237; page 594 [608])

In this drawing, what is Guaman Poma revealing about the relationship between priests and parishioners? What does Guaman Poma suggest about the ways in which priests treat indigenous women? What does the drawing tell us about how the Andean men might have viewed their roles vis-à-vis Andean women and Spanish priests?

Figure 1.1 "A bad-tempered priest very angry at the principal leaders and their Indians. Because he [the chief] defends single women and maidens, he [the priest] kills the Indian with a stick."

20

Second Drawing (Drawing 266; page 670 [684])

This drawing focuses on the interaction between Spanish teachers and Indian children. What is happening in the drawing? What does Guaman Poma assume the relationship should be between teachers and children? Why would he use maltreatment of indigenous children in an effort to persuade the king of the malevolence of Spanish priests?

Figure 1.2 "The choirmasters and teachers of this tribute kingdom." ("The cruel choirmasters and teachers should teach their students to read and write so that they can become good Christians.")

Third Drawing (Drawing 231, page 576 [590])

Here, Guaman Poma specifically depicts the behavior of a priest while administering a sacrament—confession. Why would the setting be important to Guaman Poma? What do you think he was trying to convey by making the penitent a pregnant woman? In the caption, what is Guaman Poma revealing about the priest? Why would it matter that women older than twenty are not being confessed? What does this drawing tell us about women in Andean society?

Figure 1.3 "Bad confession that the priests and friars of the parish do. He beats the pregnant Indians, the old women and the Indians. And he does not want to confess the single women older than twenty; he does not confess them and there is no other option for them."

Fourth Drawing (Drawing 258, page 647 [661])

This line drawing refers to the economic role priests assumed within the Andean world. How so? As portrayed, the priest is using force. What might this tell us about how the indigenous community responded to the economic power of Spanish priests? In this case, a woman is at the loom. What does her role as worker reveal about Andean society?

Figure 1.4 "The Mercedarian Murúa. In this kingdom in these parishes, they are angry and severe and he mistreats the Indians and he makes them work with a stick; there is no other choice." ("The Mercedarian friar Martín de Murúa mistreats his parishioners, and he makes himself kuraka, or the local authority.")

A Bonus Drawing: Guaman Poma Revisted⁺

Figure 1.5 This t-shirt art was produced in 2002 in Cuzco, Peru, as a depiction of the reaction to the 1492 Encounter between the Spaniards and the Americans. In what ways is this drawing different from Guaman Poma's? In what ways is it similar? *El encuentro de dos mundos* means "the encounter of two worlds."

2
ARRIVAL

Introduction

They had it all figured out. They knew how the world was structured and they knew why. Theology, the Bible, and observation, along with the occasional ancient Greek, led them to the truth. But now, the Encounter with the Americas would call into question most of what Europeans believed about the world. It would challenge the security that comes from certainty.

Of the physical world, Europeans knew the earth was round; the ancient Greeks had taught them that. They knew the sun rotated around the earth; it was obvious, and the Bible confirmed it. (Joshua 10:13 says, "And the sun stood still, and the moon stopped." It could not stop if it were not already moving.) And they knew that the world was divided into three large land-masses, following the tripartite nature of the Trinity.

Of the metaphysical world, Europeans knew that there was a hierarchical structure and that they were at the pinnacle; Aristotle wrote about it. They knew that Christianity was the one and only true faith; in Spain, the myth of a seven hundred year's war confirmed that God reigned. And they knew that the spiritual world held sway over the temporal; church history repeatedly reminded them of that.

Most of these beliefs would come into play as Europeans, particularly Spaniards, grappled with Columbus's tales of what he had encountered. Some beliefs would be reaffirmed, some destroyed, and some manipulated to fit this new reality. The modern reader might find the approach that religious and political leaders took to incorporate this new information into their worldview naive—and often deadly. Such is the case with the first source, "A Gift from the Pope," which is the bull *Inter caetera*, issued by Pope Alexander VI on May 4, 1493. King Ferdinand and Queen Isabella had turned to the pope shortly after Columbus returned with tales of his discovery. They were seeking authority over the New World in exchange for Christianizing it. Alexander readily granted their request; after all, one of his sons was married to the king's cousin. For the pope and the monarchs, his actions made perfect sense because temporal authority, even in lands never exposed to Christianity, had to be granted by papal approval. The pope, however, inadvertently created a conflict, largely economic in nature, between Spain and Portugal, which would only be resolved by a subsequent treaty. The Most Catholic Monarchs understood fully that this particular papal approbation brought with it untold riches.

A papal blessing of a largely secular endeavor, however, was not enough in the eyes of many to justify the wars waged on the Native Americans. By 1513, a Spanish legal scholar, Juan Lopéz de Palacios Rubios, was tackling that concern. He had created the *Requerimiento* (Source Two, "Justifying the Unjustifiable"), which was a legal document read to the Indians in Spanish outlining the Indians' obligation to the Spaniards and the latter's right to wage war on the former if such obligations were not met.

Simply laying out Spain's justification of its conquest did not guarantee that those being conquered would acquiesce to the demands of their oppressors. Rather, as Source Three, "A God Compromises," makes clear, very often native peoples found ways of combining their worldview and their faith with those of the Spaniards, much to the chagrin of some of the conquerors.

Source Four, "The Virgin Speaks to Juan Diego," is the story of the apparition of the Virgen de Guadalupe to the Indian Juan Diego in Mexico. It provides a further example of how the mixing of the New World and the Old produced unexpected circumstances. But unlike in "A God Compromises," in this story it is a Christian symbol—the Virgin Mary—who directs the Indian.

Challenges to Spanish hegemony were not limited to the New World or to Native Americans. In Spain, Francisco de Vitoria, a well-respected jurist and theologian, did not accept the pope's authority to grant the Spanish monarchs' conquest rights over the New World. In the pattern typical of his day, Vitoria refuted the pope's assertion point by point, finally concluding that his claim to temporal authority was fallacious. Source Five, "A Scholar's View," is a series of excerpts from his lectures on the Indies. It shows Vitoria's challenge to a commonly held view of the Indians' obligations and of the pope's power.

There were also challenges to how colonists executed the pope's grant, often coming directly from eyewitnesses in the Indies. The excerpts found in

Source Six, "An Entire People in Hell?" are examples of threats to European control made by non-Indian clergy living in the Americas. Antônio Vieira, a Jesuit living in Brazil, preached an angry sermon on the first Sunday of Lent, 1653, calling down the fires of hell on the heads of those colonists abusing Indians. Needless to say, his remarks were not well received, and he was forced to return to Portugal for several years. Nevertheless, he continued his fight on behalf of the Indians for the rest of his life.

Several of these sources reflect efforts to understand new realities in light of the conquest of the Americas. As you read them, look for ways in which Europeans and Native Americans responded in similar manners. How did religion play a role in forming new concepts of how the world must function? The final two sources also reflect new attitudes created as a consequence of the encounter between two worlds. In what ways do Vitoria and Vieira reveal assumptions about faith and humanity that run counter to those in most of the other documents? Which other sources reflect similar assumptions?

Taken together, all these sources demonstrate the challenges and responses to the arrival of the Spaniards in the Americas. But they also provide a glimpse into the changing nature of Christianity as it was also reshaped by the Encounter.

Source One
A Gift from the Pope

Introduction

By the time Columbus set sail for the East by going west, Portugal had developed fairly extensive trading networks with the East by going east and around Africa. Explorers such as Bartholomeu Dias and Vasco da Gama had propelled Portugal into being a major supplier of goods for European markets. Spain, which had been busy defeating the Moors, had been largely absent from "the age of discovery" until the end of the fifteenth century. While Isabella and Ferdinand were deeply religious, as we saw in the first chapter, they were not immune to the allure of great wealth that access to the riches of the East would provide. So, Isabella sponsored Columbus on his journey west.

What Columbus reported when he returned was not what Isabella expected. The "discovery" of a new world required immediate action on the monarchs' part. They did what any good European ruler would do: They went to the pope. Pope Alexander VI, a Spaniard himself, issued three bulls in 1493 dealing with the divisions of recently "discovered" and as yet to be "discovered" lands between Portugal and Spain. The third one, which is reproduced here, superseded the others. In it, Pope Alexander granted Spain "all rights, jurisdictions, and appurtenances" to any lands west of a line of demarcation one hundred leagues—roughly equivalent to three hundred miles—west and south from the Azores and Cape Verde. There was one caveat: The lands could not be in the possession of any other Christian ruler. Portugal reacted almost immediately with the threat of war, claiming that the pope had given too much away to Spain. The former feared that given the prevailing winds, its access to Africa was in jeopardy. The argument was settled with the Treaty of Tordesillas (1494), which moved the line of demarcation another 270 leagues further west. All the lands remaining to be discovered by the Europeans were now divided between Portugal and Spain. It is, in fact, the Treaty of Tordesillas that resulted in Brazil ultimately becoming a Portuguese colony.

As you read this selection, contemplate how the Europeans understood conquest. What role did religion play in that definition? Why would the pope exclude "all persons of whatsoever rank" from entering these lands for the "purpose of trade or any other reason"? Think about the balance between economic and spiritual gains outlined in this source.

The Text*

Alexander, bishop, servant of the servants of God, to the illustrious sovereigns, our very dear son in Christ, Ferdinand, king, and our very dear daughter in Christ, Isabella, queen of Castile, Leon, Aragon, Sicily, and Granada, health and apostolic benediction. Among other works well pleasing to the Divine Majesty and cherished of our heart, this assuredly ranks highest, that in our times especially the Catholic faith and the Christian religion be exalted and be everywhere increased and spread, that the health of souls be cared for and that barbarous nations be overthrown and brought to the faith itself. Wherefore inasmuch as by the favor of divine clemency, we, though of insufficient merits, have been called to this Holy See of Peter, recognizing that as true Catholic kings and princes, such as we have known you always to be, and as your illustrious deeds already known to almost the whole world declare, you not only eagerly desire but with every effort, zeal, and diligence, without regard to hardships, expenses, dangers, with the shedding even of your blood, are laboring to that end; recognizing also that you have long since dedicated to this purpose your whole soul and all your endeavors—as witnessed in these times with so much glory to the Divine Name in your recovery of the kingdom of Granada from the yoke of the Saracens—we therefore are rightly led, and hold it as our duty, to grant you even of our own accord and in your favor those things whereby with effort each day more hearty you may be enabled for the honor of God himself and the spread of the Christian rule to carry forward your holy and praiseworthy purpose so pleasing to immortal God. We have indeed learned that you, who for a long time had intended to seek out and discover certain islands and mainlands remote and unknown and not hitherto discovered by others, to the end that you might bring to the worship of our Redeemer and the profession of the Catholic faith their residents and inhabitants, having been up to the present time greatly engaged in the siege and recovery of the kingdom itself of Granada were unable to accomplish this holy and praiseworthy purpose; but the said kingdom having at length been regained, as was pleasing to the Lord, you, with the wish to fulfill your desire, chose our beloved son, Christopher Columbus, a man assuredly worthy and of the highest recommendations and fitted for so great an undertaking, whom you furnished with ships and men equipped for like designs, not without the greatest hardships, dangers, and expenses, to make diligent quest for these remote and unknown mainlands and islands through the sea, where hitherto no one had sailed; and they at length, with divine aid and with the utmost diligence sailing in the ocean sea, discovered certain very remote islands and even mainlands that hitherto had not been discovered by others; wherein dwell very many peoples living in peace, and, as reported, going unclothed, and not eating flesh. Moreover, as your aforesaid envoys are of opinion, these very peoples living in the said islands and countries believe in one God, the Creator in heaven, and seem sufficiently disposed to embrace the Catholic faith and be trained in good morals. And it is hoped that, were they instructed, the name of the Savior, our Lord Jesus Christ, would easily be introduced into the said countries and islands. Also, on one of the chief of these aforesaid islands the said Christopher has already caused to be put together and built a fortress fairly equipped, wherein he has stationed as garrison certain Christians, companions of his, who are to make search for other remote and unknown islands and mainlands. In the islands and countries already discovered are found gold, spices, and very many other precious things of diverse kinds and qualities. Wherefore, as becomes Catholic kings and princes, after earnest consideration of all matters, especially of the rise and spread of the Catholic faith, as was the fashion of your ancestors, kings of renowned memory, you have purposed with the favor of divine clemency to bring under your sway the said mainlands and islands with their residents and inhabitants and to bring them to the Catholic faith. Hence, heartily commending in the Lord this your holy and praiseworthy purpose, and desirous that it be duly accomplished, and that the name of our Savior be carried into those regions, we exhort you very earnestly in the Lord and by your reception of holy baptism, whereby you are bound to our apostolic commands, and by the bowels of the mercy of our Lord Jesus Christ, enjoin strictly, that inasmuch as with eager zeal for the true faith you design to equip and dispatch this expedition, you purpose also, as is your duty, to lead the peoples dwelling in those islands and countries to embrace the Christian religion; nor at any time let dangers or hardships deter you therefrom, with the stout hope and trust in your hearts that Almighty God will further your undertakings. And, in order that you may enter upon so great an undertaking with greater readiness and heartiness endowed with the benefit of our apostolic favor, we, of our own accord, not at your instance nor the request of anyone else in your regard, but of our own sole largess and certain knowledge and out of the fullness of our apostolic power, by the authority of Almighty God conferred upon us in blessed Peter and of the vicarship of Jesus Christ, which we hold on earth, do by tenor of these presents, should any of said islands have been found by your envoys and captains, give, grant, and assign to you and your heirs and successors, kings of Castile and Leon, forever, together with all their dominions, cities, camps, places, and villages, and all rights, jurisdictions, and appurtenances, all islands and mainlands found and to be found, discovered and to be discovered towards the west and south, by drawing and establishing a line from the Arctic pole, namely the north, to the Antarctic pole, namely the south, no matter whether the said mainlands and islands are found and to be found in the direction of India or towards any other quarter, the said line to be distant one hundred leagues towards the west and south from any of the islands commonly known as the Azores and Cape Verde. With this proviso however that none of the islands and mainlands, found and to be found, discovered and to be discovered, beyond that said line towards the west and south, be in the actual possession of any Christian king or prince up to the birthday of our Lord Jesus Christ just past from which the present year one thousand four hundred and ninety-three begins. And we make, appoint, and depute you and your said heirs and successors lords of them with full and free power, authority, and jurisdiction of every kind; with this proviso however, that by this our gift, grant, and assignment no right acquired by any Christian prince, who may be in actual possession of said islands and mainlands prior to the said birthday of our Lord Jesus Christ, is hereby to be understood to be withdrawn or taken away. Moreover we command you in virtue of holy obedience that, employing all due diligence in the premises, as you also promise— nor do we doubt your compliance therein in accordance with your loyalty and royal greatness of spirit—you should appoint to the aforesaid mainlands and islands worthy, God-fearing, learned, skilled, and experienced men, in order to instruct the aforesaid inhabitants and residents in the Catholic faith and train them in good morals. Furthermore, under penalty of excommunication . . . we strictly forbid all persons of whatsoever rank, even imperial and royal, or of whatsoever estate, degree, order, or condition, to dare, without your special permit or that of your aforesaid heirs and successors, to go for the purpose of trade or any other reason to the islands or mainlands, found and to be found, discovered and to be discovered, towards the west and south, by drawing and establishing a line from the Arctic pole to the Antarctic pole, no matter whether the mainlands and islands, found and to be found, lie in the direction of India or toward any other quarter whatsoever, the said line to be distant one hundred leagues towards the west and south, as is aforesaid, from any of the islands commonly known as the Azores and Cape Verde; apostolic constitutions and ordinances and other decrees whatsoever to the contrary notwithstanding. We trust in Him from whom empires and governments and all good things proceed, that, should you, with the Lord's guidance, pursue this holy and praiseworthy undertaking, in a short while your hardships and endeavors will attain the most felicitous result, to the happiness and glory of all Christendom. But inasmuch as it would be difficult to have these present letters sent to all places where desirable, we wish, and with similar accord and knowledge do decree, that to copies of them, signed by the hand of a public notary commissioned therefore, and sealed with the seal of any ecclesiastical officer or ecclesiastical court, the same respect is to be shown in court and outside as well as anywhere else as would be given to these presents should they thus be exhibited or shown. Let no one, therefore, infringe, or with rash boldness contravene, this our recommendation, exhortation, requisition, gift, grant, assignment, constitution, deputation, decree, mandate, prohibition, and will. Should anyone presume to attempt this, be it known to him that he will incur the wrath of Almighty God and of the blessed apostles Peter and Paul. Given at Rome, at St. Peter's, in the year of the incarnation of our Lord one thousand four hundred and ninety-three, the fourth of May, and the first year of our pontificate.

Gratis by order of our most holy lord, the pope.

Source Two
Justifying the Unjustifiable

Introduction

By 1513, when the *Requerimiento* was written, the debate about the maltreatment of the indigenous peoples of the Americas was well underway. Priests such as the Dominican Antonio de Montesinos had already condemned the colonists in Hispaniola for their abuses of the Indians. Bartolomé de Las Casas was beginning the personal transformation that would eventually lead to his being named the "Protector of the Indians." And even the crown had instituted new laws in an attempt to curtail the worst abuses of the conquistadores. Yet none of this changed the zeal with which the Spaniards conquered the Americas. What these concerns did accomplish, however, was an awareness of the need to justify the conquest. One of many undertaking this task was Juan López de Palacios Rubios, a noted jurist whose power extended to being a member of the Council of Castile, which served in an advisory capacity to the crown. His efforts to justify the conquest resulted in the *Requerimiento*. Not only did it present the reasons for the conquest, but it also absolved the Spaniards of all blame for any harm that befell the Indians.

Before engaging in battle, the conquistadores would read the *Requerimiento* aloud to the Indians, sometimes in *sotto voce* so as not to alert the Indians to their presence, but always in Spanish and without the benefit of a translation. If they "refused" to accept the sovereignty of the Spanish crown and the dominion of the pope, then the invaders were justified in waging war, enslaving, and if need be, causing "deaths and harms" to the Indians, which would all be the result of the indigenous people's intransigence. By mid-century the Spaniards had ceased using the document.

As you read this selection, think about the nexus of the legal, the spiritual, and the economic. What assumptions about the Indians, about the law, about the church, and about Spain are buried in this document? Also contemplate ways in which the *Requerimiento* echoes attitudes evident in Source One, "A Gift from the Pope." How do these two sources work together to assuage any guilt the crown and its jurists might have felt about the conquest?

The Text[†]

On behalf of King Don Ferdinand and of his daughter, Doña Juana, queen of Castile and León, subduers of barbarian peoples, we their servants notify and let you know to the best of our abilities, that God our Lord, who is one and eternal, created heaven and earth, and a man and a woman from which we and you and all others in the world have been and still are his descendants, begotten from them, as will be true of any others who will come after us. But since the people who came from them have multiplied from five millennia ago, and even more, when the world was created, it was necessary that some would go to one region and others to another, and be divided into many kingdoms and provinces, since they could no longer support themselves and carry on life in a single one.

Among all these people God our Lord commissioned one whose name was St. Peter, so that he would be lord above all in the world, and all should obey him, so that he was the head of the entire human race, no matter where people lived or under what law, sect, or belief. And he gave him the entire world as his kingdom and jurisdiction, and he ordered that his see be in Rome, as the best place to rule the world and to judge and govern over all people, Christian, Moors, Jews, gentiles, or people of any other sect or belief. This one was called pope, which means admirable, great father and ruler of all people.

Those who lived at that time obeyed and accepted St. Peter as their lord, king, and ruler of the universe. In the same regard, others who after him were elected to the pontificate have been held, and so has it been until now, and will continue to be until the end of the world. One of these past pontiffs who succeeded St. Peter to that office and see that I have already mentioned as lord of the world, granted these islands and mainland on the Ocean Sea as well as all that is in them to the above mentioned king and queen and to their successors as rulers of these kingdoms. This is stated in certain writings which they issued about this subject, and as you may see if you wish.

So, their majesties are sovereigns and lords of these islands and mainland by virtue of that donation. As such, they have been received in others and almost all the islands where this proclamation has been read. They have received their majesties and have obeyed and served and still do serve as all subjects should, with goodwill and without resisting as well as without delay. As they were informed of these things, they obeyed and received the religious men whom their highnesses sent to them so that they would preach to them and teach them our holy faith. And all of them out of their own free and good will, without any reward or condition, became Christians and still are, and their majesties received them joyfully and kindly, ordering that they be treated as their other subjects and vassals. And you are expected and obliged to do likewise.

Therefore, to the best of our abilities, we beseech and require of you that you understand very clearly what we have told you and take as much time as is justified to understand it and to decide on it, and that you acknowledge the Church as your lady and ruler over the entire universe, and the supreme pontiff, called Pope, in her name, and the king and the Queen Doña Juana, our lords, in their place as rulers and sovereigns of these islands and mainland, by virtue of the above mentioned grant, and that you will agree and make it possible so that these religious fathers may declare and preach to you all of the above.

If you do this, you will be doing what is good, as well as that which you are expected and obliged to do. And their highnesses and we in their name will receive you with all love and charity, and will leave you your women and children and your properties free of lien and without any servitude, so that with them and with yourselves you may freely do whatever you wish and consider to be good. And they will not force you to become Christians, except if you yourselves being well informed of the truth wish to convert to our Holy Catholic faith, as almost all the inhabitants of the other islands have done. Besides this their majesties will grant you privileges and exemptions, and will grant also many other mercies to you.

Figure 2.1 Vilcabamba was one of the last redoubts of Incan power.

And if you do not do this, or if you were to delay doing this with evil intent, I certify that with the help of God we will come mightily against you and we will make war on you wherever and in whatever way we can, and we will hold you to the yoke and obedience of the church and of their majesties, and we will take you as well as your women and children and make you slaves. As such we will sell and dispose of you in any way that their majesties command, and we will take your possessions, and we will do to you as much harm and evil as we can, as is due to vassals who do not obey or wish to receive their lord and resist and contradict him. And we declare that the deaths and harms that may follow from all of this are your fault and not that of our majesties, or ours, or of these gentlemen who come with us. And we ask and require of the scribe who is present that he provides us with a sealed witness, and we ask all present to bear witness to it.

Source Three
A God Compromises

Introduction

Bartolomé de Las Casas, the author of the excerpt below, was a Spaniard who participated in the settlement of the Caribbean and was richly rewarded by the crown for his efforts. Within a few years, however, as he became concerned with the atrocities Indians were experiencing at the hands of other colonists, he renounced his wealth. He began advocating on behalf of the oppressed, was eventually ordained, and finally joined the Dominican order in 1522. He worked tirelessly raising awareness of the conditions under which Indians lived, primarily through a prodigious amount of writing, until his death in 1566 at the age of eighty-two. For his efforts, he was given the official title "Protector of the Indians."

This brief excerpt from Las Casas's extensive summary of the history of the Indies comprises the reaction of Pachacama, the Incan creator god, to the conversion of his followers to Christianity and his instructions to them to "worship and serve both" him and the Christian god. The mixing of the practices from two different religions (syncretism) was an abomination for the Spaniards. In fact, in order to wipe out all traces of ancient religions in the Andes, the Spanish priests conducted extensive extirpation campaigns, resulting in the death and torture of untold numbers of Indians.

Given how Spaniards viewed the blending of religions, why would an apologist such as Las Casas include this story in the history of Peru? What does it tell us about how the Spaniards understood Catholicism? What does the excerpt reveal about how Spaniards viewed the Indian gods and the power attributed to them by the Indians? Think of ways in which these attitudes might have affected how the conquerors treated the Indians and their understanding of what they—the Spaniards—were doing. Are similar attitudes reflected in the two previous documents of this chapter? If so, in what ways? If not, why not?

Even though this document comes from a Spanish source, think about what it might indicate about how Indians viewed the relationship between their religion and Christianity. How might this have affected the evolution of religion in the region?

The Text[‡]

The Spanish believed—and that must have been the case—that the demon entered that idol and would speak to them [the Indians]. The idol had created earth and brought forth and kept all that exists in it. Thus, in their language "Pachacama" means "creator of the earth." They also believed that with the arrival of the friars and their preaching it pleased God that some among them would be converted, and at that point Pachacama angrily went to the mountains or to hell, which he always carries with him, and for many days he would not speak to them. But seeing that this was a losing proposition, he decided to follow another path, and would appear to those whom he had frequented before, that is, the priests, whom he knows how to deceive, as has already been stated, and said to them: "I have been very angry with you, because you have left me and taken up the god of the Christians. But my anger is now past, because now the god of the Christians and I have agreed that you will worship and serve both of us, and it is pleasing for us that this be done." This shows that in order to carry souls away with him, this ill-fated idol is most clever and sly. He knew well that along this path and with such practice not only did he not lose anything, but he even gained much more. This was so because when people who were baptized were also worshiping the idols they were bringing greater offense to God, as well as greater torments for those who were thus deceived. And that the idol actually used this deviousness must be believed, for it is clear that our friars have researched the matter.

Source Four
The Virgin Speaks to Juan Diego

Introduction

It was December 1531 when the Virgin Mary appeared to Cuauhtlatoat-zin, an Aztec, who upon his conversion to Christianity in his early fifties was given the name Juan Diego. He was on his way to catechism class early that morning when he walked near Tepeyac Hill and heard his name called. There, on the hill, was a dark-skinned Virgin Mary dressed as an Aztec princess and speaking Nahuatl. Our source contains much of the legend of the encounter between the Virgin, the Indian, and the Spanish bishop.

As you read this account it would be helpful to remember several things: First, in pre-Columbian times, Tepeyac Hill had been dedicated to Tonan-tizin, the Aztec mother-goddess. Second, the Virgin Mary—in this form—has become closely tied with the Native population of Mexico. Third, the Virgen de Guadalupe, as this particular apparition is known, would become the patron saint of Mexico in 1746. Fourth, in 1810 she was on the battle standard carried by Miguel Hidalgo y Costilla's soldiers in their struggle for independence.

It is also important to keep in mind that there is no mention in any historical record from 1531 of such a meeting between the Virgin and Juan Diego. When a group dedicated to her is mentioned—certainly by the 1550s—her primary devotees were not Indian; they were Spaniards. And it was not until much later that veneration of her spread throughout New Spain, going beyond the confines of Mexico City and its environs. Yet she is quintessentially Mexican.

You will need to read the Virgen de Guadalupe's story from two perspectives. Let the first one be that of the legend itself. As you do so, ask yourself what it meant that the Virgin Mary chose to speak to an Indian and to speak in Nahuatl. How might an Indian under colonial rule interpret her actions? How might the bishop? What significance is it that she sought out a "poor man of the people" to instruct a powerful Spanish official? How might an Indian understand the bishop's actions in taking the cloak from Juan Diego and placing it in his private chapel?

The second approach to employ when reading this source is to consider the use of the legend. Why did she become the symbol of Mexico over against Spain? What might those seeking independence find in her to further their cause? What does Hidalgo's battle standard tell us about the use of religion and the church in the country's struggle for independence? Also, think about the fact that today the image of the Virgen de Guadalupe routinely appears in portions of the southwestern United States. What new role is she playing for her adherents?

The Text[§]

Here it is told, and set down in order, how a short time ago the Perfect Virgin Holy Mary Mother of God, our Queen, miraculously appeared out at Tepeyac, widely known as Guadalupe.

. . . a few days into the month of December, it happened that there was a humble but respected Indian, a poor man of the people; his name was Juan Diego. . . .

It was Saturday, not yet dawn; he was coming in pursuit of God and his commandments. And as he drew near the little hill called Tepeyac it was beginning to dawn.

. . . he heard someone calling him, from the top of the hill, someone was saying to him: "Juan, Dearest Juan Diego."

Then he dared to go to where the voice was coming from, his heart was not disturbed and he felt extremely happy and contented, he started to climb to the top of the little hill to go see where they were calling him from.

And when he reached the top of the hill, . . . a Maiden . . . was standing there, who spoke to him, who called to him to come close to her. . . .

He prostrated himself in her presence. He listened to her voice [her breath], her words, which give great, great glory, which were extremely kind, as if she were drawing him toward her and esteemed him highly.

She said to him, "Listen, my dearest-and-youngest son, Juan, where are you going?"

And he answered her: "My Lady, my Queen, my Beloved Maiden! I am going as far as your little house in Mexico-Tlatilolco, to follow the things of God (everything that makes God be God) that are given to us, that are taught to us by the ones who are the images of Our Lord: our priests."

Then she talks with him, she reveals her precious will, and she says to him: "Know, be sure, my dearest-and-youngest son, that I am the Perfect Ever Virgin Holy Mary, mother of the one great God of truth who gives us life, the inventor and creator of people, the owner and lord of what is around us and what is touching us or very close to us, the owner and lord of the sky, the owner of the earth. I want very much that they build my sacred little house here, in which I will show him, I will exalt him on making him manifest;

"I will give him to the people in all my personal love, in my compassionate gaze, in my help, in my salvation, because I am truly your compassionate mother, yours and of all the people who live together in this land, and of all the other people of different ancestries, those who love me, those who cry to me, those who seek me, those who trust in me, because there I will listen to their weeping, their sadness, to remedy, to cleanse and nurse all their different troubles, their miseries, their suffering.

"And to bring about what my compassionate and merciful gaze is trying to do, go to the residence of the bishop of Mexico, and you will tell him how I am sending you, so that you may reveal to him that I very much want him to build me a house here, to erect my temple for me on the plain; you will tell him everything, all that you have seen and marveled at, and what you have heard.

"And know for sure that I will appreciate it very much and reward it, that because of it I will enrich you, I will glorify you; and because of it you will deserve very much the way that I reward your fatigue, your service in going to request the matter that I am sending you for.

"Now, my dearest son, you have heard my breath, my word: go, do what you are responsible for [in this effort]."

And immediately he prostrated himself in her presence; he said to her: "My Lady, my Beloved Maiden, now I am going to make your venerable breath, your venerable word, a reality. I, your poor Indian, am leaving you for a while."

Then he came down (from the hill) to put her errand into action; he came to get onto the causeway, he comes straight to Mexico City.

When he reached the center of the city, he went straight to the palace of the Bishop, the Governing Priest, who had just recently arrived; his name was Don Fray Juan de Zumárraga, a Franciscan Priest.

And as soon as he got there, he then tries to see him; he begs his servants, his helpers, to go and tell him he needs to see him.

After a long time, when the Reverend Bishop ordered that he enter, they came to call him;

And as soon as he entered, first he knelt before him, he prostrated himself, then he reveals to him, he tells him the precious breath, the precious word of the Queen of Heaven, her message, and he also tells him everything that made him marvel, what he saw, what he heard.

And having heard his whole story, his message, as if he didn't particularly believe it to be true, he answered him, he said to him: "My son, you will come again. I will still hear you calmly, I will look at it carefully from the very beginning, I will consider the reason why you have come, your will, your desire."

39

He left; he came out sad, because the errand entrusted to him was not immediately accepted.

Then he returned, at the end of the day, then he came straight from there to the top of the little hill.

He had the joy of meeting the Queen of Heaven; there exactly where she had appeared to him the first time, she was waiting for him. . . .

"[Juan Diego reported:] The way he answered me, I could clearly see that he thinks your house that you want them to build for you here, maybe I'm only making it up, or that maybe it is not from your lips.

"I beg you, my Lady, Queen, my Beloved Maiden, to have one of the nobles who are held in esteem, one who is known, respected, honored, (have him) carry, take your dear breath, your dear word, so that he will be believed.

"Because I am really (just) a man from the country, I am a (porter's) rope, I am a backframe, a tail, a wing, a man of no importance: I myself need to be led, carried on someone's back, that place you are sending me to is a place where I'm not used to going to or spending any time in, my little Virgin, my Youngest Daughter, my Lady, Beloved Maiden. . . .

The Perfect Virgin, worthy of honor and veneration, answered him, "Listen, my youngest-and-dearest son, know for sure that I have no lack of servants, of messengers, to whom I can give the task of carrying my breath, my word, so that they carry out my will.

"But it is very necessary that you personally go and plead, that my wish, my will, become a reality, be carried out through your intercession.

"And I beg you, my youngest-and-dearest son, and I order you strictly to go again tomorrow to see the bishop.". . .

[The following day,] although he told him [the bishop] absolutely everything, and that in everything, he saw and marveled that it appeared with absolute clarity that she was the Perfect Virgin, the Kind and Wondrous Mother of Our Savior, Our Lord Jesus Christ.

Nevertheless, it still didn't happen (his message was still not believed).

He [the bishop] said that not simply on the basis of his [Juan Diego's] word would his petition be carried out, would what he requested happen, but that some other sign would be very necessary if he was to believe how the Queen of Heaven in person was sending him. . . .

[The Queen of Heaven instructed Juan Diego the following day.] She said to him: "Go up, my dearest son, to the top of the hill, to where you saw me and I told you what to do;

"There you will see that there are different kinds of flowers. Cut them, gather them, put them all together; then come down here; bring them here, into my presence."

Juan Diego climbed to the top of the hill right away.

And when he reached the top, he was astonished by all of them, blooming, open, flowers of every kind, lovely and beautiful, when it still was not their season, because really that was the season in which the frost was very harsh.

They were giving off an extremely soft fragrance; like precious pearls, as if filled with the dew of the night.

Then he began to cut them, he gathered them all, he put them in the hollow of his tilma [outer cloak]. . . .

And immediately he came back down, he came to bring the Heavenly Maiden the different kinds of flowers which he had gone up to cut.

And when she saw them, she took them with her precious hands.

Then she put them all together into the hollow of his tilma again and said: "My youngest-and-dearest son, these different kinds of flowers are the proof, the sign that you will take to the bishop.

"You will tell him from me that he is to see in them my desire, and that therefore he is to carry out my wish, my will.

"And you, you who are my messenger, in you I place my absolute trust.

"And I strictly order you that you only open your tilma alone in the presence of the bishop, and show him what you are carrying.

"And you will tell him everything exactly, you will tell him that I ordered you to climb to the top of the little hill to cut flowers, and everything that you saw and admired, so that you can convince the governing priest, so that he will then do what lies within his responsibility so that my temple which I have asked him for will be made, will be raised.". . .

When he arrived at the Bishop's residence, the doorkeeper and the other servants of the Governing Priest went to meet him.

And he begged them to tell him how much he wanted to see him, but none of them was willing. They pretended they didn't understand him, or perhaps because it was still very dark; or perhaps because they felt by now that all he did was bother them and keep on insisting, and their companions had already told them. . . .

For a long, long time he waited for his request to be granted. . . .

They went immediately to tell the Governing Bishop what they had seen, and how much the lowly Indian who had come other times wanted to see him, and that he had been waiting a very long time there for permission, because he wanted to see him.

And as soon as the Governing Bishop heard it, he realized that this was the proof to convince him to get started on what the humble man was asking him for.

He immediately ordered that he come in to see him.

And when [Juan Diego] had come in, he prostrated himself in [the bishop's] presence, as he had done before.

And again he told him what he had seen and admired, and his message.

He said to him, "Your Excellency, sir! I have done it. I have carried out your orders.". . .

And then he held out his white tilma, in the hollow of which he had placed the flowers. . . .

And just as all the different Castilian roses fell out upon the floor.

Then and there, the beloved Image of the Perfect Virgin Holy Mary, Mother of God, became the sign, suddenly appeared in the form and figure in which it is now, where it is preserved in her beloved little house, in her sacred little house at Tepeyac, which is called Guadalupe. . . .

[The bishop] untied Juan Diego's garment, his tilma, from his neck where it was tied, and on which the Queen of Heaven appeared, on which she became the sign.

And then he took it and placed it in his private chapel.

Source Five
A Scholar's View

Introduction

The encounter with the Americas posed profound questions for the Spanish world. As we have seen in our previous documents, the church and the state, often in concert, developed a variety of arguments to bolster the right to conquer and profit from the New World. Columbus's voyage posed no less a question for those immersed in theology and the study of theological constructs of the world. Perhaps chief among those dealing with the theological implications of the conquest and conversion of the Americas was Francisco de Vitoria, a professor at the Universidad de Salamanca, Spain's premier university. In the early sixteenth century, he and his students grappled with many of the issues concerning the New World, applying theological principles to ethical questions: Were the Indians human? According to Aristotle's definition, no. According to Vitoria, almost, but not quite. Does the pope have temporal powers over Indian lands? The church says yes; Vitoria says no. Does Spain have just cause for its conquest of the Indians? For the jurists, such as Palacios Rubios, yes. For Vitoria, no.

The excerpt that follows is Vitoria's refutation to the pope's claim to temporal authority and its extension to the lands of the "barbarian" Indians. Note that Vitoria followed the pattern typical of the age: thesis, antithesis, and synthesis. He posed a proposition with its supporting arguments (the thesis). He then presented the contrary arguments (the antithesis). Finally he drew his conclusion (the synthesis).

As you read Vitoria's words, think about the delineation he made between temporal and spiritual papal authority. How does that compare to what the pope himself assumed in the bull *Inter caetera* ("A Gift from the Pope")? What arguments might Vitoria's opponents use to support their position? In what ways might those arguments be advantageous to the conquering powers? On what basis did Vitoria attack the idea of the conquest? What, if any, arguments for conquest could follow from his views? Finally, imagine how the encounter might have been different if Vitoria's views had prevailed.

The Text*

The second reason that is given, often with great ardor, to justify the possession of those provinces, is the authority of the Supreme Pontiff.

They say that the Supreme Pontiff is the ruler of all the world, including in temporal matters, and therefore he could and actually has appointed the rulers of Spain as lords of those barbarians and regions.

On this matter several students of law hold that the pope has absolute and universal temporal jurisdiction over the entire earth, and they add that all authority of any other secular ruler comes from the authority of the pope. . . . On this matter, [canon jurist] Silvestre affirms great wonders, for instance, that the authority of the king and of every other who rules is delegated from the authority of the pope. That such authority comes from God through the pope and it is entirely dependent on the pope. That Constantine granted the lands to the pope as a sign acknowledging the temporal dominion of the latter, and in response the pope gave Constantine the empire, so that he might enjoy it in compensation. Furthermore, he declares that Constantine did not grant anything, but simply returned to the pope that which had been taken away from him. He claims that the reason why the pope does not employ temporal jurisdiction beyond the lands belonging to the church is not because he does not have authority to do so, but rather to avoid scandalizing Jews and therefore in order to promote peace among all. Likewise he goes on with many other foolish remarks and absurdities.

The entire argument of these people is that "Yours is the Lord's and all that is within it" and "all power has given to me in heaven and on earth," and that the pope is the vicar of God and of Christ. . . .

Having established this foundation, the defenders of this opinion claim: First, that the pope, as the supreme temporal lord, can declare the kings of Spain to be rulers of the barbarians, and second, that even supposing that this were not true, the barbarians' refusal to acknowledge the temporal power of the pope over them would be reason enough to declare war on them and to subject them to other rulers. Both things have taken place, for in the first place the Supreme Pontiff gave those lands to the kings of Spain. And in the second place, the Indians have also been told and explained that the pope is the vicar of God and his representative on earth, inviting them to acknowledge him as their superior. Therefore, if they refuse to accept this, this is already sufficient and just cause to make war on them, occupy their lands, etc. . . .

[To this Vitoria responds with several propositions.]

First, the pope is not the civil or temporal lord of the entire universe, if one speaks of civil power and dominion in the proper sense. . . . If Christ himself did not have temporal dominion . . . much less would the pope have such, for he is no more than his vicar. . . .

Furthermore, it may be seen that the pope is not lord of the entire earth, because the Lord himself said that at the end of the world, there would be "one flock under one shepherd." This clearly shows that at present not all the sheep belong to a single flock. . . .

Second proposition: Even if the Supreme Pontiff had such secular power over the entire universe, he would not be able to pass it on to secular princes.

This is obvious because if the pope had such power it would be part of the papacy itself, and the pope would not have the authority to separate it from his own authority, nor would he be able to take such authority away from his successor. A pope cannot be inferior to his predecessor. And if a pontiff were to give this authority to another, such a gift would be invalidated or could be withdrawn by the next pontiff.

Third proposition: The pope has temporal power in the realm of things spiritual, that is, in as much as such temporal power is necessary to administer spiritual things. . . .

The goal of spiritual authority is the final happiness, while the goal of the civil authority is social happiness. Therefore, there is no doubt that temporal is subject to spiritual authority . . . Indeed, no true Christian would deny that the pope has this authority. . . . I do not doubt even that likewise the bishops have temporal authority in their bishoprics, for exactly the same reason.

This may serve as a new argument favoring the first proposition, for if the pope were lord of the entire earth, the bishops would also be temporal lords in their bishoprics, for they too in their own dioceses are vicars of Christ. But this not even my adversaries would accept.

Fourth conclusion: The pope has no temporal power over those barbarians or over any other nonbelievers. This clearly follows from the first and third propositions, for the pope has authority only in spiritual matter . . . as may be seen from the words of St. Paul [1 Cor. 5:12: "What have I to do with judging those outside?"]. Therefore, nor does he have temporal authority.

From which follows this corollary: Even if the barbarians do not wish to acknowledge the dominion of the pope, this is no reason to make war on the barbarians nor to take their possessions. This is evident since such dominion does not exist.

This is clearly confirmed. For . . . if the barbarians do not wish to acknowledge Christ as their lord, that is not a sufficient reason to make war on them or to cause them any discomfort. Therefore, there is nothing more absurd than what these people teach, that even though the barbarians may reject the dominion of Christ with impunity, they are however forced to accept the dominion of the vicar under penalty of being forced to accept it by means of war, being deprived of their goods, and even condemned to torture or death.

Source Six
An Entire People in Hell?

Introduction

Father Antônio Vieira was angry; he was very angry that Sunday. In fact, he had been angry for so long that he felt compelled to accept an invitation to preach the first Sunday of Lent, 1653, in Maranhaõ, Brazil. It was no surprise that he was asked to fill the pulpit. After all, he was known as a great orator and statesman following his success as a preacher and his years of service to the Portuguese crown. But one can only speculate that the parishioners were not aware of Vieira's anger when they invited him. They were left in no doubt, however, once he began to preach on the temptations of Christ, for his anger was directed at them.

Vieira was a Jesuit, born in Portugal in 1608 but raised in the state of Bahia in Brazil. By the time he was in his late teens, he had taken his vows; and by the time he was twenty-seven, he was ordained as a priest. For the next few years he worked among the native population and with black slaves

45

before leaving for Portugal in 1641. Finally in 1652, he returned to Brazil primarily because he had overstayed his welcome in Portugal by advocating lenient treatment of Jewish converts to Christianity. His stay in Brazil was also cut short after that Sunday because of his outspoken advocacy for the Indian population; he left for Portugal once more in 1653. Vieira would return again to Brazil, where he spent the last sixteen years of his life—until his death in 1697—continuing his work on behalf of Brazilian Indians, especially Tupí-Guaraní speakers.

In that infamous Sunday sermon, translated below, how did Vieira see his responsibility as a preacher? Did he fulfill that responsibility? Vieira used the temptation of Christ from Matthew 4 as his text for the sermon. In relating that text to the lives of the colonists he both made an argument and rejected another. What injustice did he decry? For what was he pleading? As you read Vieira's condemnation of the Brazilian settlers, think about his view of the Native Americans and how that might have put him at odds with those who heard his sermon.

The Text[+]

Oh fearful day! Oh joyful day! We are at the day of the temptations of the devil, and in the day of the victory of Christ. The day in which the devil openly dares to tempt the very son of God, "If you are the son of God." Oh fearful day! If even God himself can be tempted, who will not fear being overcome? . . . There were three temptations with which the demon accosted Jesus. . . . Of all these temptations from the devil, I have chosen only one to be discussed today, because in order to overcome three temptations, one hour is little time. And how often an instant suffices to be overcome by them! The one I chose of the three was not the first, nor the second, but rather the third and last, because it is the greatest, because it is the most universal, the most powerful, the most befitting this land in which we are. . . . Let us begin by supposing that in his offer the demon was speaking truthfully and that he was able to give the world. Suppose further that Christ had not been God, but a mere man and so weak that he could or would fall before the temptation. I ask: if such a man were to receive the entire world and to remain its lord and in exchange for that would give his soul to the devil, would he be a good trader? Would this be a good deal? In another occasion Christ himself said: "What does it profit one to be lord of the whole world if one's soul is captive to the devil?" Oh divine word! Alexander the Great and Julius Caesar were lords of the world, but now their souls are burning in hell, and they shall burn for all eternity. . . .

46

How very different is the price that today the devil pays for souls, from that which he offered for them in ancient times! Now I tell you this on this our land! There's no market in the world where the demon can buy souls more cheaply. In our Gospel text he offered all the kingdoms of the world for a single soul. But in Maranhaõ the devil does not need to offer so much in order to buy all the souls. It is not necessary to offer worlds. It is not necessary to offer kingdoms. It is not necessary to offer cities, nor even towns or villages. All that the devil needs to do is to wave a thatched-roof hovel and two Tapuias [natives] [at you], and he will immediately be worshiped on bended knees: "All these I will give you, if you fall down and worship me," says the devil. Oh what a cheap purchase! A black man for a soul, and the latter blacker than the former! This black man will be your slave the few days that he will live, and your soul will be my slave for all eternity, for as long as God is God. This is the contract that the devil has made with you, and you not only accept this contract but even pay money for it.

Gentlemen, the Gospel forces us to enter into the gravest and most useful subject in this state, a subject which involves the salvation of the soul or the medicine of life. See how serious and how useful it is. . . . But because it is also the least appealing, I had decided never to speak to you of it, and for that reason also, never to climb to the pulpit. To climb to the pulpit in order to displease is not what I like to do and even less in the case of people for whom I desire all joys and all goods. But on the other hand to climb to the pulpit and not speak the truth goes against the office, against the obligation, against conscience. This is particularly so in my case, for I have spoken so many truths and with such freedom and to such great ears. For that reason I decided to exchange one service of God for another, and went out to teach the Indians in their villages.

I was following this resolution until Thursday, when some people whom I respect very much forced me to agree to preach in the city this Lent. I once promised to do so, and I have repented from it many times, because once again I found myself in the same perplexity. It is true that in the mind of those of good judgment there was no danger that they would suspect my good intentions. I now ask you: who is the better friend, one who warns you of danger or one who in order not to cause you pain allows you to fall into it? Which doctor is a better Christian: one who warns you of your death, or one who, in order not to cause you grief, allows you to die without the sacraments? All these things I thought within me and would not cease debating them. On Friday I went to say Mass for guidance from God in this tension, so that God would show me what would be to his greater glory. And upon reading the epistle, God told me what he wished me to do: ". . . cry out, oh preacher and cease not, raise your voice as a trumpet, undeceive my people, announce their sin to them, and tell them in what state they are." . . .

Do you know, Christians? Do you know, nobility and people of Maranhaõ, what is the fast that God wishes from you during this Lenten season? That you will untie the chains of injustice, and that you allow to go free those whom now you have as captives and oppressed. These are the sins of Maranhaõ. These are the things that God commands me to proclaim: "announce their stains to my people." Christians, God commands me to undeceive you, and on his behalf I do so. You are all in mortal sin. You all live and die in a state of damnation, and you are all going directly to hell. Already there are many there, and you also will be there with them soon if you do not change your life.

Then, God help me! An entire people in sin? An entire people in hell? Whoever is surprised by this does not know what unjust captivities are. . . .

What did God do, what took place, when the captive Israelites were fleeing and King Pharaoh himself went after them with all the power of his kingdom in order to return them to their captivity? The Red Sea was opened so that the captives could cross dry-footed (for God knows how to do miracles in order to free the captive). Do not think that the Hebrew people deserved this by reason of their virtue, for they were worse than those Tapuias. In a few days they would be worshiping a calf. And of the six hundred thousand who left, only two entered into the promised land. But God so favors freedom that what they did not merit because they were evil, they attained because they were unjustly held captive. After they crossed to the other side of the Red Sea, Pharaoh followed the same path which was still opened, with the sea to each side as if held by walls, and then the waters fell upon him and his army, and all were drowned. . . .

Anyone who holds and will not relinquish the freedom of others will certainly be damned. All, or almost all, in Maranhaõ are debtors who have taken the freedom and the services of others and, even though they could make restitution, they do not do so. Therefore, all or almost all are damned. Perhaps you will tell me that even in that case, these people did not care, or did not know, or that they will be saved by their good faith. I deny this.

. . . Some are condemned by their certitude, others by their doubt, and others by their ignorance. Those who are certain are condemned because they avoid restitution. Those who have doubts are condemned because they did not examine the matter, and those who are ignorant because they did not know what they had obligation to know. . . .

All the Indians in this state either serve as slaves or live in the villages of El-Rei as free, or they live as wild in their natural and greater freedom. People follow the rivers in order to go and buy or rescue them as they claim, giving the pious name of "rescue" to a sale that is forced and violent and that may well be done with a pistol aimed at their chests. As for those who serve you, all those in this land who are inherited, taken, or possessed in bad faith, would do much by forgiving you all this service that they have given you in the past. Even so, they would do it readily. However, after they have been told that such forgiveness is a condition for their freedom, some may decide voluntarily and spontaneously to serve you and remain in your house, because they have been doing domestic work and have grown up in your house and with your children. Such, if they actually wish to remain, may not be severed from your service. And what would be done with those who do not wish to continue in such subjugation? They would be forced to go to live in the villages of El-Rei, where they will still also serve you in a manner that we shall soon see. As to the wilderness, you could go in once a year in order to rescue those who are, so to speak, in chains, ready to be eaten, and those who have done such things will have that cruelty commuted into perpetual captivity. Likewise those who were sold as slaves without any violence on the part of their enemies, who were taken in just war, would also be captives. This would be judged by the governor of this state, the general overseer, the vicar of Maranhaõ in Para, and the prelates of the four orders: Carmelites, Franciscans, Mercedarians, and Jesuits. All who by the judgment of these people are declared to be truly captive will be distributed among the settlers for the same price for which they were bought. And, what will be done with those who cannot be proven to have been taken in just war? They will all be settled in new villages or divided among the villages that already exist. There, distributed like all the other Indians among the settlers [the Portuguese], they will serve them alternately for six months in the year, retaining the other six months to deal with their own work and families. In this manner, all the Indians in this state will serve the Portuguese, be it as their proper and complete captives, which is the case with those who are slaves, those taken in just war, and those who freely and willingly wish to serve, as was said earlier, or they may serve as half-captive, which is the case with all in the earlier and newer villages. For I know that even though they are free, for the good and the preservation of the state, they will be subject to serve and help us during half of the time throughout their lives. . . .

Let the world know. Let heretics and gentiles know. God was not deceived in making the Portuguese the conquerors and preachers of his holy name. Let the world know that there is still truth, that there is still fear of God, that there is still a soul, that there is still a conscience, and that self-interest is not such an absolute and universal master of all as it would seem. Let the world know that there are still those who, for the love of God and their salvation, trample on their own interests. Furthermore, gentlemen, this is not losing interests, but rather multiplying them, increasing them, planting them, and giving them out in usury. Tell me, Christians, if you have faith: the goods of this world, who gives and distributes them? You tell me that it is God. I therefore ask: What is the best way to move God to give you many goods, serving God or offending him? Obeying and keeping his law, or breaking every law?

. . . Lord Jesus, this is the spirit, this is the resolution on which from now on stand all your faithful Catholics. There is no one here with any other interest than serving you. There is no one here who seeks any other convenience than loving you. There is no one here who has any other ambition than being eternally obedient and surrendered at your feet. At your feet is the wealth, at your feet are the interests, at your feet are the slaves, at your feet are the children, at your feet is the blood, at your feet is life, so that you may do with all whatever is more fitting to your holy love. Is it not so, Christians? It is so. This I say and this I promise to God in the name of all. Victory therefore to Christ. Victory! Victory against the greatest temptation of the devil. Death to the devil. Death to his temptations. Death to sin. Death to hell. Death to ambition. Death to interests. And life only to the service of God. Life to faith. Life to Christianity. Life to conscience. Life to the soul. Life to the law of God and what it commands. Life to God. And may we all live in this life with great abundance of goods, particularly of the goods of grace.

3
SHAPING

Introduction

Several factors made life in the Americas fairly malleable, at least by Spanish standards. First, even after the conquest, the New World and its civilizations were largely unfathomable to the Spaniards, making it difficult to impose completely their culture on their colonies. Second, the Americas were quite far away from the center of colonial power, making the crown slow to respond to conditions in its colonies, thus in a sense liberating the colonies to respond to their own situations. Third, in the late sixteenth and early seventeenth centuries, there was an influx of settlers—some willing, others not—bringing with them all manner of differences. And fourth, those settlers fashioned lives that made sense to them in the reality that was the New World.

These factors made it impossible for Spaniards to replicate Spanish life in the colonies. The truth, however, was that "Spanish life" did not even exist in Spain. Attitudes, expectations, beliefs, and religious practice—among other aspects of life—varied widely in Spain, as they did in Latin America. But those who governed in the New World preferred to believe that there was one way to be Spanish. Life in the Americas would prove that belief to be fallacious.

The collection of documents we will examine in this chapter reveals how Spaniards in particular tried to understand, function within, or rail against the world they found in the Western Hemisphere. From a Jesuit priest trying to learn of—and share knowledge about—the world of the Indians, to a Mexican nun of Spanish extraction chafing at the gender confines of her world, to a Brazilian accused of witchcraft and tried by the Inquisition, we shall encounter people being shaped by the world around them as well as shaping the religious life they practiced every day.

Trying to understand the Indies was a task often undertaken by priests as they searched for the best way to convert the Indians. Our first source, "A Priest Reports," a selection from *Historia natural y moral de las Indias* (*Natural and moral history of the Indies*) by Jesuit José de Acosta, is the result of just such an effort. Acosta was charged by his superiors to gather information and observations about the Native Americans and their history. He could not, however, refrain from placing what he learned in the context of the conquest, as our source reveals.

The intersection between American reality and the Spanish world is also clearly exemplified in Source Two, "On Becoming a Saint." This is an excerpt from the ultimately successful process to canonize Martín de Porres (or Porras, as he is called in the document). A mulatto born in Lima, as a young man Porres was accepted into the Dominican order as a lay brother. There he was known for his kindness, humility, and charity. The testimonies given here bear witness not only to how a devout Catholic might cross the social and racial barriers of seventeenth-century Lima but also to how the church itself might unwittingly facilitate that crossing.

Boundaries, however, were not only along social or racial lines in colonial Latin America. Women, too, experienced enormous restrictions in their choices. Sor Juana Inés de la Cruz, the author of Source Three, "Theology in the Kitchen," was a woman who fought against the constraints placed on her by society, particularly those dictating that her intellectual gifts—which were quite prodigious—should be secondary to "womanly" virtues. These included traits such as piety, obedience, serenity, and subservience to males. But she routinely found men far less intellectually inquisitive than she. As we read this excerpt, we shall find once again that the church became a place in which social mores could be circumvented.

There was a boundary, however, that the church maintained much more vigilantly than it did that of male/female or black/white: that of the heretic and the apostate. Source Four, "The Inquisition at Work," is an excerpt from an *Auto de la fe* held in Lima, January 23, 1639. It outlines the charges, the findings, and the final disposition of an Inquisition case against Manuel Bautista Peréz, who was accused of being a crypto-Jew—that is, a Jew who had ostensibly converted to Christianity only to revert in secret to his old faith.

The Inquisition was not reserved solely for those who turned their backs on the Christian faith. Those who perverted it were equally—if not more so—subjected to the conforming powers of the church, although often given fairly mild sentences. Guiomar d'Oliveira of Brazil found that out. All she wanted was for her husband to love her as he once did. Her choice of remedy for her intolerable situation of a loveless marriage created another undoubtedly intolerable situation: a trial in front of the Tribunal of the Inquisition. Our reading, "Magic and Love," is her confession to the charges of witchcraft.

Our selections in this chapter reflect two distinct visions of religious practice in the Americas. The first is that of orthodoxy in which adherence to dogma and the "right" way is paramount. The second is one in which particulars of the faith (e.g., words uttered at a ceremony) are used as tools to achieve a desired outcome with little regard to orthodoxy. These sources also reveal ways in which the seventeenth-century church in Latin America was instrumental in creating the complex society of today's Latin America.

Source One
A Priest Reports

Introduction

The book *Historia natural y moral de las Indias* was nothing short of groundbreaking when it was published in 1590. Jesuit José de Acosta's compilation of his observations and knowledge gathered during his years in the Americas—fifteen in Peru and one in Mexico—immediately caught the European public's attention, and within a few short years it was translated from Spanish into several other European languages and Latin. Here was a book that explained the Indians in terms of their natural history (geography, climate, etc.) as well as in terms of their moral history (customs, mores, beliefs, etc.). It cautioned that ignorance of the Indians and their history had led to brutal, ineffective attempts at conversion. Only by understanding how to communicate in terms that were relevant to the "heathens" and "barbarians" whom the church was trying to convert would the conversion itself be true. In fact, Acosta's ideas were used by missionaries in regions of the world far from Latin America.

The selections below are from two different chapters in Acosta's book. The first comes from chapter "*Que es falsa la opinion de los que tienen á los Indios por hombres faltos de entendimiento*" (That the opinion of those who believe that the Indians are lacking in understanding is false). As you read this portion of the text, notice that Acosta is concerned with more than just conversion. Why else does Acosta believe it is important that Indians be understood as people of reason and intelligence? What attitude does he advocate toward the Indians?

The second selection is drawn from the chapter, "*De algunos milagros, que en las Indias ha obrado Dios en favor de la Fé, sin méritos de los que los obraron*" (On some miracles in support of the faith that God has worked in the Indies, without merit on the part of those who worked them) and includes accounts of God's intervention in the conquest when all seemed lost. Consider why Acosta would retell these incidents. How do they reflect the myth of the reconquest of Spain? How might these divine interventions assuage guilt over the conquest itself?

Acosta himself indicated that he was highly influenced by the writing of Vitoria—as were many of his fellow Jesuits. In these excerpts, where do you see Vitoria's influence? Where does he depart from Vitoria? And finally, how would you reconcile what we might call the "two faces" of the church reflected in Acosta's writing?

The Text*

Libro sexto capítulo primero (Sixth book chapter one)

(That the opinion of those who believe that the Indians are lacking in understanding is false.)

Having discussed the religion of the Indians, in this book I intend to write about their customs, policies, and government, with two ends in mind: the first is to correct the false opinion commonly held about them, that they are a brutish and bestial people with no understanding or with so little of it that it can barely be called such. The result of this error is that they receive many and profound injuries, being used as less than animals, and scorning any kind of respect that one could have for them. . . . I see no better way to undo this very injurious opinion than explaining the order and manner of living that they followed when they were under their own law. And although there were many things that were barbaric and without foundation, there were also many others worthy of admiration. The latter clearly shows that the Indians have a natural capacity to be well-taught and that to a large degree they are ahead of many of our republics. . . . The other end that may be attained by knowing the laws, custom, and policies of the Indians is to help them and to rule them by those laws, customs, and policies. Since in those things in which they do not contradict the laws of Christ and of his holy church, they are to be governed according to their own systems, which function as their municipal laws. By reason of this ignorance many previous mistakes have been made, for those who judge and those who govern do not know how they are to judge and to govern their subjects. Which, besides the injury and senselessness of what is done, results in grave loss, for we are hated as men who in everything, both good and bad, are and have always been against them.

Libro séptimo capítulo XXVII (Seventh book chapter 27)

. . . In the city of Cuzco, when the Spaniards were besieged and surrounded and in such a difficult situation that without the help of heaven it would have been impossible to escape, trustworthy people tell, and I heard them say, that as the Indians threw fire on the roof of the dwelling of the Spaniards, which is the place where the main Church now stands, and while the roof was made out of thatch straw which they call *chicho*, and while the torches that they threw were very big, still nothing burned or caught on fire because a Lady who was on high would put the fire out immediately. The Indians clearly saw this and declared it with great surprise. On the basis of the accounts of many and many stories that are told about it, it is known for certain that in several battles where the Spaniards were engaged, both in New Spain and in Peru, the opposing Indians saw in the air a knight with sword in hand, astride a white horse, fighting on the side of the Spaniards. This is the reason why the glorious apostle St. James has been held and still is held in great veneration throughout all the Indies. In other cases they saw in such conflicts the image of our Lady, from whom Christians of those regions have received great benefits. And were all of these stories of interventions from heaven to be told completely as they actually took place, they would result in a very long tale. It suffices to mention this in connection with the great mercy of the Queen of Glory to our people when they were sorely oppressed and persecuted by the Mexicans. All this has been said so that it be understood that our Lord has taken care to favor the Christians' faith and religion, defending those who follow it, even though they might not deserve such gifts and favors from heaven for reason of their works. In this connection, the things which the first conquerors of the Indies did should not be condemned as absolutely as some learned and religious men have done, no doubt with good zeal, but to an extreme. For, although most of them were covetous and uncouth and very ignorant of how they should act among nonbelievers who had never offended Christians, it cannot be denied that there were also on the part of the infidels many evil acts against God and against our people. These acts forced the conquerors to turn to sternness and punishment. Furthermore, the

Lord of all, even though the faithful were sinners, wished to favor their cause and their side for the good of the nonbelievers themselves who would later be converted to the holy gospel by this means, because the paths of the Lord are high and his ways marvelous.

Figure 3.1 The earliest biography of Martín de Porres was written by his fellow Dominican Fr. Bernardo de Medina some thirty years after Martín's death.

Source Two
On Becoming a Saint

Introduction

Trying to have someone canonized requires a great deal of patience. It took more than three hundred years for fray Martín de Porres to become the first black saint from the Americas. ("Fray" is the title given to men within certain religious orders, much like the English "brother.") In 1657, almost twenty years after Martín's death, permission was granted by the diocese of Lima to begin gathering evidence in support of the cause for his beatification, the first step toward canonization. Over the course of the next decade, testimonies from those who knew Martín or who had some divine experience of him were taken. Eventually an apostolic process (one conducted by the Vatican) was opened in 1678, resulting in Martín de Porres's beatification in 1837 and canonization in 1962.

Martín de Porres was the illegitimate, though recognized, son of a Spaniard and a free black woman. At a young age, Martín became a servant in a Dominican priory. Most likely because of laws barring those of mixed race from joining religious orders, Martín was never more than a lay brother, although there is some disagreement as to that. Nevertheless, his reputation for holiness, for fervent service to the order, and for skill as a healer spread widely throughout Lima. He continued his work with the poor of the city, founded orphanages, and created schools for poor children. He was also known for his profound humility in the face of cruelty even from other members of his own order and for his excruciatingly austere lifestyle, far beyond the standards of the day. He extended his healing to all who sought it, including animals. In one of the most loved stories about San Martín, he created a shelter for homeless animals and cured any that were injured or ill. At the time of his death in 1639, he was revered by many from all strata of society in Lima.

Below are three of the testimonies gathered in 1670: the first from a woman of some standing in the community as denoted by the title *doña*, the second from a fellow Dominican brother, and the last from a local laborer. The selections tell us much about how people in seventeenth-century Lima viewed holiness. What in Martín de Porres's life provided proof to his fellow Limeños that he should be canonized? Why would they go to such trouble for so long? In San Martín's time, race played an important part in Lima's social structure, yet he managed to transcend those barriers to heal the sick and to minister to rich and poor alike. How did the church provide him that chance? What about San Martín, as revealed in the testimonies, made it easy for some in white society to accept him while he lived and others to work for recognition of his saintliness after his death? What does that tell us about the intersection of race and the church? Remember, however, as you think on these issues, that San Martín was truly unique. His experience of acceptance—to whatever limited level it extended—was not that of most people of color in seventeenth-century Lima. Extreme forms of racism—both legal and *de facto*—were much more common, even for San Martín de Porres.

The Text[†]

Testimony of Doña Ursula de Medina, 1670

When she was approximately twelve years old, she attended the funeral of said venerable brother fray Martín de Porras, accompanying him with other women. And when she reached the cemetery of the convent, she perceived a very strong aroma that did not seem to come from this world. This witness says that when she entered the church she looked everywhere to see if there was anything that could produce such a scent and saw nothing. This led her to the conclusion that it came from the body of the said servant of God. She knows this and it is nothing but the truth publicly and widely known. On the basis of the oath that she had already made, after this was read, she affirmed and ratified it by signing it with her name.

Testimony of Fray Juan de la Torre, 1670

. . . On the second and other questions that were put to him, he said that what he knows is that around the year 1629, before the abovementioned servant of God fray Martín de Porras died, he knew him for all this time and saw in him a great holiness adorned by all sorts of virtues. He [Martín] was indefatigable in continuous prayer day and night and such a man of penance that he fasted throughout the year, excepting only Sundays. Every night he did scourge himself three times, and that for this he was entirely naked, spacing his lashes so that the penance would be more deeply felt.

His attire was most humble and poor, for he only wore a black woolen coat which reached to his knees and over that he wore the habit, with no undercloth that he wore next to his flesh because he preferred to be constantly surrounded by rough haircloth. And his bed was a coffin with a straw mat to serve as a mattress and a piece of wood as a pillow. And in spite of this rigor, he used this bed seldom, for most nights he would be content with a short nap on a wooden or stone bench at the feet of a patient. The witness said that he was convinced that fray Martín should be justly known as fray Martín of Charity, which he practiced with all sorts of people, feeling their needs and trying to help them with all care, solicitude, and diligence. He said that Martín shared so profoundly in the pain of humanity that half an hour before he died he was told that a black man was full of lice. When he heard this he was so disturbed that he repeatedly struck his breast: "fray Martín, where is your charity?" Thus, he felt the needs of others so deeply that even at the moment of his death he mourned them. And even with animals he was also very charitable, healing and feeding them. And in this regard many notable events took place.

This same witness declared that he had heard the now deceased Father fray Miguel de Mejorada, also of the Order of Preachers, say that when he was in the convent in Lima, he had an accident in which he was profusely bleeding from the mouth. When he went in quest of the servant of God, fray Martín de Porras, in the infirmary, so that he might heal him, he did not find him. After ringing the bell that was used to call the infirmarian three times, and still not seeing him, he went to the chapter house where Martín usually prayed. Before he entered there, the said servant of God said to him from inside, "Go to the water trough and go into it naked, and you will be healed." Said Father fray Miguel was puzzled that even though it was night and Martín had not seen him, he knew what his need was and told him how to remedy his illness. He went into the trough and was immediately healed.

Testimony of Joseph Pizarro, 1670

He said that what he has to declare is that when he was working in the convent as a carpenter joiner, he went, as he often did, to the cell of venerable brother fray Martín de Porras, between eight and nine in the morning to ask the friar to give him something to eat. As he arrived there, he saw that Martín left with some medications, so that he seemed to be on the way to heal somebody. This witness saw him enter a cell in the infirmary of the convent, where he was an infirmarian, and so as not to detain him with his own request, he let him go and decided to await him at the entrance to his cell, outside of it, for the door was open. And after he had been there waiting for him for some time, without any distraction he saw the said venerable brother fray Martín de Porras come out from his own cell, from the inside, calling this witness by name. Having seen this, the witness was overcome with awe, seeing that the venerable brother fray Martín de Porras was able to enter his own cell without the witness seeing him, for he had been awaiting him there. Martín gave him his food and the witness left. And in order to learn how said venerable brother was able to enter his cell, he examined and walked all around it in order to see if there was any other door through which he could have entered. He found that there was no other than the one main door where he had been waiting for Martín.

He also declared that when he told of this event to many people in the convent, they told him that this was nothing new, for the venerable brother would often appear without anyone knowing how he had entered. Every day he appeared in the novitiate of the convent, even when the doors were closed and at strange hours of the night, in order to meet their needs and cure their afflictions. He also knows that the venerable brother was a man of great charity, which he showed not only with his neighbors but also with brute beasts, for in many occasion he saw Martín returning from the street and bringing with him dogs that had been wounded or were ill, and bringing them to his cell. For these he cared with as much will and love as if they were rational beings. When they were healed he told them to leave, and they would obey.

Source Three
Theology in the Kitchen

Introduction

To this day Sor Juana Inés de la Cruz is perhaps Mexico's most loved poet of the Baroque era.[‡] Her work reveals the tensions she herself felt: reason and religion; male and female; obedience and rebellion. In her own day, she was known as a child prodigy. Years later, she was a great poet and intellectual who steadfastly pursued the life of the mind even while in the convent. Such a pursuit was deemed inappropriate for women, which may have led to her disregard for men.

She made her opinion of men clear in her seventeen-stanzas-long poem "Silly, you men," of which two stanzas are as follows.

> Silly, you men—so very adept
> at wrongly faulting womankind,
> not seeing you're alone to blame
> for faults you plant in woman's mind.
> . . . .
> With you, no woman can hope to score;
> whichever way, she's bound to lose;
> spurning you, she's ungrateful—
> succumbing, you call her lewd.[§]

Marriage was not an option Juana Inés would contemplate—unsurprising given her attitude toward men. By the age of sixteen she had realized that her only escape from the confines of matrimony was the convent, where she spent twenty-eight years until her death in 1695. Even there, she bristled at the limits placed on her.

Our selection is from her letter to "Sor Filotea." The letter, however, was not to another nun, as the title suggests, but was a response to an earlier letter received from the Bishop of Puebla, Fernández de Santa Cruz. He, along with her superiors in the convent and many of her fellow nuns, criticized her for her constant quest for knowledge—much of it scientific, but not exclusively so. Eventually she would be forced to surrender her beloved library, which she had accumulated while in the convent, and all her scientific instruments. In her spirited defense of her passion for learning, Sor Juana explained why she joined the convent, why she felt she *must* study, and what had been the response to her efforts.

As you read her words, remember that Sor Juana's choices represent what was possible for a woman in seventeenth-century Mexico. But also remember that she would be remarkable in any age. Not many of us would be fascinated by the physics of a ball thrown by children or contemplate the chemical change that occurs when an egg is boiled. This is exactly what she did when the church denied her the right to continue her studies. Think about what function the church played for Sor Juana. Did it provide an escape, or did it prove to be as much a prison as marriage? The reaction to her endeavors tells us that her superiors—male and female—as well as some of her sisters found her a threat. Why? What was it about her choices that challenged social norms to the point that she had to be suppressed? What world did Sor Juana Inés de la Cruz so want to see?

The Text*

. . . I joined the religious order even though I knew that there were in it many things—I refer not to the formal matters, but rather to those that are ancillary—that were abhorrent to my nature. Even so, given my total rejection of marriage, this was the least outlandish and the most acceptable that I could choose in matters having to do with the certainty of my salvation, which I sought. This being the most important goal, this was also the first consideration to which all the objections of my own nature had to bend and obey. Those objections had to do with wishing to live alone, not having to be forced into any task that would hinder my freedom to study, nor having to deal with community rumors that might impede the peaceful silence of my studies. This made me hesitate on my decision, until some learned people made me see that this was a temptation. I overcame it with divine help, and I took the solemn condition [of being a nun], which I now hold so unworthily. I thought that I would be fleeing from myself. But, woe is me! With me I brought my own self as well as the greatest enemy I had in this calling, an

61

enemy that is either a punishment or a boon given to me from on high. The result was that when this tendency to study was smothered or hindered with all the practices that the religious life requires, I would burst like gunpowder, and it became true of me that *privatio est causa appetitus* [privation causes desire].

I returned (although I have misspoken, for I had never abandoned it) to the studious task of reading and more reading, studying and more studying, with no other teacher than the books themselves. (Although while I say that this was a task for me, in fact it was a rest which I took whenever I could spare some time from my religious obligations.) One can imagine how difficult it is to study only on the basis of those writings without a soul, without the live voice and explanation of a teacher. But all of this toil I was able to bear with pleasure out of love for knowledge. Ah, if this had really been done for the love of God, as was proper, how great merit I would have gained! Even so, I attempted to raise my studies as much as I could, directing them to God's service, for my goal was to study theology. It seemed to me a great short-coming that, even while being a Catholic, one would not know all that can be attained in this life about the divine mysteries by use of natural, rational means. It seemed to me that, being a nun and not a secular woman, I should profess in letters, precisely for reason of my ecclesiastical state. This was even more being the daughter of a St. Jerome and a St. Paula, for it was a great fall from such great parents to have an idiotic child. This I said to myself, and it seemed to make sense, even though the truth was that I really wanted to embellish and applaud my own inclination, making what was a pleasure appear to be a matter of obligation.

. . . Since I owe to God a soft and affable nature—among many other moods—the nuns love me much. At the same time, since they are good, they do not consider my faults and enjoy my company. Knowing this and moved by the love which I have for them—with greater reason than they have for loving me—I very much enjoy their company. Thus, I would take whatever free time we had and devoted it to console them and to rejoice in their conversation.

. . . I confess that I am very distant from the limits of knowledge, and that I have tried to follow it even from a distance. But the result has been to get closer to the fire of persecution, the crucible of torment, and this to such a point that they [who are concerned about my studies] have even requested that I be prohibited from studying.

They once managed to convince a very holy and very simple-minded prelate, who believed that study was a matter for the Inquisition, and she ordered me not to study. I obeyed her for the approximately three months that she was in authority, and I did not take a book in hand. But not studying at all is not something that I can really do, nor could I do it then. Even though I did not study in books, I did study all the things that God has made, using them as letters, and the entire machine of the universe becoming a book. Nothing did I see without reflecting, nothing did I hear without thinking, and this even in the least and most material things, since there is no creature, no matter how low, in which one cannot acknowledge *me fecit Deus* [God made me]. There is not one of them that does not overwhelm the mind, if it is properly considered.

. . . For, what could I tell you, my lady, of the natural secrets that I have discovered while cooking? . . . Had Aristotle cooked, he would have written much more.

. . . For, why could not an elderly woman, learned in letters and of holy customs and conversation, take charge of maidens? But instead of that, these [maidens] are lost either by lack of teaching or by being taught by such dangerous means and by male teachers. It would be much less perilous for them to commit the indecency of sitting by an elder lady who would blush even when her own father looks into her face than for them to sit by a male stranger who deals with them with inappropriate familiarity and condescension. The shame itself of dealing with men and their conversation should be enough not to allow this. I cannot believe that this manner of teaching men and women can be without danger except in the severe tribunal of the confessional or in the distant teaching of the pope, or in the remote knowledge of books. But everyone knows that this is true and that it has to be allowed simply because there are no elder wise women. Therefore, it is a great evil that there are no such women. This should be a matter for consideration for those who, tied by the *Mulieres in Ecclesia taceant* [let women be silent in church*], condemn the notion that women might know and teach.

Source Four
The Inquisition at Work

Introduction

On January 23, 1639, a grand religious procession wended its way through the streets of Lima. Crosses held aloft led the group of penitents, for this was an *auto de la fe* (a procession of those found guilty—for any number of different crimes—by the Inquisition). These were followed by a large number of priests, sacristans, and other clergy. Then came the seventy-two penitents: first, those convicted of minor crimes, of witchcraft and bigamy; next the Judaizers in their *sambenitos* (penitential garb); and finally those who were to be "relaxed to the secular arm" (put to death by the government) because of their refusal to admit their crimes and accept reconciliation with the church. This last group had thick ropes around their necks, wore the sambenito with dragons, demons, and flames depicted on them, upon their heads was the *coroza* (conical-shaped hat), and they carried crosses. It was among this last group of eleven people that Manuel Bautista Peréz walked that day. He had been convicted of being an unrepentant crypto-Jew (a person converted from Judaism to Christianity but who then reverted secretly to the "old religion"), a charge that he resolutely denied.

The historical context for Manuel Bautista's trial and execution is important, for it provides us a broad perspective in which we can place what happened to him and others like him. The crowns of Spain and Portugal were united from 1580 to 1640. During that time, Portuguese—among them New Christians (converts to Christianity)—were allowed to travel freely within the Spanish empire, and many ultimately found their way to the New World. New Christians and their descendants, whether in the colonies or in the metropolis, were often suspected of not being "Christian enough." Prejudices against them were such that they were not allowed to hold certain public offices, could not join religious orders, and could not attend certain schools or pursue particular professions. Manuel Bautista Peréz must have felt he had escaped all of that oppression by living as an Old Christian in Lima, but then circumstances turned against him. The Dutch, who practiced religious tolerance, had occupied a portion of northeastern Brazil (Pernambuco), thereby opening that region to anyone from Holland. A sizable Jewish community made the transatlantic journey and settled there. Spanish authorities in Peru were sure that New Christians in Peru were conspiring with Jews in Pernambuco to overthrow the Spanish. Manuel Bautista Peréz got caught in the whirlwind of frenetic activities to tear out root and branch any Portuguese/Jewish threat.

Our source is the summary of the findings against Manuel Bautista Peréz. What was the evidence against him? As you read that evidence, search for other reasons why the state might have been interested in prosecuting Manuel Bautista Peréz. What threat might prominent New Christians face? How was religion used as a political weapon? What elements of the *Reconquista* myth do you see here?

The Text[5]

Manuel Bautista Perez is a New Christian in his entire lineage, . . . a resident of this city [Lima] married to his cousin Doña Guiomar Enriquez, who is a New Christian, and whom he brought from Seville, and living also with children in this city. Among the Hebrew nation, he is a man of great respect, taken as an oracle, and called the great Captain. He was always understood to be the leader in the observance of the law of Moses. The gatherings in which that law was discussed, and over which he presided, took place in his home. He had many spiritual books and discussed theologians of Portuguese background regarding several theological matters on which he gave his opinion. He was most ostentatious both in his person and in his wife, children, and home. The carriage in which he traveled was among the goods that the Inquisition took from him and was sold on the 19 of February of this year for 3,800 of today's pesos which come to 30,400 *reales*, which shows how rich and expensive it was. Manuel Bautista Perez was much esteemed by clergy, friars, and laypeople. In the royal university itself many writings were dedicated to him with much adulation and praise, and he was always given the foremost seats. Outwardly he seemed to be a great Christian, following the feasts of the most holy sacrament, hearing mass and sermons, particularly if they dealt with one of the stories of the Old Testament. He went to confession and took communion frequently, met with the rest of the church, and reared his children with priests as teachers (although he was so attached to his own land that he had them baptized by a Portuguese). Finally, he also performed such good deeds pertinent to a good Christian that he dazzled even those who were very attentive to make certain that there was no deception in such actions. But he was not able to do the same with the Holy Office of the Inquisition, which arrested him as a judaizing Jew on August 11 of 1635. Imprisoned and bereft of all goods, he was always negative. Seeing that he was being accused by more than thirty witnesses and that there was no way in which he could refute the evidence of guilt, in his very cell he tried to kill himself with a dagger. He stabbed himself six times in the belly and the groin, producing two or three deep wounds. He wrote in code to his brother-in-law Sebastian Duarte who was in his own cell, persuading him to renege on his confession and to remain obdurate, with the result that the said Sebastian recanted and took the attitude that led to his death, always claiming outwardly that he was a Catholic, while it was most evident that he was a Jew, for he believed that by doing it secretly he was able to fulfill the observance of the law. He was turned over to the secular arm for his resistance and punished with the confiscation of all his property. He gave signs of his depraved soul and Jewish deceitfulness in the kiss of peace that he gave to his brother-in-law Sebastian Duarte, after having been turned over to the secular government, in his scaffold, and also in the signs of wrath which he gave with his eyes to those of his own house and family who had confessed. And he was there wearing a sambenito, heard his sentence with much severity and majesty, and died impenitent, asking the executioner to do his work.

Source Five
Magic and Love

Introduction

By all accounts, marriage was supposed to be a blessed union, filled with love, happiness, and children, or so the sacrament of marriage seemed to imply. That was not the case for Guiomar d'Oliveira of Brazil. Her marriage was a source of pain and heartache for her. So she turned to an old friend from Lisbon, Antonia Fernandes. Unfortunately, Antonia's solution was to invoke the devil and to use potions—solutions that, for the most part, Guiomar embraced.

Our selection below is from Guiomar's confession to the Inquisition in 1591. We—and most likely she—do not know who her accusers were. She also probably never saw the witnesses brought against her. And while she indeed learned the final disposition of the case, we do not have that information. What we do have is a summary of her words and her explanation as to why she chose to follow her friend's suggestions.

Summaries of Inquisition trials were compiled by scribes present during the interrogation. These documents follow set patterns, with the accused being asked set questions, and are not verbatim accounts of answers. These types of documents pose unique issues for historians. We must remember that Guiomar's responses were summarized by a male working for the Inquisition. While seeing Guiomar's world through the prism of an interlocutor may distort the picture, we can nevertheless learn much about the place of religion in daily life.

As to the outcome of her trial, an intense level of repentance and confession of an accused would often mitigate the punishment: death or not; permanent banishment or exile for a set number of years; or any combination of banishment, public penance, loss of privilege. But in the vast majority of cases, if a person was found guilty, at the very least, that person's personal property would be confiscated, and he or she would be forever "stained," as would any relative.

As you read the selection below, consider why Guiomar would risk the wrath of the church in order to pursue black magic. Historian Carole Mycofski tells us that persons in the colonial period often turned to magic—love magic in particular—in order to attain the promises that the church made to them through its sacraments. Was Guiomar doing that? If so, how and why? In her confession, the accused tells us that there were actions Antonia wanted her to take but she refused. Why? For these two women, what role did the demons play? What power did they understand to reside in holy oil or in the Eucharistic words of consecration? What does that say about their understanding of the power of demons? What role did the church play? What was religion's relevance to Antonia and Guiomar?

The Text*

She says that she is of Old Christian stock from the city of Lisbon, daughter of Isabel Jorge and her husband Christóvão d'Oliveira, who was a sailor in ships to the Indies, both dead at approximately thirty-seven years of age, and she is married to Francisco Fernandes, a Christian of old stock and a carpenter living in this city.

In her confession she declares that some four years ago a woman who was punished by the Inquisition and whose name is Antonia Fernandes, an Old Christian, . . . a widow of some fifty years of age, came to this land. She [Guiomar] declares that approximately fifteen years back she knew this woman, then living in . . . Lisbon, working in a tavern . . . and having been punished [by the Inquisition] for hiding her own daughter, whose name was Joana de Nobrega.

Thus coming here, Antonia befriended Guiomar on the basis of their former acquaintance in Lisbon. So Guiomar and her husband took her in and honored her by giving her a bed and many meals in their home. As this friendship grew and Antonia saw that Guiomar's marriage was not going well, she told Guiomar that she spoke with the demons and ordered them to do as she pleased, and that once she told them to kill a man, and they did. This was because she in turn did what they asked of her, and in Santarem she had given the demons a writing in blood from her finger in which she gave herself up to them. They then taught her many incantations to achieve what she wanted. She told Guiomar that if she wished she would perform and teach her witchcraft with which to make her marriage good, and Guiomar consented.

Antonia then taught her to take three hazelnuts (or instead of hazelnuts, three of the pine nuts from this land that serve as purgatives) pierced with a pin and emptied. Then they should be filled with hair from all her body, and pieces of her fingernails and toenails, and of scrapings from the soles of her feet, and with a piece of the nail of Antonia's small right toe. Having thus filled the said nuts, Guiomar was to swallow them, and having expelled them she was to give them to Antonia. All of this Guiomar did, and Antonia told her to wash the three nuts that she had swallowed and expelled, and took them and turned them into a powder that Guiomar placed in a pot of chicken soup. . . .

Likewise the said Antonia Fernandes gave her other powders of unknown origin and others of the bones of a dead person, which she then mixed in wine and gave to her husband Francisco Fernandes so that he would be her lover and they would be happily married. She did all these things even though the said Antonia Fernandes had told and declared that they were devilish and that she had learned them from the demons.

She also taught her that she had learned from the demons that a man's semen given to him to drink would make him love her very much. It was to be the semen of the man whose love one sought, taken from the woman after carnal union. Such semen, given to drink to the same man who ejected it, would make him love greatly. And this she did, giving it to her husband to drink mixed in wine.

Being guilty of all these things and of performing such witchcraft in the hope that they would avail her even though they were demonic, she begs forgiveness and mercy from this tribunal. . . .

Antonia also encouraged Guiomar to have a dishonest relationship with a clergyman in the cathedral of this city, and that she would perform acts of witchcraft so that this would happen. After they became lovers she would be able to get from the clergyman some of the baptismal oils, which she [Antonia] greatly desired in order to give them to the demons. She also wished to anoint her lips with such oils, so that when she was in intercourse with laymen she would kiss their mouth (or, in the case of clergy or friars, their tonsure) and after that they would never be able to leave her. But Guiomar would not agree to this.

She also taught her that if in the midst of a dishonest carnal act one would pronounce into the mouth of the other the five words of consecration—*hoc est enim corpus meum*—this would make that other person stronger with love. . . . But she [Guiomar] never did this.

68

Figure 3.2 An *auto de la fe* included a procession of penitents and accompanying clergy. The former were marked by distinctive signs such as the garments known as *sambenitos*. There was also ample seating for spectators.

4
REFORMS

Introduction

At the end of the seventeenth century, Spain was in turmoil; indeed all of Europe was. The War of Spanish Succession engulfed the continent in war. At stake was who would control Spain and all its patrimony: the Indies, the Philippines, the Spanish Netherlands, Sicily, Naples, and others. Among the rival factions, the one that ultimately prevailed would control significant portions of Europe and have the power that came with the wealth of the Indies. When the war ended in 1713, Spanish lands were divided among many of the claimants, and the Bourbon Dynasty of France came to power in Spain itself. Its challenge would be to confront the changes occurring throughout the continent during the eighteenth century. Perhaps the most profound intellectual challenge for Europeans came from the Enlightenment, which would lead to constitutions, to new attitudes toward the church and science, and, once in the hands of the masses, to revolutions. But in Spain the Enlightenment had less of an impact than in other parts of Europe. In a very real sense Spain was an amalgam of royal absolutism and selected Enlightenment thought: increasingly powerful monarchs coupled with loss of status of the church, an emphasis on economics, and the search for practical solutions to the country's troubles.

As a whole, the Bourbons of the latter half of the eighteenth century brought some of the most profound changes to affect Spain and its American colonies. Our study of the reforms of the 1700s will begin with "The Royal Throne and the Holy See," a series of selections from the agreement on the *patronato real* signed by Spain and Rome in 1753. Through this document, Ferdinand VI asserted his royal patronage over the church in Spain and its colonies. In real terms it meant that the king named all the candidates for ecclesiastical benefices of any size in the Spanish domain. The *patronato real* was certainly a very successful salvo by the crown for control of the church. Within a few years, there would be another, and this one came from Charles III, perhaps the most effective of the Bourbon kings and the one principally responsible for what are known as the Bourbon Reforms.

Rivals to the monarchy who commanded much of the loyalty of the people, who controlled immense wealth, and who had sworn allegiance not to the king but to the pope were not to be tolerated. In 1767, Charles rid himself of those rivals, namely, the Jesuits. Source Two, "Cloak and Dagger," is the order issued throughout the Spanish realm for the expulsion of the Jesuits. For several reasons, the king viewed that religious order as one filled with troublemakers of questionable loyalty to the crown. This document reveals the extent of the secrecy the crown employed to ensure its instructions were followed by local government officials in order to minimize conflict and disruption.

Controlling ecclesiastical appointments and ridding the kingdom of recalcitrant Jesuits were not the Bourbons' only forays into control of the church. With the promulgation in 1776 of the *real pragmática*, or royal pragmatic (Source Three, "Who Can Say, 'I Do'?"), the crown asserted control over marriage, specifically who could marry whom and who had the right and responsibility to approve of such unions. No longer did the church, often in the form of parish priests, have the final say. That right now rested with parents or guardians. Families often used marriages as a tool in cementing political and social alliances, in preserving wealth, and in accumulating power. Many a parish priest, though, was more interested in the parties' willingness to marry: Were the two people involved being coerced? Was this a marriage of choice? Charles III clearly believed that parents were more useful proxies for building the social order he wanted than was the church.

Often, however, conflicts between the church and the state took on a local flavor. In Source Four, "Correction or Abuse?" a 1780 letter written by the Franciscan Junípero Serra to Governor Don Felipe de Neve of New Spain, we can see that the two disagreed on the treatment of Native Americans. Serra, who led the expeditions that established missions in what is today California, argued for the continuation of harsh treatment of wayward Indians. Neve clearly did not think such actions were either beneficial or effective.

Our final source, "Travels in Brazil," is an excerpt from Henry Koster's observations of Brazil at the beginning of the nineteenth century. His account of the interaction among the church, slaveholders, and slaves reveals how slave masters used religion and the church to sanction and justify a "peculiar institution" just at the time that much of Western Europe was moving toward abolition. (England outlawed the importation of slaves to its colonies in 1807, ultimately ending the practice in the mid-1830s. Other countries followed suit. Brazil would not eliminate slavery until 1888.)

As you read through these selections, consider how the church's power manifested itself in progressively smaller arenas: the entire Spanish empire, specifically the institution of marriage, upon one religious order, within missions in California, and finally within slavery and with the individual slave. Also think about how that power was curtailed in some places and remained steadfast in others. The eighteenth century was clearly a time of reform for the church.

Source One
The Royal Throne and the Holy See

Introduction

By the middle of the eighteenth century, the Bourbons were exerting control over the Spanish realm and its various institutions, including the church. The power, wealth, and independence of the church ran counter to the growing trend toward regalism, in which supremacy in all matters was concentrated in the monarch. Efforts to bring the church, and by extension Rome, to heel began with the first Bourbon, Philip V, but it would be Ferdinand VI, almost fifty years later, who would succeed. By 1753, the Spanish crown had successfully negotiated a new concordat—after several others—on the *patronato real*, clarifying its right of presentation or nominating individuals for ecclesiastical appointments. While the right was of nomination, in fact, as the pope would choose only from the names given to him by the Spanish crown, in effect the king chose the church hierarchy of his realm.

This new version of royal patronage over the church extended the king's rights to all but fifty-two benefices, and those were in Spain itself. The crown now claimed its right to name those who would fill ecclesiastical posts in terms stronger than in any previous concordat. Spain had succeeded in curtailing Rome's power in the Indies, at least in terms of the church hierarchy.

A few years later (1768), in a consultation between Charles III and his council, the aims of controlling the church were made clear:

> In such remote countries [the Indies] the bases of a well observed Religion are the strongest bonds to maintain people in subordination; therefore, the clergy, secular as well as regular, having the most influence on the masses, should be placed under orderly surveillance by the Government, with healthy principles of obedience and love to Your Majesty, and the aim of educating and strengthening this way of thinking, as well as educating the Regulars, and the natives and residents in the Indies.*

As you read this document, consider what interests were being guarded for the crown, for the clergy, and for the pope. Where do you see the crown claiming its power over the church? What did the crown have to gain? Much of this source refers to monetary compensation for the pope. Why would the crown be willing to pay the church so much money? What does that willingness tell you about what the crown expected to gain in return? Finally, think about what the role of the church, its power, and its wealth must have been for the crown to go to such efforts to curtail it.

The Text†

Since there is no doubt that the Catholic Monarchs of the Spains have the royal patronage, that is, the right to nominate those who will occupy archbishoprics, bishoprics, monasteries and benefits as written and appraised in the books of the Ministry as may become vacant in the kingdoms of the Spains; since this right is supported by bulls and apostolic privileges and other reasons that have been given; and since there is no doubt that the Catholic Monarchs have the right to nominate those to occupy those archbishoprics, bishoprics, and benefits that become vacant in the kingdoms of Granada and of the Indies, as well as those to occupy other positions, it is hereby declared that the royal crown will remain in peaceful possession of the right to nominate occupants in the case of vacancies, as has been done up to now. And it is also agreed that those nominated to occupy archbishoprics, bishoprics, monasteries and benefits will continue to receive from Rome the necessary bulls, in the same manner and fashion in which it has been done until now, without any changes. . . .

Third. That the practice will continue of conferring parishes and other positions of pastoral care through a process of competition. This will be done not only in the case of parishes that become or have been vacant, but also in the case of new ones. In every case the right of presentation belongs to the king, and the ordinary in charge of the diocese or other jurisdiction will receive in nomination the name of the person whom the patron considers most worthy among three whom the synodal examiners have considered most fitting and approved for the care of souls. . . .

Seven. That in order to safeguard the ordinary authority of bishops it is agreed and declared that, even though the rights of nomination, presentation, and patronage have been given to the king, this is not to be understood as conferring either him or his successors any ecclesiastical jurisdiction over the churches included in these agreements, nor over the persons presented or nominated for the various churches and benefits. Those people presented or nominated by the king for these churches and benefits will be just as subject to their respective ordinary supervisors as all others. They must not claim any exception from that jurisdiction, except in those cases when the supreme authority of the Roman pontiff, as shepherd of the church universal, has over all churches and ecclesiastical persons, and excepting also the royal prerogatives that pertain to the crown as a consequence of the protection which the crown offers, particularly over churches under royal patronage.

Eight. Since his Catholic majesty considers that the rights of patronage thus granted to him and to his successors would leave the apostolic see and chancery without the use of the income of these positions, which would produce a heavy burden on the pontifical treasury, the king decides to give to Rome by way of recompense, and only once, a capital of 310,000 Roman *escudos* which will be placed at the disposal of his Holiness. On the basis of three percent, this capital will produce an annual income of 9,300 *escudos*, which has been determined to be the product of all the rights hereby granted. . . .

Likewise, his Majesty the Catholic King, by reason not only of the devotion to the Holy See which he has inherited but also of the particular affection in which he holds the sacred person of His Beatitude, has agreed to provide a onetime help which will at least in part lessen the burden on the pontifical treasury of the expenses of the ministers named above. Therefore he commits to sending to Rome 600,000 Roman *escudos*, which at three percent will produce an annual income of 18,000 *escudos*. . . .

And his Majesty, as a gift to the Holy See, commits to deposit in Rome a onetime donation of a capital of 233,333 Roman *escudos* to be placed at the disposal of His Holiness. This amount, at three percent, produces an annual income of 7,000 *escudos*. Furthermore, his Majesty agrees that in Madrid 5,000 *escudos* will be assigned every year to be placed at the disposal of His Holiness in order to support the apostolic nuncios.

Source Two
Cloak and Dagger

Introduction

If one were a mid- to late-eighteenth-century Spanish monarch trying to amass power, surely one would rid the realm of any rivals, even if those rivals were found within the church. Charles III was just such a king, and the Madrid riots of 1766 gave him the excuse he needed to expel the Society of Jesus, a religious order for which he held profound animus.

Jesuits swore allegiance to the pope, not the king. They controlled enormous wealth, and they had been implicated, however erroneously, in a Guaraní Indian uprising in Paraguay. Their place within Spanish territory was tenuous at best. In fact, Charles was not the first European monarch to expel the Jesuits. Portugal expelled the order in 1754 and France in 1762. It was only a matter of time before they faced a similar fate in Spain, and that time came in 1766.

In that year, riots gripped Madrid, spreading to other Spanish cities. More than likely, those conflicts were the result of a failing economy and rising food prices. Nevertheless, a report—written by advisors to the king who shared his view of Jesuits—detailed the causes of the uprising and laid them squarely at the Jesuits' feet. This was just the excuse the king needed. By February 1767, Charles had issued the decree ordering the ouster of all Jesuits from every corner of Spain and its kingdoms.

As you read this source, pay special attention to the secrecy that surrounded the expulsion of the Jesuits. Why was that necessary? What did the crown fear? What does that fear on the part of government officials reveal about the place of the Jesuits in the Spanish world? Why would it be dangerous for the public to know what was happening? The document also makes it clear that secular clergy were to take control of the educational institution previously run by the Jesuits. (Secular clergy are priests who are not also members of a religious order; regular clergy are.) Why would Charles trust the secular clergy and not the regulars? How might the expulsion of the Society of Jesus function as a tool of control over the entire church? Finally, as you read this source, think about what motives are implicit.

The Text[‡]

Instruction for Those Commissioned to Execute the Sequestration and Occupation of the Goods and Properties of the Jesuits in These Kingdoms of Spain and Adjacent Islands, According to What Has Been Decided by His Majesty

This instruction shall remain sealed until the day prior to its implementation. The executor of the instruction will be well informed of each of its headings, and will then, without letting it be openly known, take charge of the troops present or nearby, or if not, he is to find other sources of help that he considers satisfactory. Then with valor, boldness, and caution, before the day dawns he will take possession of the roads leading to the house or houses of the Jesuits. To this end, the previous day he will seek to learn by himself what is the layout of these institutions, both inside and out. This practical knowledge will make it easier for him to prevent anybody from going in or coming out without his knowledge.

The executor will not let anybody know about his plans until early in the morning, before the doors of the Jesuits are opened at the normal time. At that point he will use some pretext to arrive before such opening, giving orders so that his troops or helpers will take possession of all the entrances, and he will not allow the doors of the church to be opened, for this is to remain shut this particular day and as many as necessary while the Jesuits are still within the compound.

His first step will be to gather the entire community, not exempting even the brother who does the cooking. To that end he will require in the name of His Majesty that the Superior ring the interior private bell that is used to summon their gatherings. And thus, in the presence of the notary in charge and with paid secular witnesses, he will read the Royal Decree of sequestration and occupation of all the properties, writing down the names and ranks of all the Jesuits present.

He will require them to remain in the chapter house and will learn who among them are permanent residents of that house and who are passing by. Regarding the latter, he will inquire what their places of residence are. He will make a list of the names and addresses of those lay people who serve the house either living in it or attending during the day. He will not let those who live in the house depart, nor will he allow those who only work during the day to enter, except for the most serious reasons.

He will then proceed to the actual sequestration with particular care. Having previously acquired the keys, with great caution he will take possession of all the valuables of the community and everything else of importance that may be there, either in deposit or as rents received.

Within twenty-four hours, beginning from the time of the announcement of the sequestration, or in any case as soon as possible, all the Jesuits from each of the houses are to be moved to temporary holding places or houses of residence that will be set for them. The necessary means of transportation will be taken from the town or its vicinity.

Each of these houses of residence will be under a special commissioner named by myself, whose responsibility will be to tend to the Jesuits until the time when they can leave the kingdom by sea, and meanwhile to make sure that they have no communication with the outside by either written or spoken word. Such communication will be forbidden from the very first moment when these steps are taken. They will be told so by the executor who has responsibility for each house. Even the least transgression in this regard will be dealt with through the most exemplary punishment.

There may be some elderly or ill Jesuits who cannot be moved immediately. In their case, the necessary time will be allowed until they improve or perish from their affliction. In any case, no fraud or collusion will be allowed in this regard.

In those towns in which there are Jesuit houses or seminaries of education, at the very instant when the Jesuit directors and teachers are deposed, they will be substituted by secular clergy who do not belong to their order. This will be done until the necessary information is available to determine how these schools are to be run. The purpose is that these substitutes will make it possible for seminaries and schools to continue. As to secular teachers, nothing will be changed in their teaching responsibilities.

Source Three
Who Can Say, "I Do"?

Introduction

How often have parents disagreed with their children's choice of marriage partners! It is an age-old point of contention, particularly during those times when marriage functioned in large part as a political, dynastic, social, or economic tool. Obviously such considerations were most often the purview of those social classes and families for whom sheer survival was not the primary concern. Nevertheless, the choice of a spouse also had profound implications for society as a whole—at least that is what Charles III of Spain thought. In 1776, he issued a royal pragmatic (an official decree that becomes the law of the land) requiring parental consent before any marriage of those younger than twenty-five could take place. At last, parents had veto power over a child's choice of marriage partner, and, as defined by the Pragmatic, the objection was to be based on inequality. That is not to say that parents or guardians did not exert enormous control and power prior to the Pragmatic, but now they had legal recourse if a child acted against his or her parents' wishes. Before the Pragmatic, a priest in any parish could perform a marriage as long as both parties agreed to it, or he could refuse to consecrate a marriage if either party was unwilling. In either instance, he need only consider the desires of the proposed bride or groom. And if there was a conflict between parents and their offspring, it was an ecclesiastical court that would decide the matter. Now, the desires of the children were secondary to those of the parents, and the latter used their newfound legal power with abandon.

In using it, parents tended to stray from the new ruling's strict definition of "inequality," which was limited to racial differences: black with white or Indian with black (not white with Indian). Rather, parents also used the idea of inequality to refer to those they deemed to be morally or socially inferior. The secular courts, which now heard the cases pitting children against their parents and which required parents to state their reasons for objections, tended to support the parents' position, no matter their definition of "unequal." Furthermore, as ideas of race and class became increasingly solidified over the course of the eighteenth century, the law also evolved. By the early nineteenth century, parents no longer had to state the reasons for their objections. With the sole exception of performing the marriage, the church no longer had a voice in who married whom.

In our first document for this chapter we saw how the Bourbon kings of Spain were increasing their control over the church in general, ensuring that Rome did not interfere in the workings of the state. As you read this document, think about the reasons why the state wanted to wrest control over marriage choices from the church. Why was the crown so interested in assuring that it was parents who made choices about marriages? Consider the fact that controlling marriage choices is a form of social control. In what ways was the crown reinforcing social structures? What social order did the crown want to support or create? Why do you think Charles III saw the church as incapable of maintaining the "desired" society? What points of tension between the church and the state are revealed by this document? What might have been happening to make such a decree necessary in the eyes of the state?

The Text[§]

Taking into account the consultations of my Councils of Castile and of the Indies regarding the law of marriage issued on 23 March 1776, as well as later orders and resolutions and various reports that I have received, I order that neither sons of less than 25 years of age, nor daughters younger than 23, no matter of what social condition, will be able to marry without permission from their fathers, who will have no obligation to give reason nor cause for their refusal to allow such a marriage. Sons who are 25 years of age, and daughters of 23, shall be free to marry as they choose, without having to ask advice nor consent from their father. If there is no father, the mother will have the same authority, although in this case the sons and daughters will have the freedom to decide on their marriage a year earlier, that is, a male at 24 years of age and a female at 22. If there is no father or mother, the paternal grandfather will have the same authority. The maternal grandfather will have it in cases in which there is no paternal grandfather. But in this case, the minors will have the freedom to marry two years before those who have a father, that is, the males at 23 and the females at 21. If there are neither parents nor grandparents, the guardians will have the authority to oppose the marriage of minors. And if there are no guardians, the judge of the area will have this authority. These will have to explain the reason for their opposition. But in this case, the males will be free to marry at 22 and the females at 20. Those who [because of their social status] must only marry with my permission, or by requesting it from the chamber, from the governor of the Council or from their respective judges, and who are younger than the appointed ages, will only be granted such license after their parents, grandparents, or guardians have also agreed, explaining why such permission has been granted. And the same official permission must be obtained by those who are above the ages already mentioned, expounding the circumstances of those whom they wish to marry. Nevertheless, the parents, grandparents, and guardians of those who are below these ages will also have to give cause for not consenting to the marriages which they seek. If they belong to the class that requires my royal permission, they may come to me or to the governing chamber of the council or to those who have such an obligation, so that by means of the reports which I may receive the license may be granted or denied so that these marriages may take place. . . . Ecclesiastical vicars who authorize the marriage of those who are not qualified as stated above will be exiled and all their possessions will be taken. Those who join in such a marriage will also suffer the same penalty of exile and confiscation of property. No ecclesiastical or secular tribunal in my kingdoms will accept any marriage not celebrated by people capable of marrying according to the requisites, as attested by a public document. . . . All marriages that have not yet been contracted upon the publication of this my royal decree will obey it without seeking to change, interpret, or comment on it in any other way. . . . Given in Aranjuez on 10 April, 1803. . . . This decree is to be published in Madrid and in all my cities and places in my kingdoms, in the accustomed form, and I charge archbishops, bishops and other ecclesiastical prelates who are in ordinary jurisdiction over their respective dioceses and territories, and to their officials, representatives, vicars, fiscal promoters, parish priests, and their representatives . . . and any others having to do with this decree, that they observe and execute it as stated without allowing any pretext contradicting what is ordered in it, for this is my will. . . . I, the King.

Figure 4.1 Recumbent Christ in the church of San Sebastián, Álvaro Obregón, México. No matter what the king decreed or said, the heart-broken appealed to the suffering Jesus for intercession. The many hearts are signs of either requests or thanksgiving.

Source Four
Correction or Abuse?

Introduction

Tension between the state and religious orders did not end with the expulsion of the Jesuits. In fact, they continue—off and on—to this day. In our fourth source, we see more of the strain that arose between governing officials and religious orders during the colonial period. In this case, it is between Don Felipe de Neve, the governor of Las Californias (Alta California and Baja California), and Fray Junípero Serra, a Franciscan friar sent to establish missions in Alta California. Initially it had been the Jesuits who were charged with such endeavors. Following their removal from the empire, however, Charles III designated the Franciscans to go into the northwestern portion of his American colonies.

In May 1769, Serra, five other friars, and a band of explorers celebrated mass in San Diego. By December of that year, they had arrived at San Francisco Bay. Eventually, there would be twenty-one permanent missions in Alta California. Following the establishing of these missions were the Spanish settlers who populated the region already occupied by perhaps as many as three hundred thousand Native Americans.

It should come as no surprise that the confluence of these three groups created tension not only among themselves but also with Spanish officials, usually located far away. The letter we have before us now is one in a long series of communications between Neve and Serra and focuses on Indian self-government. From the letters we know that Neve had much more faith in the Native Americans' ability to "manage satisfactorily" their own affairs than did Serra. Specifically, the governor trusted the Indians' right to hold elections for their own leaders, known as *alcaldes*. Serra disagreed. Yet in this letter, Serra claimed that the governor had changed his views and that he now believed the Indians incapable of holding successful elections for their own officials.

As you read this letter, think about reasons why the government might have wanted to limit the friars' involvement with the elected officials of the Indian community. How did Serra justify his actions? What does that justification reveal about his attitude toward the Indians? How does what you see here compare to what you saw in "A Tragedy in Pictures," in chapter 1? Why was Serra so concerned about Indians deserting the mission and moving to the mountains? What economic impact might such desertions have had for the friars? What other controls did Neve want Serra and the other religious to relinquish? Why? How did Serra defend his Franciscan community against Neve's charges? Why would Serra employ that particular defense?

A statue of Junípero Serra stands in the United States Capitol's Statuary Hall representing the state of California. He was chosen by the state because of his tireless work in bringing the missions, and the many important cities that sprang from them, as well as the diverse agricultural products he introduced to the region. Yet, there is much controversy and debate over this choice. Why do you think that is the case? On what side of the debate would you stand? Why?

The Text*

Letter written January 7, 1780 by Fray Junípero Serra, Franciscan priest, to Don Felipe de Neve, Governor of California

Hail Jesus, Mary, Joseph!

Colonel and Governor Don Felipe de Neve.

My dear Sir:

. . . I put it down that the high ideals which Your Lordship entertained in their [the Indians'] regard were responsible for the hopes you formed. But now that we have seen them frustrated, I take it, in consequence, that, as you rely on us for the good conduct of the elections, so you should likewise leave to us the guidance, correction and the direction of those who are elected. In that case it might be that the new ones would turn out better than the first group. . . .

Baltasar, while in office as *alcalde*, once aware of his privileges and exemption from correction by the Fathers, began to do just as he pleased. He had a son by one of his relatives, and had a California Indian flogged because he carried out an order from the Father missionary, as I reported to Your Lordship at the time. There is no need to speak of his neglect of duty while in office. And now, everyone sees and knows in what circumstances he is living—deserter, adulterer, inciting the people here, meeting personally those who leave here with permission, and thereby trying to swell the numbers of his band from the mountains by new desertions of the natives of this mission.

Since this is the state of affairs at present, can there be any doubt that if with the newly elected, we try to introduce the so much needed betterment in the behavior of the people here, it will happen that one day, because they are punished or reprimanded, another day, because they fear punishment, and yet another day, because they have friends over there, little by little they will flee there, and that it will multiply our enemies as I said? And while the situation appears to be as I have described it, it also would seem that the best method to rid ourselves of all annoyances would be the previous arrest and punishment of the entire group of malcontents. . . .

In your aforesaid letter, Your Lordship pays homage to the religious belonging to these missions—God repay you for it—and you add: "With the elections and the establishment of a New Commonwealth, His Majesty's designs will have been carried into effect, as far as these countries are concerned. And, guided by our more seasoned experience, the natives of these parts will, in the course of time, develop into useful vassals for our religion and for our State."

Such is the desire we all foster, Sir, and we hope to accomplish it not from any capabilities or efforts of our own but with the help and grace of God. To His Divine Majesty belongs all the glory for having brought this ambitious scheme to full realization in the missions of the Sierra Gorda, which His Majesty—God keep him—had been pleased to entrust to our Apostolic College of San Fernando. Everyone in the country knew of our good work, and the Court knew it. And, of the religious who worked there for not a few years, there are today seven, laboring in the work of conversion in these new territories. Now those of us who worked in that mission field know that as soon as any Indian fled to the woods and a religious wanted to go in search of him—it was an occurrence that happened frequently—there was never anyone to make objections; an escort was always supplied for the reason that, there, the soldiers were militia-men, and were not paid a salary.

And in the matter of correcting the Indians, although we allowed them the distinction and title of being governors, *alcaldes* and *fiscales*, nevertheless, when it appeared to us that punishment was deserved, they were flogged, or put into the stock, according to the gravity of their offense. In consequence, they took particular pains to carry out their respective duties. And the diligence I have observed, in all parts of the Kingdom which I have visited, among such officials, in the fulfillment of orders from their missionaries or pastors, is a proof to me that everywhere the same method should be observed. For instance, one day in Acayucán, a big town in the diocese of Oaxaca, I saw, with my own eyes, punishment such as this inflicted on an Indian governor, in front of the church.

The parish priest, the first vicar, and four other assistant priests—all of them priests of such high character as I would wish to see every parish in the Kingdom manned by—were present to witness it. Furthermore, there were two companions of mine and myself—all three engaged in giving a mission in the town. One of the audience, too, was the *alcalde mayor*, who, ordinarily, would hand the staff of office to the Indian governor. But no difference was made, or special treatment given, because of his rank. And I feel sure the same is true in most parts of the Kingdom.

That spiritual fathers should punish their sons, the Indians, with blows appears to be as old as the conquest of these kingdoms; so general, in fact, that the saints do not seem to be any exception to the rule. Undoubtedly, the first to evangelize these shores followed the practice, and they surely were saints.

In the life of Saint Francis Solano, who has been solemnly canonized, we read that, while he had a special gift from God to soften the ferocity of the most barbarous by the sweetness of his presence and his words, nevertheless, in the running of his mission in the Province of Tucumán in Peru—so we are told in his biography—when they failed to carry out his orders, he gave directions for his Indians to be whipped by his *fiscales*.

Now the *alcaldes* are likewise sons to the missionary Fathers, and as such they are likewise under their care. Seeing that they are no less in need of direction, correction and training, I do not see by what law, or what line of reasoning, it can be argued that they should be exempt.

The whole world is aware of the fact that, when the famous Fernando Cortés permitted himself or, to speak more accurately, saw to it that he should be flogged by the Fathers, in full sight of the Indians, he took this course of action not merely to impress those who had no staff of office, but to set an example to all. The lesson he wished to teach was that, no matter how distinguished any Indian might be, he never would be on an equal footing with himself. And yet, they saw him subject himself to this humiliating treatment.

For these and other reasons, it was always a cause of surprise to me to observe that Your Lordship should consider this practice among other evil customs which the Fathers from San Fernando passed on to the Reverend Dominican Fathers in Old California [now Baja California]. The Fathers of our Order, without any doubt, were practicing what they knew from before, and in that lies the whole explanation.

I am willing to admit that in the infliction of the punishment we are now discussing, there may have been inequalities and excesses on the part of some Fathers and that we are all exposed to err in that regard. But that argument equally applies to those who are not *alcaldes*. Now, in respect to both classes, the good standing in which we are universally regarded may be gathered from the consideration that when we came here, we did not find even a single Christian, that we have engendered them all in Christ, that we, everyone of us, came here for the single purpose of doing them good and for their eternal salvation; and I feel sure that everyone knows that we love them.

Source Five
Travels in Brazil

Introduction

Like many well-to-do nineteenth-century Europeans, Englishman Henry Koster ventured far from home. At sixteen years of age, in 1809, he set sail for Brazil, where his father had business ties, and there he would remain until 1815. His keen observations, both of flora and fauna as well of society and culture, were put to good use when he published his travelogue, following his return to England. At the time, travel accounts were often met with great popularity—such was the curiosity and sense of adventure among the general public.

In this excerpt from Koster's accounts, we examine his observations about the intersection between slavery and Catholicism. As you read, remember that like the Aztecs who recounted their creation story to Fr. Bernardino de Sahagún (chapter 1, "Ancient Beliefs"), the information we have is filtered through the eyes of a European and, in this instance, intended for an inquisitive European readership. How would that context affect what Koster wrote? What do you think he might have missed or misinterpreted? How are we, as twenty-first-century readers, to understand his words? In what places might we "read between the lines"?

Once again, we must read a source from two distinct perspectives in order to mine as much as we can from it. First, as you read the document, remember who wrote it and its audience. Second, use the information Koster actually gives us and analyze it with the first perspective in mind. From his viewpoint, how were religion and slavery reconciled? What role did he see Christianity playing in the lives of the slaves? He wrote of the Christian church existing in an "impure state." What evidence did he give of that?

Koster also remarked on baptism. How was it used to define humanity? What does the combination of baptism with branding on the chest tell us about the expected connection between faith and subjection to Spain? In earlier readings, particularly the *Requerimiento* (chapter 2, "Justifying the Unjustifiable"), the Christian faith and subjugation were linked. How are the attitudes in that sixteenth-century document similar to or different than those expressed by Koster?

Koster also wrote of ways in which slaves co-opted Christianity for themselves, primarily through the religious brotherhoods. Where do you see evidence of syncretism? What connections do you see with the story of the Virgen de Guadalupe? What advantages might the slaves have experienced through the brotherhoods? What role did these play in the lives of the slaves?

It was the slave owner, however, who most benefited from the nexus of the church and slavery. In what ways? How did the masters use the church to their advantage in terms of their enslaved population? How did the church itself function as slave owner? And this brings us back to our first question: How were religion and slavery reconciled?

The Text[+]

All slaves in Brazil follow the religion of their masters; and notwithstanding the impure state in which the Christian church exists in that country, still such are the beneficent effects of the Christian religion, that these, its adopted children, are improved by it to an infinite degree; and the slave who attends to the strict observance of religious ceremonies invariably proves to be a good servant. The Africans who are imported from Angola are baptized in lots before they leave their own shores, and on their arrival in Brazil they are to learn the doctrines of the church, and the duties of the religion into which they have entered. These bear the mark of the royal crown upon their breasts, which denotes that they have undergone the ceremony of baptism, and likewise that the king's duty has been paid upon them. . . .

The slaves are not asked whether they will be baptized or not; their entrance into the Catholic church is treated as a thing of course; and indeed they are not considered as members of society, but rather as brute animals, until they can lawfully go to mass, confess their sins, and receive the sacrament.

The slaves have their religious brotherhoods as well as the free persons; and the ambition of a slave is very generally aimed at being admitted into one of these, and at being made one of the officers and directors of the concerns of the brotherhood; even some of the money which the industrious slave is collecting for the purpose of purchasing his freedom will oftentimes be brought out of its concealment for the decoration of a saint, that the donor may become of importance in the society to which he belongs. The negroes have one invocation of the Virgin (or I might almost say one virgin) which is peculiarly their own. Our Lady of the Rosary is even sometimes painted with a black face and hands. It is in this manner that the slaves are led to place their attention upon an object in which they soon take an interest, but from which no injury can proceed towards themselves, nor can any through its means be by them inflicted upon their masters. Their ideas are removed from any thought of the customs of their own country, and are guided into a channel of a totally different nature, and completely unconnected with what is practiced there. The election of a King of Congo . . . by the individuals who come from that part of Africa, seems indeed as if it would give them a bias towards the customs of their native soil; but the Brazilian Kings of Congo worship Our Lady of the Rosary, and are dressed in the dress of white men; they and their subjects dance, it is true, after the manner of their country; but to these festivals are admitted African negroes of other nations, creole blacks, and mulattos, all of whom dance after the same manner; and these dances are now as much the national dances of Brazil as they are of Africa. . . .

The slaves of Brazil are regularly married according to the forms of the Catholic church; the banns are published in the same manner as those of free persons; and I have seen many happy couples (as happy at least as slaves can be) with large families of children rising around them. The masters encourage marriages among their slaves, for it is from these lawful connections that they can expect to increase the number of their creoles. A slave cannot marry without the consent of his master, for the vicar will not publish the banns of marriage without this sanction. It is likewise permitted that slaves should marry free persons; if the woman is in bondage, the children remain in the same state; but if the man is a slave, and she is free, their offspring is also free. A slave cannot be married until the requisite prayers have been learnt, the nature of confession be understood, and the sacrament can be received. . . .

The sugar plantations which belong to the Benedictine monks and Carmelite friars, are those upon which the labour is conducted with the greatest attention to system, and with the greatest regard to the comfort and ease of the slave. I can more particularly speak of the estates of the Benedictine monks, because my residence at Jaguaribe gave me daily opportunities of hearing of the management of one of their establishments. . . .

The slaves of the Jaguaribe St. Bento estate are all creoles, and are in number about one hundred. The children are carefully taught their prayers by some of the elder negroes, and the hymn to the Virgin is sung by all the slaves, male and female, who can possibly attend, at seven o'clock every evening; at this hour it is required that every person shall be at home.

. . . Almost every description of labour is done by piece-work; and the task is usually accomplished by three o'clock in the afternoon, which gives to those who are industrious an opportunity of working daily upon their own grounds. The slaves are allowed the Saturday of every week to provide for their own subsistence, besides the Sundays and holidays. Those who are diligent fail not to obtain their freedom by purchase. The provision-grounds are never interfered with by the monks, and when a negro dies or obtains his freedom, he is permitted to bequeath his plot of land to any of his companions whom he may please to favour in this manner. The superannuated slaves are carefully provided with food and clothing.

. . . The conduct of the younger members of the communities of regular clergy is well known not to be by any means correct; the vows of celibacy are not strictly adhered to. This circumstance decreases the respect with which these men might otherwise be treated upon their own estates, and increases much the licentiousness of the women. . . . The monks allow their female slaves to marry free men, but the male slaves are not permitted to marry free women. Many reasons are alleged in favour of this regulation. One is that they do not wish that a slave should be useless in the way of increasing the stock of the plantation; likewise the monks do not wish to have a free family residing among their slaves (for obvious reasons), which must be the case if a man marries a free woman; they have less objection to a man, because he is during the whole of the day away from their people, or is perhaps employed by the community, and thus is part dependent upon it, and he merely comes to sleep in one of the huts; besides, a stranger is contributing to the increase of the stock.

5
TURMOIL

Introduction

As you may recall from the last group of readings, during the eighteenth century the church in the Americas underwent a great many changes, losing much of its independence and power to a more powerful state. Nevertheless the church remained a tool of the state. In the nineteenth century we see the church grappling with different problems.

The nineteenth century opened with many of Spain's American colonies gaining their independence. As is often the case, institutions that thrived during the colonial period were frequently the target of repression and anger once independence was achieved. In some of our readings in this chapter we will see the church, in the form of an encyclical from Pope Pius VII and in the regulations governing Cuban slave owners, struggling to assert its power and guard its place in the society. Yet in other selections the church is clearly "on the run." Many of the new governments of Latin America turned against the church and the colonial systems of which it was a part. Clearly, the church's continued support of old social orders and cultural patterns, even after independence, put it at odds with many of the liberal movements of the nineteenth century. (A word of caution: Nineteenth-century "liberalism" is not the same as modern-day "liberalism." The earlier version of liberalism included a belief in a written constitution, in basic human liberties, and in a *laissez-faire* attitude toward the economy. Likewise, it held that all were equal before the law, an assumption that went against the old privileges [*fueros*] that the church and other sectors had enjoyed for centuries. Fueros allowed certain groups to be held accountable to their own laws and judged by their own courts, not by those of the country. This effectively put the members of those groups beyond the laws enacted by the state.)

During the nineteenth and early twentieth centuries, the Catholic Church in Latin America had to find new ways to make its presence felt in society while, paradoxically, continuing to represent tradition and authority. It was not lost on the new governments of the region that the church could be an effective tool to maintain power, as it had been for the colonial authorities. By laying claim to what they called *patronato nacional*, states were trying to assert their version of the *patronato real* that the crown had enjoyed during the colonial period. They declared they had authority over the church as heirs to the Spanish empire that Charles III had created.

Source One, "Submit and Be Good," is Pope Pius VII's 1816 encyclical *Esti longissimo terrarum*. This was his effort to encourage Catholics throughout Latin America to remain loyal to the Spanish crown during the wars of independence. Undoubtedly he feared that independence would bring further loss of power for the church. Our second source, "*El Supremo*'s Temper Tantrum," is part of a letter from José Gaspar Rodríguez de Francia, the ruling caudillo of Paraguay from 1816 to 1840, to Bishop Don Fray Pedro García de Panes. It reveals the extent to which a government would go to suppress a "meddlesome" church. But Source Three, "A Slave Code," promulgated in 1844 for the planters in Cuba, tells us that the church continued to be a powerful tool in the hands of the dominant social class.

Source Four, "Faith in a Healer," is a collection of testimonials written on behalf of healer Miguel Perdomo Neira. It puts a twist on the idea that it was only the old, elite order that espoused traditional patterns. Here it was the masses who supported a continuation of some colonial ways, particularly regarding medicine and healing. These sources do remind us that facile explanations rarely give us complete pictures.

Source Five, "An Alternate Creed," and Source Six, "A Last-Ditch Effort," are both from Mexico. Perhaps more than most other Latin American countries—but by no means the only—Mexico's church suffered many vicissitudes after independence and into the twentieth century. Sometimes, the church was favored by the government. Other times, it became the object of suppression. These two documents reveal the contempt with which the church was held by more radical forces at play in the country as well as the church's efforts to maintain some semblance of control.

As you read these sources, remember that even after independence the church was very often supported by those who had been in power during the colonial period. In which documents and in what ways is that evident? What tools did the church use to bolster its power? What tools did secular society use to bolster its own power?

The church's alignment with this wealthy class continued well into the twentieth century. Why would that be the case? Yet, simple assumptions as to which portion of society took which "side" belie the complex reality of the period. Thus, after all the efforts to suppress its presence in society, the church continued to have power, albeit often not as the holder of that power but rather as the weapon of the powerful.

Source One
Submit and Be Good

Introduction

Pope Pius VII had to do something. The Spanish king needed his support in the wars of independence, which were taking place in the American colonies. If only the pope would condemn the struggles, then many loyal Catholics would surely work to suppress the rebellions. Pope Pius thought so. In 1816, he issued an encyclical calling the bishops and archbishops of Latin America to encourage their parishioners to remain loyal to Spain.

In truth, the pope had little choice. If he did not declare his alliance with the cause of the crown, then a schism with Spain would surely occur. For all his attempts to find the way most advantageous to the church, however, Pius VII would ultimately have to come to terms with the failure of his efforts. Good Catholics fought in the wars of independence. In some cases, priests were the leaders of the cause against Spain, and symbols important to the church, such as the Virgen de Guadalupe in the case of Mexico, were used to break the ties to the Old World.

As you read this source, try to determine what it was that the pope wanted. How did he understand the role of the church in the independence process in Latin America? Why would he have thought it necessary to issue such an encyclical? What do his actions indicate about his assumptions about the nexus of faith and politics and about the role of the church in everyday life? What did all this portend about how people in Latin America might view the role of the church after independence? Also ask yourself what the encyclical shows about the relationship between the Spanish crown and the papacy. How did that relationship differ from what we have seen in previous documents? How was it the same? At what points do you see the role of the church shifting?

The Text*

Venerable brethren Archbishops and Bishops, and beloved children of the clergy of Catholic America, subject to the king of Spain. Pius VII, pope. Venerable brethren and beloved children, greetings. Although a long distance of lands and seas separate us, we are well aware of your piety and your zeal in the religion we profess. Venerable brothers and beloved children, this is well known to us.

And since among the most beautiful and important precepts of this religion is the one that prescribes submission to higher authorities, we have no doubt that in the upheaval in those lands that have been so bitter to our heart, you have constantly inspired your flock to abhor such sedition.

However, since in this world we represent the god of peace, who in order to relieve humankind from the tyranny of demons announced peace through his angels, it has seemed proper to us, following our apostolic role, to encourage you even more, even though you do not need it with this letter to make every effort to destroy to its very root the tares of sedition that the enemy has sown in those lands.

Venerable brothers, you will easily achieve this holy end if each of you most zealously shows your flock the terrible and most grave cost of rebellion, expounding the virtues of our beloved son in Christ, Ferdinand, Catholic king of Spain as well as yours who seeks above all the faith and happiness of his subjects. Finally, this will be accomplished if they are shown the sublime and immortal examples that Europe has received from those Spaniards who forsook life and property in order to show their invincible adherence to the faith and their loyalty to their king.

Therefore, venerable brothers and beloved children, who seek to respond willingly to our paternal exhortations and wishes, ever most strongly commending the loyalty and obedience due to your king, this do for the good of the people entrusted to you. Increase the grace that both our sovereign and we bestow on you. And your efforts and care will receive in heaven the reward promised by the one who declares that peacemakers are blessed and God's children, and which in heaven will be fulfilled. Meanwhile, we convey to you with the greatest love our apostolic benediction, assuring you of the most complete success in this fruitful and important enterprise.

Issued in Rome in Santa Maria Maggiore, with the Fisherman's seal, on the thirtieth of January of 1816, and the sixteenth year of our pontificate.

Source Two
El Supremo's *Temper Tantrum*

Introduction

By most accounts, Dr. José Gaspar Rodríguez de Francia was a bit beyond the pale. His tight-fisted control of Paraguay for almost twenty-five years brought dramatic and, in some instances, devastating changes to the country, at least from the perspective of the Roman Catholic Church. Espousing Enlightenment ideals, Francia seems to have embraced most heartedly its dislike of religion. As the country's first post-independence ruler, he abhorred the church's tie to the old colonial elite and its effort to preserve traditional ways. But it was clear from early in Francia's rule that he held a special animus for the church, particularly religious orders. His first action directed against the church was to deny clergy the right to participate in politics, which—as we have seen in earlier documents—was something priests routinely did. He also demanded that members of religious orders swear allegiance to the state and that such orders could only be governed by those who were Paraguayan-born. Francia would eventually declare that the religious orders served no purpose other than to protect loose-living friars from the laws of the land. By 1824, he had confiscated lands belonging to religious orders, forced the secularization of their members, and taken control of their finances.

Lest one be left with the impression that Francia's actions were directed only at the church, we must remember that "*El Supremo*," as he called himself after becoming dictator for life in 1816, largely isolated his country from the outside world. Although he encouraged internal trade and development, he eschewed foreign contact. He established a secret police to monitor his supposed enemies and executed those whom he suspected of disloyalty. His actions, however, failed to raise much public outcry because his attacks were directed primarily at those who had controlled the country prior to independence. The poor and the peasants found little to dislike.

As you read Francia's letter to the bishop written in 1816, remember that it was written at the beginning of his dictatorship. From the tenor of the letter, what might have been his relationship with the bishop? Were they cordial to each other? Were they working together to control the orders? Why did he attack the religious orders so early in his rule? What was he trying to achieve by controlling the election of monastic officers? What was the point of freeing religious orders from obedience to their superiors in other countries? Think back to Charles III's attempts to wrest control from the church. How do

Francia's efforts compare? Did they have the same goal? Whose approach do you think might have been the more successful?

The Text[†]
Excerpt of letter from Dr. José Gaspar Rodríguez de Francia to the Most Reverend Don Fray Pedro García de Panes, July 2, 1816

Most illustrious sir:

So that the religious communities are able to have a stable government in the future, and may thus be able to respond in a timely fashion to the urgent needs of their houses, convents, services, and economic management without the obstacles, difficulties, and dissension that have taken place in the present conditions, on this date I have decided on a resolution determining what follows:

"Since the present circumstances and the state of the republic require that the religious communities existing within its territory be exempt from all interference or exercise of jurisdiction by prelates or foreign religious authorities from other countries, I forbid and where necessary I undo and make null any use of authority or supremacy of the abovementioned authorities, judges, or prelates residing in other provinces, or any governments over the religious convents of this republic, their communities, individuals, goods of any kind, fraternities, or brotherhoods attached to them or depending upon them. In this manner the abovementioned religious communities are free and absolved of any obedience and are to be entirely independent of the authority of provincials, chapters, or general visitors from other states, provinces or governments, thus forbidding that they may receive from them titles, appointments, charters, waivers, or any document establishing order, lodging, government, discipline, or any other religious policy. Therefore from now on they will be ruled with this independence, following their own rules and institutions under the direction and authority of the most illustrious bishop of this diocese in matters both spiritual and temporal, being managed with the following precepts:

The communities of each order will gather in their respective convents in this city every three years in order to elect their local prelates and to appoint those to serve in the various positions within each house or convent—after the usual exams or proof of ability and suitability. And all those friars who are in sacred orders will be able to hear confessions, as long as this is possible and compatible with the needs of the convents. Those elected as well as those named to such positions will not be able to fill them until they obtain approval from this government.

Each of these chapters will be presided over by the meritorious and most suitable friar of the particular order, who will be named by the illustrious bishop. When such chapters are to be called, prior permission will be obtained from this government, so that, taking into account all that is convenient, a decision will be made as to which magistrate or other qualified person will be named to attend in representation of the supreme authority so as to keep order.

In these chapters the decisions will be made declaring the graduation of the friars, their retirement, and the customary privileges within each order. These will take effect after being confirmed by the illustrious bishop.

When it is necessary to fill positions between the triennial chapters that are hereby established, the following procedure will be observed: Due notice must be given to the most illustrious bishop. The council of seniors or the fathers of the council of the principal convent—presided over by a respected local prelate—will verify that the necessary formalities have been fulfilled. Any appointments suggested by the council must be approved by the prelate and by the government. These councils will also have authority to grant admissions and retirements as needed, for which all that will be required is the approval of the most illustrious bishop.

In general, the association or incorporation of religious coming from other provinces or governments into the houses of orders already existing within the territory of the republic will be allowed, always after the approval of this government.

The taking of the monastic habit and the subsequent professions will be granted by the triennial chapters, as well as by the prelates of the major convents, in agreement with the abovementioned council of seniors or governing body. But when it comes to receiving orders, both minor and major, the friars who are candidates for such orders will be referred to the most illustrious bishop. He will determine their suitability and having received the necessary reports, he may confer upon them orders without any other requirement than what the bishop considers convenient.

The present decree will be valid until the decision is made regarding the creation and appointment of a general provost or chairman for all the monastics in the republic. If in obeying it there were to appear any doubts or difficulties, I reserve the right to explain the matters or to resolve them with further declarations. And so this may be understood and observed, let it be communicated to the abovementioned most illustrious bishop and to all the prelates, communities, and convents in the republic."

All of this I now send to Your Most Illustrious Lordship, expecting that in as much as he is able he will see that it has the appropriate effect. Let God guide Your Most Illustrious Lordship. Asunción, July 2, 1816
José Gaspar Francia

To the most illustrious and most reverend lord bishop Don Friar Pedro García de Panes.

Source Three
A Slave Code

Introduction

While much of the rest of Latin America was gaining its independence in the early nineteenth century, Cuba became known as "the ever faithful island" for its continued loyalty to Spain. (In fact, Cuba would not gain its independence for almost another century—in 1902.) There were reasons why the island wanted to remain a colony. Some historians point to the very large slave population, which grew dramatically in the late eighteenth/early nineteenth centuries. As that population increased, eventually free blacks and slaves outnumbered whites. For the minority, having Spanish troops on the island provided a sense of security. As independence spread throughout other regions of Latin America, Spain's large military presence on the island and the elites' close ties to it, along with an unease experienced by all whites, resulted in tranquility not seen elsewhere. Additionally, Cuba's powers-that-be worked at maintaining the traditional social and cultural structures that were the underpinnings of colonial society. Among these was the church.

As we hope is clear by now, the church was evident in almost every facet of colonial life. Certainly the Koster document from the previous chapter ("Travels in Brazil") and the story of San Martín de Porres ("On Becoming a Saint") from chapter 3 indicate that the church played an important role in race relations, generally acting as a suppressive force. Our document, the Cuban Slave Code of 1844, was more than likely a response to chronic slave unrest on the island. As historian Robert Paquette points out, with masters focusing on increasing profits, they neglected the institutions that made slaves tractable, including religious indoctrination. Instead, the masters and their overseers resorted to physical punishment as a means of control. By 1842, Captain-General Gerónimo Valdés, the most powerful Spanish official on the island, looked for ways to rein in the increasing number of rebellions.

His solution was a new slave code that curtailed physical punishment and encouraged other means of control.

Read this document with an eye toward the role of the master in the spiritual life of the slave. Why do you think the first five articles of the code deal with religious practices? What does that tell us about the role of religious life and instruction in the plantation economy of Cuba? How was the master supposed to balance "spiritual formation" and work? What was given priority? And what does that reveal about the role of the church in the life of both slave and planter? In what ways had the church's purpose changed from the conquest period? How had it remained the same?

The Text‡

Article 1

Every owner of slaves must instruct them in the principles of the Roman Catholic and apostolic religion so that those who are not baptized may be so. In emergencies, they will be given the healthful water of baptism, for it is known that in such circumstances anyone may do so.

Article 2

The instruction to which the previous article refers is to be given in the evenings after work is done, and immediately they shall be made to pray the rosary or some other devout prayers.

Article 3

On Sundays and special feast days, once they have fulfilled their religious duties, the owners or overseers of farms may employ their laborers for up to two hours in cleaning houses and workshops. But they must not take more than this time or use them in the various works of the hacienda unless it is in harvest time, or there are other matters that cannot be delayed, for in such cases they are to work as on regular days.

Article 4

The owners are responsible for seeing that slaves who have been baptized and who are of necessary age receive the sacraments as the holy mother church has decreed, or as they are necessary.

Article 5

Their owners will work as diligently as possible in making the slaves understand the obedience they owe to established authorities, their obligation to revere priests, respecting white people, behaving well with those of color, and living in harmony with their fellow slaves. . . .

Article 23
On feast days owners shall allow their slaves to amuse and enjoy themselves in honest fashion, once they have fulfilled their religious duties. But this must be done without leaving the farm, nor joining the slaves of other farms, and always in an open place and in plain view of their own masters, stewards, or foremen, until the sun sets or there is a call to prayers. . . .

Article 29
Slave owners must prevent illicit contact between [enslaved] men and women and encourage marriage. They shall not hinder those who marry slaves belonging to a different owner, and they will make arrangements so that the couple may live under the same roof.

Article 30
In order to assist this reunion and to allow the couple to fulfill the purpose of marriage, the wife shall follow her husband. The latter's owner shall purchase her for a price agreed to with her owner. If not, the price may be set through a thorough assessment by experts from both sides, and a third in case the two do not agree. And if the owner of the husband does not agree to buy the wife, her owner will have the option of buying the husband. If neither of them is able to make the appropriate purchase, the couple shall be jointly sold to a third party.

Source Four
Faith in a Healer

Introduction
Faith healing or comparable practices had long been the hallmark of popular piety. Often frowned upon by the institutional church, it was frequently the manifestation of deeply held views about sin and illness and about healing as an act of charity. By the nineteenth century, the art of healing was subsumed into the liberal versus conservative struggles, with traditional healing pitted against scientific healing. In Colombia we find a prime example of the fight that surrounded medicine.

Healer Miguel Perdomo Neira was the cause of an 1872 riot in Bogotá. It was, however, not the first time that Perdomo had been the reason for public unrest.[§] In Quito, in 1867, a constellation of events—including his arrest and a charge of practicing medicine without a license—had Perdomo's followers marching in the streets, publishing supportive testimonials, and demanding justice for the healer of the poor. An eventual quick exit from the city in December spared Perdomo any other unpleasantness there.

By the time Perdomo showed up in Colombia in 1872, his reputation as a healer was widespread. As historian David Sowell points out, Perdomo's practices brought him into conflict with "professional physicians, medical students, and certain members of the official political community" but also brought him the support of "broad segments of the city's populace."[*] Perdomo claimed that his surgeries caused no pain or bleeding. He used traditional methods of treating illness, incorporating herbs and other medicinal plants, and he did not charge for his services. He never claimed to be a faith healer or that his cures were miraculous. Yet, as the testimonies below indicate, many of his patients found hope and healing in him precisely because he combined religious faith and traditional medicine.

Although not in Bogotá, Perdomo remained in Colombia through 1874, at which point he returned to Ecuador. There he remained until his death on December 24 of that year, most likely the result of smallpox or yellow fever contracted while treating a patient. After his death, his devotees continued to revere him as Christ-like, even reporting that his tomb had been found opened and he was seen walking on the road to Quito.

The texts included in this source are divided into three parts, each one representing a different publication in which the work of Perdomo Neira was discussed.

As you read these excerpts, look for places in which the witnesses ascribed to Perdomo the qualities of a faith healer. Also, many of his patients were clergy. What do their testimonies reveal about the continued power of traditional medicine, particularly as an act of charity, over against scientific methods? How would they position Perdomo vis-à-vis the church? Where do you see the popular church in these documents? Are there statements that might make the institutional church uncomfortable? Why might political leaders and those involved in modern medicine find the religious-like devotion of his patients a problem? Where do you see class and economic divisions in the way people responded to Perdomo's healing?

Perdomo Neira himself made no mention of the church in his defense, as the last excerpt in this source reveals. Why would he not claim special gifts from God in defending his medical practice? To what did he turn to explain the animosity he faced? Where is the link between his political views and the divine healing powers ascribed to him by his followers?

The Texts

Part A[+]

. . . Mr. Gabriel Jiménez under oath as is required, declares that there is no way he can sufficiently thank Mr. Miguel Perdomo in payment for having left him hale and healed from a serious and very bad sickness. Because of that sickness he spent all his resources, during more than twenty years, on various doctors in the nation, and none of them had been able to cure him from a urinary problem that caused him great suffering. Medicines had served only as palliatives. Today he is totally restored and is certain that he will not get worse, thanks to God and to the marvelous medicines with which Mr. Miguel Perdomo Neira has healed him. And therefore, with great feeling of gratitude he offers the present document and signs it jointly with the judge certifying it in Quito on November 15, 1867. [signed] Gabriel Jiménez and Nicanor Chiriboga, central judge. . . .

I, Antonio Muñoz, judge in the parish of Chillogallo, hereby certify under proper oath that having suffered for more than six years from a serious and bothersome disease that included pneumonia, liver irritation, serious stomach pain, so that I suffered beyond words, I had need to go to several doctors in the capital asking for a cure. Even having done all the things they prescribed, I did not improve at all. I was lying in bed and already given up on by the doctors who were attending me. I sent word to Mr. Miguel Perdomo who had mercifully come to the capital, and he kindly and generously agreed to come to visit me in this parish. Finding me lying in my bed of pain and with no hope for life, after a careful examination and without asking even a single question, he declared that I had a great complication involving the ills that I have already expressed. He also noticed that I had an obstruction in my intestine. Despite this, he offered to take care of me and heal me, which actually did take place after ten days of using the prescriptions that he ordered. I was cured and healthy. This was to such an extent that after fifteen days I was once again able to ride on horseback and to carry out all the various functions of my ministry as a judge and of the agricultural work which I do. At present I am still healthy, thanks to the abovementioned Mr. Perdomo. And fulfilling a duty of eternal gratitude which my heart feels for my good benefactor, I issue this document in this parish of Santiago de Chillogallo on November 8, 1867. [signed] Antonio Muñoz, parish judge. . . .

Likewise citizen José Hurtado who lives in this capital city came to me and after making the legal oath he declared that he was grateful to Mr. Miguel Perdomo Neira. Therefore it was proper for him to offer the present certificate in payment for the favor that he has received from Mr. Perdomo Neira. [The healer restored] his health, healing him from a strong nervous breakdown that resulted in keeping him in bed without being able to move and with pain in his legs so that he was not able to take one step. They were contracted to such a point that when he was touched in order to turn him on his bed from one side to another, it made him cry quite loudly. In that condition he called on a doctor in this capital and another very able practitioner. Neither one nor the other was able to make him any better. On the contrary, the patient declares that he was left even worse than he was before. After some days, making great efforts with crutches, he went to Mr. Perdomo, who examined him and gave him six prescriptions with which he has been anointed. Now he is healthy and walking on his own feet without crutches. As a payment to this kindness from Mr. Perdomo, he signs the present document jointly with the judge who certifies it in Quito, on November 2, 1867.

At the request of the deponent, who is unable to write, and also serving as witnesses, [signed] Benigno Navarro and Santiago Herrería, parish lieutenant.

Baldomira Estupiñan, who also lives in this capital, likewise appeared and declared that she found herself suddenly in bed with a violent pain in her stomach which was complicated by a pain in her back that seemed to go across her body. She recognized that she was about to die. This came to such a point that those who saw her went after a confessor and doctors, and she was immediately examined. They tried to alleviate her pain, but it was not possible to hear her confession nor to make her better. Immediately afterwards, at ten o'clock at night, at the suggestion of the dying woman, Mr. Miguel Perdomo Neira was called. Mr. Perdomo prescribed a medicine that the woman's mother, Ramona Estupiñan, gave her. After taking it she began improving, speaking, and giving thanks to heaven. Those who were around her were alarmed and declared that "This is a miraculous resurrection." The next day Mr. Perdomo gave her another prescription that she took, and the patient declares that today she is completely healed and in good health, as strong as she was before. As a result of her gratitude, she offers the present document which she signs together with the judge that certifies it in Quito, on November 1, 1867. Furthermore, she declares that the doctor who visited her was the best in this place. He ordered that leeches be applied to her and that she be bled of eighteen ounces, for if she was not bled she would surely die. The patient did not agree and was healed with the medicine offered by Mr. Perdomo, whom she accordingly thanks. At the request of the deponent, who does not know how to read and write, and as a witness to the above [signed] Manuel Soberon and Santiago Herrería, parish lieutenant.

Part B'
The newspaper printed the following report from the village of Serrezuela [Colombia]:

From the evening of the 25th we have here Mr. Perdomo, who after residing some weeks in Guaduas and Villeta, most unexpectedly came to this village, establishing here what could well be called his headquarter for the area. The news immediately spread through the neighboring towns, and by the dawn of the following day one could see a multitude of curious and ill people coming by all the paths that meet in this village. Some [came] in improvised carriages, others riding pitiful nags, and the rest in decent carriages or on lively horses. This has continued without any decline, rather increasing notably. The scene the curious spectator thus witnesses is odd. The borders of the plaza, the immediate streets, the yard, and the rooms in the house where Mr. Perdomo came to dwell are flooded with people. The movement and excitement that come with the advent of so many travelers, the many beasts of burden tied wherever possible, the ladies who show off their luxuries everywhere, the peasants in their Sunday-best, the groups of riders and the beggars, and people suffering from all kinds of handicaps, contrast greatly with the normal quiet of this town. This singular spectacle begins again every morning with the cheerful tolling of bells and five or six consecutive masses.

Meanwhile Mr. Perdomo is ceaselessly busy visiting the sick who cannot come to him, offering consultations, distributing medicines, and operating in his house, almost constantly invaded during the daytime hours by three to four hundred people. . . .

This would be a good opportunity to offer judgment about the aptitude and efficiencies of Mr. Perdomo. But we are mere chroniclers and should not therefore go into such depth. We should only say that Mr. Perdomo's ability as a surgeon is evident and that one cannot deny that he has a great natural understanding or perhaps an intuition in the exercise of medicine. As such, it would be very desirable for the distinguished members of the medical profession who live in Bogotá to receive him benevolently as a compatriot who, despite his humble origins and lack of academic studies, has gained for himself an estimable reputation by means that are irreproachable.

Part C*

Today I address the people of Colombia in order to appeal to it and to register a complaint. I address the people, the true people, the working and patient multitude who are the essential part of the nation, the powerless and disinherited masses that even despite their powerlessness carry on their shoulders the life of all, the weight of the efforts and sacrifices needed to sustain the existence of the nation. I address the entire people of Colombia where I am well known in order to complain about the manner in which I have been received and treated in the capital of the republic, our motherland. . . . Even before arriving at Bogotá, I already knew that some of the professors of medicine in that highly educated city were set against me. I knew that some of them claimed that I would not dare come to the capital of Colombia and practice in a city where they were. They, the intellectuals, the professors of official teaching, and the mentors of youth, surrounded by their many disciples! I knew of all this, and for that very reason was even more interested in going to Bogotá. I wanted these gentlemen to see that even in front of them I could do what I had and am still doing in front of hundreds of thousands of rational beings who, without any doubt, are worth more than a few doctors, no matter how eminent. I had barely reached Bogotá when the people, as elsewhere, favored me with their faith and with their sincere and simple kindness. Those who were poor and ill were all in my favor. The same was true of the healthy portion of our middle class, artisans of all political inclinations in the capital, as well as the well-to-do dwellers of the surrounding country. Among the higher and most educated part of society, I also had the support of many respectable people and the goodwill of many of the finest families in Bogotá. But I had against me scientific skepticism and the jealousy of some doctors and the mockery and animus of the students. And above all, I had against me the envy and jealousy of the authority, moved by political reasons, who opposed me because they knew that I am a conservative.

 . . . Well now: I, in God's name and witnessing to the truth, affirm with a clear and tranquil conscience before the Lord of all light and all truth; I swear also in the presence of all, that I possess substances that make it possible for me to practice the most serious surgical operations without producing hemorrhage, pain, inflammation, or suppuration. Even though I cut into the great arteries and veins, even though I may cut all the way through them, it produces no hemorrhages. Even though I may wound the most sensitive parts of the nervous system, it produces no pain. And even though I cut into the most irritable and delicate tissue in the body, I produce no inflammation or suppuration. Yes, I operate using my own preparations, which draw on the hemostatic [stopping bleeding], anesthetic, and antiphlogistic [counteracting inflammation] virtues and properties of certain plants that are a treasure in the vegetable kingdom. These medicines are better than those that European science now has. This is much more than the science of the disbelieving gentlemen doctors in my own land. And I formally call on and challenge them to come to see me practice these operations, to see me mutilate the human body in both its upper and lower extremities, and even in the more delicate organs without any hemorrhage, absolutely without any bleeding, without causing the patient any pain, and without any subsequent inflammation or suppuration. I invite them to watch me do this in front of impartial witnesses and with all the necessary solemnity.

. . . These are the truths; these are the documents and testimonials and the positive facts that I will take to learned Europe. Its chemists, doctors, and truly competent naturalists may examine these plants. By analyzing them they may find out what are the active chemical agents that give these important substances their marvelous properties. I shall do this so that Europe, the present representative of the scientific spirit, may present them to science and give them as a patrimony to all humankind. Humanity is the rightful owner of all scientific truth, of every discovery in the sciences and the arts, and of all progress within the human family. . . .

There is no other alternative: Either Miguel Perdomo Neira is a charlatan, a liar and a public thief, an infamous deceiver, or he is a man deserving the respect and particular consideration of others. Either he is a public evil doer, or he is a benefactor of humanity. There is no possibility between these two extremes, because what Perdomo does is too important and even critical in its very nature. If he is an imposter, a swindler of the people, and a progressive poisoner of public health, he is a criminal. If this is proven, he must be immediately punished, cast away from the bosom of society and from the rest of humanity. But if he is not but is instead a sincere and truthful man, a lover of humanity, and servant of the people, surely the national spirit and conscience will favor this man. In that case, the action and the unanimous opinion of all should protect this man and shield him from evil passions. And the doctors and the intellectuals and the teachers of youth and the apostles of truth and the professors of science, and the authorities who above everybody else represent public order and human right—the highest majesty and dignity of all association of rational and moral beings—those authorities instead of persecuting and insulting him, as they did in Bogotá, must join the doctors in respecting him a bit more than any man deserves.

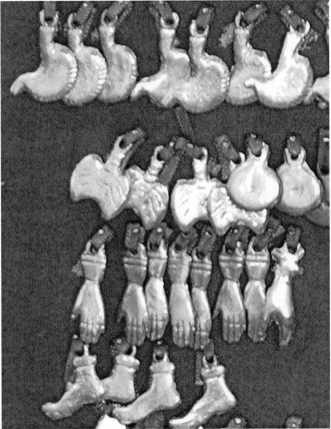

Figure 5.1 The connection between faith and healing has continued from pre-Columbian times to the present. Votive offerings such as these are frequently available for sale outside holy sites where the faithful present them as requests for healing or signs of gratitude. They normally represent the body part in which illness has occurred.

Source Five
An Alternate Creed

Introduction

The early years of the twentieth century were no calmer than had been much of the nineteenth. Country after country experienced wars between conservatives and liberals. Conservatives wanted to maintain much of the colonial structure that had benefited them, including the preeminence of the church. Liberals were concerned with the abolition of privilege and the suppression of traditional patterns. Mexico was no more immune to these conflicts than was any other area of the region. By 1910, the Mexican Revolution was in full swing, lasting off and on for ten years.

The following brief document is a parody of the Apostle's Creed, a second-century formula initially used in baptisms but nowadays recited regularly by Roman Catholics and many Protestants in worship services. The Apostles' Creed reads:

> I believe in God, the Father Almighty,
>> creator of heaven and earth.
> I believe in Jesus Christ, his only Son, our Lord:
>> who was conceived by the Holy Spirit,
>> born of the Virgin Mary,
>> suffered under Pontius Pilate,
>> was crucified, dead, and buried;
>> he descended to the dead.
>> On the third day he rose again;
>> he ascended into heaven,
>> is seated at the right hand of the Father,
>> and will come again to judge the living and the dead.
> I believe in the Holy Spirit,
>> the holy catholic church,
>> the communion of saints,
>> the forgiveness of sin,
>> the Resurrection of the body,
>> and the life everlasting. Amen[**]

What does the cooption of the Apostles' Creed tell us about the power of liturgy and the rebels' understanding of the society they were trying to change? Why might the rebels have followed the style of the creed? What was their purpose? What did they hope to accomplish? How might the Creed of the Liberals be offensive to Christians—Catholics and Protestants alike?

The Text[††]

I believe in one free and powerful country, cradle of a noble and eminent people, and in Juárez, its great son, our Lord who was conceived by the Virgin of America, suffered under the power of Roman clergy, was excommunicated, died, and buried; on the second day he rose again from the dead, ascended into heaven, and is seated at the right hand of Sublime Right, from there he will come to judge the bigoted and the rich; I believe in Liberal Thought, Holy Universal Peace, the communion of heroes, the shame of traitors, the redemption of the people, [and] the happiness of the poor. Amen.

Source Six
A Last-Ditch Effort

Introduction

On Saturday, August 21, 1926, an unprecedented interview took place in Chapultepec Palace in Mexico City. President Plutarco Elías Calles and the bishops of Tabasco and Michoacán, Pascual Díaz and Leopoldo Ruiz y Flores, respectively, sat down together to discuss the growing religious tension in Mexico. Earlier that year, the government had published a series of regulations meant to curb infractions against Article 130 of the Mexican Constitution. Among other provisions, this particularly anticlerical aspect of the Constitution denied churches legal standing within the country, limited the number of priests—all of whom had to be Mexican born—required that all priests register with the state, prohibited clergy from participation in or critique of the government, and limited worship service to within the church building proper. And President Calles was determined to enforce the anticlerical provisions. In response to Calles's actions, Archbishop José Mora y del Río of Mexico City issued an interdict in July 1926 and instructed his priests to go on strike, which ultimately lasted three years. A Catholic rebellion known as the Cristero uprising would ensue in which over thirty thousand Cristeros and fifty-seven thousand federal troops died, but not before efforts at conciliation had been made, as our document proves.

In August, attempts at bringing tranquility to Mexico resulted in the now-famous *La entrevista de la última oportunidad* (Interview of the last chance). In this exchange, the bishops proclaimed their desire for peace and their insistence that good Catholics be submissive. They insisted, however, that this did not include infringement of their religious practices or of the activities of the church. Calles remained intractable, reiterating that he would not waiver from the path laid by the Constitution.

As you read this source, think about the conversation from the perspective of each side. What do you think the president heard the bishops saying? What did they hear him saying? How might the presuppositions they each brought have affected their willingness to compromise? What was each side demanding? Who had the upper hand? Consider why both sides seemed so entrenched. What evidence do you find of a shifting relationship between church and state in Mexico?

The Text‡‡

The Bishop of Tabasco: We are very grateful to you Mr. President, that you have been willing to receive us. For us this interview is of the greatest importance, for out of it we expect magnificent results. We had been very desirous to speak freely with you. We want to clear from your mind your prejudice that the bishops have tried to obstruct the work of the government. First of all I will tell you something you ought to know: When we had our first meetings there was a person interested in having us go to the American embassy in order to ask for their influence and intervention in seeking the solution to the religious question in Mexico. And in the minutes, which I wrote as secretary for the episcopacy, it is stated that all the bishops as in one voice interrupted the secretary who was reading the document containing such a proposition in order to reject it energetically, for we do not wish the intervention of foreigners, but rather to come to a direct understanding with those in our government. . . .

The President: I wish that the words that you now speak will eventually be translated into actions, which speak louder. But I must tell you that we are perfectly aware (for my government has ample sources of information everywhere) of what have been the activities of Catholic elements abroad, and we know very well what are the direct and indirect means they have been employing in order to seek the support of foreign governments to pressure the Mexican government. And we not only have reports on the activities of Catholic elements here but also are aware of the activities of the pope himself in the same direction. The government of Mexico will in no way disobey the laws, and these pressures that they are promoting do not concern us. We are resolved to sustain national dignity no matter the cost. As to the attitude of the clergy within the country, it is well known that it has been promoting rebellion. Among such clergy are the priests of Saguayo, and I sincerely tell you that if those priests are captured by the federal troops they will be shot, for they are responsible for having instigated rebellion, causing the shedding of blood. They are directly responsible for what took place in Saguayo, where several men lost their lives. And like them, in many other parts of the Republic Catholic priests have acted subversively in one way or another, be it through leaflets, by means of newspapers, or in their sermons. If you serenely examine these activities, you will see that in truth there has been incitement to rebellion and to disobedience of our institutions and our laws. This is something that we will not allow no matter under what circumstances. As to the registry of priests, I wish to make clear to you that this is only due to matters of statistic. It is also in compliance with the Constitution of the Republic, which establishes that church buildings belong to the nation, and as long as that constitution does not say the opposite, such buildings will continue being the property of the nation. What less can the legitimate representative of the people, which is the government, demand to know than who is administering their properties? The government is not interested in matters of doctrine or dogma. Catholics, within their churches, and as long as they do not disobey the legal ordinances, may do whatever they wish. But when it comes to the law, as long as I head the executive power of the nation I will make certain that it is obeyed. The only possible way so that all of these difficulties will come to an end is to have the clergy submit to this law. And if the law itself is contrary to their interests, they may seek ways to reform it following the path that the law itself determines to that end. This is the road I have taken, and no one will move me from it. . . .

The Bishop of Michoacán: We will have to subject in order to avoid the penalties of the laws and not to deprive the faithful of the right that they have to their worship.

The President: How has your worship been impeded?

The Bishop of Michoacán: From the very moment that we have to submit to a law even though our conscience goes against it.

The President: You have no other way than to submit.

The Bishop of Michoacán: Even against the dictates of our conscience.

The President: The law is above the dictates of conscience.

The Bishop of Tabasco: By conscience I understand that which our feelings dictate and by law I understand an ordering of reason. Therefore, when my conscience tells me a law is against reason, I have a right to follow the dictates of my conscience and not submit to that law because, being against reason, it cannot be a law. Naturally, that which I tell you here quite frankly I am not about to say to the ignorant masses because it would be misinterpreted. But here we must speak with all clarity, for otherwise our interview would not have a purpose.

The President: Laws are those that are written in the codes, and they have to be respected. They have to be obeyed.

The Bishop of Tabasco: The conflict has taken place because we had been denied the right to take steps for the reformation of the law. But now you tell us that the law itself points to a path that may be followed to that end. . . . Therefore we will obey this law and make use of the right which you acknowledge. But, how are we to do this with your help, sir, because without that help it would be impossible. If we do not coordinate our efforts, we will become more and more alienated, and the results would be tragic. . . .

The President: But I am not the one to resolve this matter, for it pertains to the legislative chambers, and quite sincerely I tell you that I am in perfect agreement with what this law says that you are trying to reform, since it meets my political and philosophical convictions.

The Bishop of Tabasco: Very well, sir, I respect you, for a man of such convictions deserves respect. A man with your characteristics deserves to be admired. I congratulate you and I move forward. The legislative chambers in their totality are formed by people who agree with your policy. There is no one to defend what we present to the chambers, because as I say, they are constituted by people who are completely opposed to our way of thinking. And it is here that we need your help. We will present our points of view. You will study them. . . .

The President: I've already told you that this is not a matter that pertains to the Executive, but to the legislative chambers. . . .I am going to speak with all sincerity. The Mexican clergy has not evolved. The intelligence of our priests is very low. They have not perceived the evolution that is taking place, and not only have they not joined this movement, but they even try to obstruct it, and naturally they will be routed. That is the truth. You are rapidly losing ground among your faithful, because in the labor movement that is developing Catholic priests have openly taken the side of those who oppress workers. . . .

The Bishop of Tabasco: Mr. President, you can point for us a way to come safely to the shore, giving us a plank of salvation.

The President: I have already told you what this way is, and it is none other than the exact obedience to the law.

The Bishop of Tabasco: And precisely there lies the difficulty.

6
PROTESTANT PRESENCE

Introduction

The end of colonial rule brought changes to Latin America far beyond independence itself. The monopoly on trade that Spain and Portugal had zealously guarded now came to an end. So did the strict control on immigration, until then permitted only from the Iberian Peninsula, with very few exceptions. Interested in promoting trade and development, most of the new governments also favored new ideas as well as new immigrants. Such policies were resisted by the more conservative elements, usually supported by the Roman Catholic hierarchy, which bemoaned the loss of its former monopoly not only on religion, but also on education, publications, and all other venues for intellectual debate.

Seeking to counterbalance such opposition, many of the new governments supported the introduction of Protestantism, which they saw as an expression of modernity at a time when Roman Catholicism embraced a radically antimodern conservatism. Thus, although most of the leaders of such governments still considered themselves Catholic, they followed policies that conflicted with the Catholic hierarchy, hoping that Protestantism would help modernize their nation and in some cases hoping also that it would help modernize the Catholic Church itself.

Source One, "The President's Visit," is a letter from the man usually considered the first Protestant missionary to Latin America. James Thomson, commonly known among Latin American Protestants as Diego Thomson, traveled extensively throughout the region. Before visiting Peru, he had been in Argentina, Uruguay, and Chile. Later he would go to Mexico and to Colombia, where he was able to found the Colombian Bible Society that was headed by a Roman Catholic priest. Even though Puerto Rico and Cuba were still Spanish colonies, and therefore he was not welcome, Thomson managed to visit and distribute Bibles in both islands. In all these endeavors he was the representative of the British and Foreign Missionary Society, and his task was to promote interest in the Bible and to distribute it. However, his point of entry was a new method of education—the Lancaster method—which at that time was considered a great advance over the earlier emphasis on memorizing and repeating by rote. In this new method, the more advanced students helped teach others, and the main textbook was the Bible. This was abhorrent to most in the Catholic hierarchy, who held that the Bible ought to be interpreted and taught following the dictates of the Church. But it was a welcome breath of fresh air for those—Catholic or not—who felt that it was time for greater openness in the exchange of ideas.

Source Two, "Unwelcomed Peddlers," is a selection from Rev. H. P. Hamilton's report on his work in Mexico on behalf of the American Bible Society. The ABS was an organization founded in 1816 whose initial international focus was on India and the Near East but which in 1826 began distributing Bibles in Mexico. Our document dates from 1897, when the American Bible Society had been working in Mexico for over seventy years. And yet, one still notes the novelty that the Bible seems to have been to many Mexicans.

Source Three, "Race and Mission," is written by Robert E. Speer (1867–1947), a Presbyterian whose missionary experience was mostly in the East and who became Secretary of the Presbyterian Mission in 1891 and retained that post until his retirement in 1937. Although he did visit Latin America in 1909, his knowledge of the area was mostly secondhand. Therefore his writing reflects the views of those who, while interested in the missionary enterprise, were not directly acquainted with Latin America.

Source Four, "A Woman's View," comes from a North American, Mrs. E. M. Bauman, who had long lived in Buenos Aires as a pastor's wife. She was addressing the Conference on Missions in Latin America that took place in New York in 1913 and was trying to convey her experiences with people, society, and culture in Buenos Aires. Thus, it is an example of how a North American who had significant experience in the region interpreted culture and conditions in Latin America.

Source Five, "A Radical Perspective," also comes from a conference but this time in Chile, in 1966. This was the second of a series of conferences organized by ISAL—*Iglesia y Sociedad en América Latina* (Church and Society in Latin America)—an organization known for its radical views on the need for social change in Latin America. It is part of the report of a committee.

Finally, Source Six, "A Poet's Fear and Faith," is a poem by Julia Esquivel Velásquez, a Presbyterian from Guatemala who suffered the pains of thirty years of brutal dictatorships and violent repressions. The poem itself was written in Switzerland in 1986, when constant death threats and an attempted kidnapping had forced her into exile.

Source One
The President's Visit

Introduction

Peru had been an independent country for scarcely over a year. Its first president and national hero, who had led the army that took Lima from the Spanish, was the Argentinean general José de San Martín, who to this day is hailed as one of the great heroes of South American independence. The letters of recommendation to which Thomson refers included a commendation from Bernardo O'Higgins, the leader of Chilean independence, who had fought against the Spanish jointly with San Martín. In Chile, O'Higgins had acknowledged the value of Thomson's work by making him an honorary citizen—a recognition he had received earlier in Argentina. Thus, as you read this letter, keep in mind who the person visiting Thomson is and what his support might mean. The Marquis of Truxillo, whom Thomson also met and whom he calls "first minister," was San Martín's right-hand man. His actual title was "Supreme Deputy," meaning that his functions were similar to those of a vice president. He would eventually become president of Peru. Thus, Thomson was being welcomed and supported by the most powerful and respected people in the new nation.

Remember that these were the very early dates of the new republics. This was a time marked by the ongoing conflict between liberals and conservatives. Read the entire document with that in mind.

Note what Thomson says about the relation between the civil and ecclesiastical authorities. What reasons might have led San Martín to view Thomson's work with such favor? What was Thomson's view of the Catholic Church and its influence on the country? What would be the reaction of the Catholic hierarchy to the attitudes and events that Thomson described, and more specifically to the decree for the reformation of education? Try to imagine the reaction of the friars in the convent of St. Thomas and of others who had been in charge of education. What objections to the decree quoted by Thomson might they have raised?

Why would the decree include the education of girls? How would liberals and conservatives react to such provisions?

Consider the matter of immigration. Why would the government promote it? Why would Thomson? How would the Catholic hierarchy view such plans for immigration? As you read between the lines, what seems to be Thomson's view of Latin American culture and society?

The letter you will be reading is one of Thomson's many reports to his supporters in Great Britain. How might this have affected his account of events? Suppose he were writing to San Martín. How would he state what he hoped to accomplish?

The Text*

Lima, 11th July, 1822

. . . On the day on which I arrived in this city, I called on San Martin, and delivered him the letters of introduction which I had brought from Chile. He opened one of the letters, and observing its purport, said "Mr. Thomson! I am extremely glad to see you;" and he rose up, and gave me a very hearty embrace. He would not, he said, be lavish in compliments, but would assure me of his great satisfaction at my arrival; and said that nothing should be wanting on his part to further the object which had brought me to Peru. Next day as I was sitting in my room, a carriage stopped at the door, and my little boy came running in crying, San Martin! San Martin! In a moment he entered the room, accompanied by one of his ministers. I would have had him step into another apartment of the house more suited to his reception; but he said the room was very well, and sat down on the first chair he reached. We conversed about our schools, and other similar objects for some time; and in going away he desired me to call on him next morning, and said he would introduce me to the Marquis of Truxillo, who is at present what is called the Supreme Deputy or Regent. I called on him accordingly next morning, and he took me with him and introduced me to the Marquis and to each of the ministers.

From all the members of the government I have received great encouragement. On the 6th current an order was issued relative to our schools, and published in the Lima Gazette of the same date. I am going to write Mr. Millar tomorrow, and shall give him a translation of this order or decree, a copy of which will of course be sent you. By this order one of the convents is appropriated to the schools, and is now in our possession. I believe the convents here will decrease in number as the schools multiply. There is no contest or balancing of powers between the civil and ecclesiastical powers on this place. The former has the latter at their nod. The ease in regard to this convent is a proof of what I have said. The order for the friars to remove was given on Saturday, on Monday they began to remove, and on Tuesday the keys were delivered up.

From all I have seen during the short time I have been here, I cannot doubt of the great benefits which this country will derive from the new state of things. San Martin and his first minister, (and also the others) seem truly anxious to characterize the times by improvements—by solid improvements. They wish to encourage foreigners, and to improve the state of the country in every point of view. I have already mentioned to you my representation made to the Chilean government just before leaving that place, regarding the bringing out of tradesmen and farmers. I showed a copy of this representation to San Martin; he read it very carefully over, and concluded by saying, "Excellent!" He then told me what was his opinion on the subject, and proposed a plan for carrying it into effect, much more likely to succeed than the one I had stated. I am to draw up this plan in order, and to present it to him, that it may be sanctioned and carried into effect. I therefore consider this matter, so far as regards Peru, as fairly begun. The particulars of the plan I may send you afterwards. In the mean time, that you may see that in these matters I am not losing sight of my chief object, I shall mention to you one sentence of the representation referred to. It is, "The men who will be most useful to South America, are men truly religious and of sound morality." The minister of Chile, upon reading this sentence, said, "That is very true;" and San Martin expressed himself in a similar manner upon my stating the same thing to him.

What an immeasurable field is South America; and how white it is to harvest! I have told you this repeatedly, but I have a pleasure in telling it to you again. I do think that, since the world began, there never was so fine a field for the exercise of benevolence in all its parts. The man of science, the moralist, the Christian, have all fine scope here for their talents. God, who has opened such a door, will surely provide labourers. . . .

"The Supreme Deputy, with the advice of the Privy Council, decrees—

"1. There shall be established a central or principal school, according to the Lancasterian system, under the direction of Mr. Thomson.

"2. The convent or college of St. Thomas shall be appropriated to this purpose. The friars at present residing in it shall remove to the large convent of St. Dominic, leaving only so many as are necessary for the service of the church attached to it.

"3. In this establishment the elementary parts of education shall be taught, together with the modern languages. The teachers necessary for this purpose shall be appointed agreeably to the arrangements which will be pointed out in the plan for the National Institute of Peru.

"4. At the expiration of six months all the public Schools shall be shut, which are not conducted according to the system of mutual instruction.

"5. All the masters of the public schools shall attend the central school with two of their most advanced pupils, in order to be instructed in the new system; and in studying it they shall attend to the method prescribed by the director of the establishment.

"6. As soon as the director of the central school shall have instructed a sufficient number of teachers, these shall be employed, with competent salaries, in establishing public schools on the same principles in the capital city of each province of the state.

"7. At the first public examination which shall take place in the central school, those masters who have been most attentive in learning the system, and shall have made such progress as to be able to conduct schools according to it, shall receive the reward of a gold medal, to be ordered for that purpose by the Minister of State.

"8. For the preservation and extension of the new system the Patriotic Society of Lima is particularly requested and commissioned to take such measures as may be considered necessary for these purposes; and they are desired to make known to the government those things in which its co-operation may be required, in order effectually to carry forward this important object.

"9. In order that the advantages of this system of education may be extended to the female sex, which the Spanish government has always treated with culpable neglect, it is particularly recommended to the Patriotic Society to take into consideration the most likely means for establishing a central school for the instruction of girls.

"10. The salary of the director, and the other expenses necessary for this establishment, shall be defrayed by the government. The Minister of State is authorized to issue all the orders necessary for the punctual fulfilment of this decree.

"Given in the government palace in Lima, 6th July, 1822.

Signed "Truxillo.

"By order of his Excellency, countersigned,

"B. Monteagudo."

As we go on in our operations, I shall communicate to you the result.

Source Two
Unwelcomed Peddlers

Introduction

Shortly after the American Bible Society was founded, most of Latin America was free from colonial rule. Therefore, although at first this Bible society had looked mostly to distant lands across the oceans, it soon found itself involved in distributing the Bible in Latin America, where the Roman Catholic Church no longer held sway. This did not mean, however, that there was no opposition to its work. While the laws and constitutions of most of the new republics allowed for freedom of expression and of thought, there were still many who believed that Protestantism was a heresy that should not be allowed to contaminate the land. Foremost among these were the Catholic clergy, as well as a good number of those among the laity who were most involved in the life of the Catholic Church and who generally identified with conservative rather than liberal parties.

In all this, the Catholic Church found itself in an awkward tension. It certainly affirmed and taught that the Bible was the word of God, but it did little to put the Bible in the hands of the faithful. While there were Bibles available in Spanish, these were so expensive that only the wealthy could afford to have one of them. Furthermore, ever since the sixteenth century the Roman Catholic Church had determined that the Bible should always be read in the light of traditions and the *magisterium* (the teachings) of the Church, and had frowned on individual believers who sought to read the Bible on their own.

Now the American Bible Society (and the British and Foreign Bible Society) was distributing Bibles at relatively low cost, so many more people could afford to purchase one. The governments were promoting literacy, and this made people eager to read all that was made available to them, particularly the Bible, a book about which they had heard so much but had never even seen.

This context in many ways explains the opposition that the representatives of the American Bible Society faced. As you read this report, note the role of the clergy. Note also how the clergy used its power to persuade landowners not to allow the distribution of Bibles in their lands. And do not forget the power of the mobs apparently stirred up by the clergy to prevent the distribution of Bibles.

Why would priests consider the Bible "evil"? What instruments did they use to prevent its distribution? As you read of people eager to buy and read the Bible in spite of the warnings of priests, what does this tell you of the relationship between clergy and laity and about the actual authority of the clergy?

What were the attitudes of Mr. Hamilton and his representatives toward Roman Catholicism? How do their attitudes compare to those of the Catholic leadership? How did they understand their own work? What did they say about traditional devotions such as that to "el Señor de Chalma"? What do you think Mr. Hamilton meant by "Bible countries"? Note that, although Mexico was not included among these, Hamilton did call it a "Christian land." How would the American Bible Society justify its work in a Christian land?

Why do you think some people were so eager to secure a copy of the Bible and found it such a significant experience even after the American Bible Society had been distributing Bibles in Mexico for seventy years? What role did social class seem to have in the availability of the Bible in Latin America?

The Text[†]

It may seem a thing incredible to dwellers in Bible countries that a few persons devoted to the one sole object of securing the intelligent acceptance of the Holy Bible by the inhabitants of a Christian land like Mexico should meet with deliberate religious hostility, the bitter enmity of the clergy, and the persistent opposition of their followers; and yet that, at the same time, thousands every year should receive and read the sacred volume in defiance of Rome.

The policy of the Pope is still the same; to the poor the Bible is prohibited. The recent public declarations in Latin letters from Rome recommending the reading of the Scriptures were not intended for the masses, nor ever reached them.

How this barrier between the people and the Bible is extended and defended, and how also it is broken down in places here and there, may be practically shown by the narration of the experiences of some of our colporteurs [Bible salesmen]. Plainer things are said to the unconventional Bible seller than to the ministers or to the professional writers. In the *incidents* of their daily work are joined their trials and the triumphs of the printed word they offer.

On the 20th of February, Hipolito Aguilar placed his little stand for the sale of Bibles in front of the cave of Chalmita, which is found in a beautiful ravine some ten leagues northwest of Cuernavaca. There, tradition says, the "crucifix image" of the "Señor de Chalma"—second only to the image of the Virgin of Guadalupe in Mexican hearts—was placed by the angels, one night in May of 1539, on the very altar so long occupied by the ancient Aztec idol, Ostotochitle, God of the Caves, which at dawn was found in pieces on the rocky floor of the cavern. Aguilar was in danger, not from the multitude of pilgrims, as they were eagerly listening to the message and purchasing Gospels; but from what they might become by a word from the priest, who sent messengers to examine the books and pronounce them "bad and prohibited." In fear, among so many thousands who might be turned against him, he gathered up his books to go, when the tax collector came past urging him to hold his post and promising protection until night. Thus he sold, at the very gates of the saint of "Chalma," scores of Gospels and Bibles, which were carried to distant towns, even to the Pacific ports.

A few days ago a picture of "El Señor de Chalma" was handed me, its edges worn off by age, and on the back of it was written: "My mother worshipped this with greatest veneration during many years; it had the richest frame and the finest altar of all our saints; but in January last she bought a Holy Bible, and in her last moments, instead of mentioning this picture, she recommended us to read the sacred Scriptures, by which she came to know the true Saviour in this last year of her life." The writer and her sister live a hundred miles from the Chalma Cave, and the Bible was sold by Cortez on his way to Lagos.

Mr. Hernandez explains why he could not sell more Bibles, saying in a letter of October 2: "Two months ago I took my books to a little market-place close by the Hacienda of Omialca. The *cura* [priest] came by and asked if I had *authority* to sell those books. I said yes, but not from 'the Church.' He opened one and was reading, until the bell calling to mass sounded out, when he let the cover fall, saying, as though commanded by some superior: 'They are evil books, and prohibited.' Later came the owner of the estate commanding me to take my books away, remarking, but in a manner as though he did not believe it, 'The cura says they are false.' Then a man who collects the rents for the spaces occupied by the sellers in the market came and tried to induce me to go by imposing a double quota for my place. Now, my neighboring tradesmen began to make signs to those who stopped before my books that something was wrong with them; and at last, toward night, drunken fellows even shouted the same to those who would listen to the gospel. The priest was first and last in all this opposition, so I gave up the *plaza* to employ again the method of going from house to house."

Moreno writes from the same state, July 31: "In Tianquistengo, a fanatical place, but one in which I had sold six Bibles, a very obstinate Romanist, who sold old books at fabulous prices, came to tell me, 'The cura calls your books very bad;' but, looking at them more closely, he continued, 'I notice that they are very new; what are the prices of new books on new religions; on this, for example?' taking up a large Bible. Following his manner I said;

'It might be worth ten dollars to one who is sick of idols; see what it says of them,' and I opened it in Exodus XX, Acts VI, and also to the words of Paul in Corinthians regarding idolatry. He listened with increasing surprise, but like a true trader offered three dollars for the book, which being the price, he became possessor of a Bible. He read his new book, for days later, when his friends charged him with having bought the 'condemned book,' he firmly declared, 'No, *this is the book that uncondemns.*'"

Opposition sometimes opens the way. Orocio writes, July 22: "The night before I left Pozos the cura sent three men to summon me before him. At first I refused to go fearing evil designs, but as one of the three had already asked me to take back a Bible which I had sold him, I finally consented on condition that all three should hear my conversation with the priest. The *padre* scolded me severely, but I answered only with simple questions, which brought us to arguments as to what constituted a true Bible. When he finally admitted that it might be the word of God, if it gave the sense to the reader, whatever the language or the name of the translator, I saw that I had gained my listeners, though he dismissed them, still holding that 'without notes and authorization by the Church it was a prohibited book.'

"The man who had asked me to take back the Bible decided to keep it, and the son of one of the others, whose Bible the priest had already burned, came out on the road after me next morning and brought another.

"In this town two of my friends were accused before the priest, by their wives, of the sin of possessing and reading Bibles, and as they refused to give them up to the priest, their wives were intrusted with the duty of burning them. They were surprised in the task by one of the husbands, who rescued the books and brought them to me but slightly damaged. They bought new Bibles, and asked me to give the old ones to persons too poor to purchase."

Cortez relates how in Puebla one came to his stall where he offered the Bible in the market and became interested in reading the New Testament. On pretence of going to bring the price he left his cloak and took the book to his priest, whom he met coming that way. The priest pronounced it "false," and was about to tear it up when the man said, "but it is not paid for, I left my cloak as surety." Then the priest handed him a piece of money to pay for the book, which, proving to be of lead, Cortez had to refuse. The priest then came up saying, "But your books are false also." "Very well," said the colporteur, "let us go to the judge and settle both questions at once." The priest however decided to pay good money and tear up the book before the crowds of people who had gathered round. The wind carried the leaves about, and many were picked up and read." That was on June 14. In December, Cortez offered his books to a woman, sitting at her sewing machine by a window in the same city; she said that she wished only one book, which she did not suppose he would have—a religious book, about *the ten virgins*. He showed a large New Testament opened at the parable, and she bought it without hesitation. He could not but ask how she came to be looking for it. She replied, taking a single leaf out of her prayer-book, "My boy found this in the *plaza* some time ago, and as it has only part of the story, I have been looking for the whole book." The leaf was of the size of the Testament torn up in the market in June. . . .

Mr. Fernandez writes: "On the 12th of December I reached the ranch Quemado, one of the poorest in Chiapas state, between Chicuasen and Copainala, and as I dismounted from my horse, was surprised to see sitting in the shade of a tree an old man of about eighty years reading a small reference Bible, full of little place marks, of paper doubled up for the use of the reader. I saluted him as a stranger, asking what book he was reading. He answered gravely, 'This is the book of God.' 'How has God a book?' I asked. 'Si Señor,' he replied, 'this is his book, *La Santa Biblia*,' and keeping his finger at the place he had been reading, he showed me the title on the back of the cover, then he opened it, inviting me to hear what Jesus says; he was reading in Mark, and urged upon his belief that every man who desired to be saved ought to procure one of these little books, and continuing, said, 'One of my sons brought this from Tuxtla, five years ago; it changed my life, and we all read it in the family. Six months ago my wife died, and she knew many passages of the Gospels by heart.' He paused a moment here, and my companion told him who I was, when he arose and embraced me, full of joy; he had never learned to pray aloud, but we prayed there, and after explaining more fully the use of the reference, I left him a Bible of larger type for family worship, and went on my journey rejoicing that one of my little Bibles had found such rich soil."

Source Three
Race and Mission

Introduction

While Robert Speer's missionary experience was not mostly in Latin America, he was the head of the American Presbyterian Mission, one of the most active missionary societies working in the region. Therefore his writing, while not reflecting much direct experience, would certainly reflect much of what he heard from those who did have such experience and would in turn help shape the opinions and attitudes of missionaries sent to Latin America by the American Presbyterian Mission, as well as by other similar agencies.

As you read this document, note Speer's attitude toward Latin American culture. To what did he ascribe what he called Latin American "backwardness"? What did he see as the influence of Indian and African stock in Latin America? What about the Spanish? When he wrote of immigration as being favorable, what sort of immigration was he envisioning? How did he compare immigration in Latin America with immigration in the Unites States? How did he compare Latin Americans with the "Teutonic race"? What notions of racial and ethnic superiority do you find here? Note how he quoted and used Charles Darwin in order to support the Protestant missionary enterprise in Latin America. How does this relate to his entire argument?

What signs of a general affinity between Protestantism and liberalism on the one hand and Catholicism and conservatism on the other do you see? How is this related to the issue of freedom of worship? What is the connection between such freedom and immigration?

Why was Speer so negative toward "Rome"? Did he blame the Roman Catholic Church for the "backwardness" of Latin America? How would this support the other reasons he gave or contradict them? Why did he devote so much attention to immigration rather than to actual missionary work? What connection between the missionary enterprise and ethnic and cultural superiority do you find here?

For several decades before Speer wrote this essay, and for several decades thereafter, Presbyterian missions had put much of their effort in establishing missionary schools in Latin America—sometimes under the name of *Colegio Americano*. What connection exists between this policy and Speer's understanding of the problems of Latin America?

Since Speer himself never actually lived in Latin America, he was for the most part reporting what he had heard from others, particularly Presbyterian missionaries in the region. What does this tell you about how those missionaries understood and reported their work?

Speer wrote for a North American audience. Imagine he were speaking in Buenos Aires or in Caracas to a Spanish-speaking audience. Would he have expressed himself differently? Had you been a Latin American living early in the twentieth century and read these lines, how would you have reacted? What basis do you see here for the assertion that Protestantism was indissolubly connected with other cultures and would forever remain a foreign presence in Latin America?

The Text[‡]

Immigration. This expansion of trade and prosperity in South America is proportionate to the introduction of energy and capacity and character from without. South American progress is not indigenous. It is imported. Those countries which have received no immigration are almost as stagnant now as they have been for generations. The northern and western nations, i.e., from Venezuela around to Bolivia, are the backward nations. There are no railroads, no banks, no great business interests in all these republics which do not depend somewhere upon foreign character and ability. And even in Chile foreign enterprise and integrity are employed in every great commercial enterprise. Even on the ships of the Chilean corporation, the Compañía Sud-Americana de Vapores, all the captains and responsible officers are foreign. And it is the scarcity of this foreign element in all these lands which accounts for their backwardness. There has been no immigration to mention to any but four of the republics and these four have been already described as the foremost nations, separated from the rest. . . . The Argentine, which is the South American wonderland in wealth and development, is predominantly foreign. Even the Spanish element has been almost overmastered by the Italian, and the Italian stock has been a good one. Argentina is becoming a new Italy, while British and German capital, and with the capital men to supervise it, have been poured in like water. . . . It is the new blood and character from without which account for the progress which South America is making. Even in Chile, where it may seem to be Chilean, the men who are leading the nation bear names that show their British or German ancestry. With us it is now the native stock that dominates and improves the imported blood. In South America the imported blood dominates and improves the native stock. The governing class is European rather than American. Beneath this governing class, of course, is the great body of people with the heavier strain of native blood, uneducated, unawakened.

Causes of South American Backwardness. It is this heavy strain of Indian blood, and of negro blood as well in Brazil, and the unfavorable climatic conditions of South America which are usually charged with the responsibility for the backwardness of South America.

But more can be made of the climate than is warranted. . . . A different people would have worked out a far different result. As Charles Darwin wrote in his "Naturalist's Voyage in the Beagle," chapter xix, after his memorable visit to South America in 1832–35, contrasting Australia even in 1836 with South America: "At last we anchored within Sydney Cove. We found the little basin occupied by many large ships and surrounded by warehouses.

125

In the evening I walked through the town and returned full of admiration at the whole scene. It is a most magnificent testimony to the power of the British nation. Here, in a less promising country, scores of years have done many times more than an equal number of centuries have effected in South America."

The fundamental trouble in South America is ethical. The people of South America have their noble qualities as truly and as conspicuously as any other people. And there are among them, as among all peoples, all types of character. Speaking generally, they are warm-hearted, courteous, friendly, kindly to children, respectful to religious things, patriotic to the very soul; but the tone, the vigor, the moral bottom, the hard veracity, the indomitable purpose, the energy, the directness, the integrity of the Teutonic peoples are lacking in them. . . .

The issue of religious liberty arose also in connection with immigration. Brazil and Argentina especially wanted immigrants from northern Europe and they soon came. But when they came the impossibility of the conditions under which they had to live emerged. The young people wished to marry. They could not do so, for there was no civil marriage. The only marriage was marriage in the Roman Church. Children were born. If born out of Roman marriage they were deemed illegitimate. They could not be baptized. There was only Roman baptism. And unbaptized they were incapable of the inheritance of property. And old people died. There were no cemeteries in which they could be laid to rest. The Roman Church absolutely controlled the burial grounds and admitted to them only Roman Catholic dead. The leading minds of South America saw at once the impossibility of the situation. As Alberdi, one of the foremost publicists of Argentina, wrote, "Spanish America, reduced to Catholicism, with the exclusion of any other cult, represents a solitary and silent convent of monks. The dilemma is fatal—either Catholic and unpopulated, or populated and prosperous and tolerant in the matter of religion. To invite the Anglo-Saxon race and the people of Germany, Sweden and Switzerland and deny them the exercise of their worship is to offer them a sham hospitality and to exhibit a false liberalism. To exclude the dissenting cults from South America is to exclude the English, the German, the Irish and the North American, who are not Catholics, that is to say, the inhabitants whom this continent most needs. To bring them without their cult is to bring them without the agent that makes them what they are, and to compel them to live without religion and to become atheists."

Under free institutions, moreover, men began to think freely. They learned more of the world and by comparison came to understand more clearly the real character and corruption of the Church. They saw also that their free institutions were doomed unless they secured them not only against Spain and Portugal, but also against a far more subtle and powerful foe, even Rome itself.

Source Four
A Woman's View

Introduction

The Conference on Missions in Latin America, which took place on March 12 and 13, 1913, had been very carefully planned. One of the leaders in that planning, and the keynote speaker at the conference, was Robert Speer, the author of our last source, "Race and Mission." The conference was attended by representatives of the entire gamut of Protestant denominations in the United States—Baptists, Presbyterians, Methodists, Lutherans, Congregationalists, and many others—as well as of organizations such as the American Bible Society, the Y.M.C.A., and the Y.W.C.A. Its purpose was to compare notes and promote collaboration among the various bodies engaged in missions to Latin America.

Among other subjects, the conference discussed issues having to do with "women's work." At that time, it was reported that there were in Latin America 392 Protestant women missionaries from the United States. Of these, 241 were married, and their task was understood as supporting their husbands' work. Of the 151 who were single, all but nine were engaged in school work, primarily as teachers.

Mrs. Bauman was one of three women invited to address the issue of women's missionary work in Latin America. Another was a missionary working on education in Valparaiso, Chile. The third was an executive from the Board of Missions of the Methodist Episcopal Church. Mrs. Bauman was a pastor's wife in Buenos Aires. While the other two speakers focused their attention on the role and work of women missionaries, Mrs. Bauman dealt primarily with the conditions in which the Latin American women lived. She claimed to base her statements on what she had seen of the condition of women in Latin America. She also claimed that, not being a teacher or a pastor, she was able to observe and to get to know these women in a way that would have been difficult for pastors and teachers. Therefore, as you read this document you are invited to look both at the condition of the Latin American women themselves and at the manner in which Mrs. Bauman interpreted that condition and the remedies she proposed. Ask also to what degree and how Mrs. Bauman could be right in her claim that, as a pastor's wife, she could see things that others would not see.

Some questions you may ask, always taking into consideration those two sides of the picture, are: What were the problems she saw in the lives of servant girls and the lower echelons of society? What problems did she see among those who were better off and better educated? What character flaws did she see in them?

How much of what she said agrees with Speer's understanding of the "backwardness" of Latin America? Did she disagree in any way? Would she recognize Roman Catholics as Christians? What did she see lacking in them? How did she propose to improve the condition of women in Latin America? How is this similar or different from Speer's proposal? (Remember: Speer was most probably present at her speech!)

The Text[§]

I am glad of this opportunity to present to you, a company of people peculiarly interested in Latin-America, the needs of the women of Roman Catholic lands, as far as I have been able to study them in five years of missionary work in the Argentine Republic. My study of the subject may bring out some features which would not have appealed to the teachers, since I, as a pastor's wife, have come into closer touch with a wider circle of women than they, whose time is necessarily almost exclusively devoted to girls, either in class or boarding department. Being a woman, I am naturally interested in women I meet, and although my years of observation may not seem long to some of the older workers, it has been my privilege to know intimately, in my own home and in their own homes, a number of representative types of Latin-American women—and I shall endeavor to tell you how they impressed me.

Shall we begin at the lowest rung of the ladder of society—the servant? The servant in an Argentine family is a drudge, pure and simple. She works from early morning until late at night, has a bare, unfurnished corner in the house, or more often in an outhouse, is almost invariably illiterate and has far fewer opportunities of brightening or bettering her life than the girl of similar position in our own, or any Christian land—although in Buenos Aires, as is the case in any large city, with its increasing number of factories and stores to tempt the uneducated girl, the good servant commands a high salary. But all of this is insignificant in comparison with the moral dangers surrounding her. She is an unprotected girl, looked upon as little more than an animal and it is in the class that we see most openly the dreadful effect of the immorality of a nation who knows no God. It is the children of the poor, betrayed servant girls who fill the foundling asylums with their thousands and thousands of nameless children—and these same foundlings, the future servants of the nation—does it not make one sick at heart to think what future lies before them? I cannot tell you how amazed and shocked I was in our first pastorate, in a small town several hours by train from Buenos Aires, to find that it was almost impossible, in the whole country region, to find a servant over 17 or 18 years old, who did not have one or several nameless children. Most pitiful of all—no one wonders at it or thinks it extraordinary in any way—it is looked upon as quite a matter of course. Do you agree with me that the servant girl needs the Gospel? For her own personal life and especially, to give her a safer, cleaner moral atmosphere?

But let us turn to a brighter picture—the better educated girls. Girls are always interesting, but those of Latin race I think especially so; they are so attractive in face and manner, so bright and intelligent and they are withal winning in personality. But—when I go into an Argentine home, unless the people are true Christians, I am always wondering how much of the cordiality and sweetness I meet is real and how much simply a matter of courtesy (for the Argentine is above all things courteous) he (or she) will promise anything you ask and agree with everything you say, rather than seem to offend by disagreeing. And this leads me to a statement which every Argentine would regret to hear me make, but which he would have to admit as true: the Latin character is lacking in one great fundamental essential, the very foundation of true nobility of character: sincerity, sincerity of word and life. The missionary teachers present will agree with me that the fault most frequently found in their pupils, and the one most difficult to eradicate, is untruthfulness. It seems to be implanted in their very natures,—a bitter fruit of Romanism. And one encounters it on every hand, and with it a resulting superficiality and artificiality of life and character—for there can never be found a high moral character based on insincerity. The little girl is not a playful, cheerful child; she is a little overdressed "senorita," [sic] taught to care more for the admiration of society than for childhood pleasures. The school girl is bright and may aim for first place in her studies, but usually not through any desire for efficiency, but to make a good impression and to outshine others. The young lady is most charming in society (not always so in her own home) but almost always lacking in high ideals, caring far more for what others will say than for the reality of a thing.

Of course I am speaking generally. There are gratifying exceptions and I have known a number of girls, not yet touched by the power of Christ, who were worthy of all regard and admiration; but they always impressed me as rare plants, growing and blooming in spite of abnormal surroundings—and I can see how these same characters, if allowed to grow and expand in the atmosphere of consecration to God and service to mankind, would be immensely strengthened and ennobled, and of infinitely greater blessing to their fellows. . . .

Finally, though by no means last in importance, comes the mother—she whom all the world delights to honor, whose task of training the family for lives of usefulness is such an exceedingly important and difficult one. Have you ever thought, my dear mothers, what it would mean to undertake that task with no reliance on a Higher Power, without knowing Him who invites us to come to Him with our cares and difficulties and Who never fails to share them with us; Who guides and leads us when we know not which way to turn?

When all is well and life rolls on smoothly and pleasantly, you will see very little difference between the Argentine home and the Christian home. There is the same self-sacrificing mother spirit, warm affection between brothers and sisters—a closer bond often than we find in many of our American homes. But it is when the storms of sorrow and suffering come, the trials that put to the test the strongest Christian heart, it is then that we can see the difference. Oh, I often wonder how the mother's heart does not break with the strain—what consolation is there in lighting the candle before an image in the bedroom—a candle which all the rest of the year is unlighted? Imagine for yourselves what it must mean to lose a loved one, with none of the comforting promises of God's word to appease the pain, with no Everlasting Arms beneath to support us through the trial. Dear mothers, if your daughter or son is willing to go to teach those who know not the Risen, Living Saviour, our ever-present and abiding Comforter—put no obstacles in their way; rather, think of your sisters bearing their burdens alone, and gladly, willingly offer God the sacrifice He is asking of you.

Source Five
A Radical Perspective

Introduction

Iglesia y Sociedad en América Latina—ISAL—was born in 1961, gathering many of the most outspoken critics of social injustice in the region. The ISAL conference of 1966 in El Tabo, Chile, took place at a time of increasing polarization in Latin America—a polarization that also rent apart believers as well as churches. The economic disorder of the postwar years, and the increasing dominance of large transnational corporations in agriculture, manufacture, and trade, led many to the conviction that revolution was the only way out. But at the same time the reports coming out of the Communist bloc led others to the conviction that the greatest danger was not social injustice but Marxist revolution. The Cuban Revolution seven years earlier had further polarized the region, for some saw in it a sign that revolution could indeed succeed, while others saw in it the violence, dislocation, and suffering that revolution would inevitably produce.

Among Christians, some favored revolution, others argued that it was best to stay out of politics, and still others formed Christian political parties whose purpose was to attain power and then lead their nations to a better future. From its outset, ISAL leaned toward the first of those three positions—revolution as a way out—and was therefore accused of promoting both Marxism and violence.

This source comes from the second continent-wide conference of ISAL. As you read it, keep in mind a continent and a church deeply divided by differing and conflicting reactions to Marxism, to social injustice, to the Cuban Revolution, to North American policies, to capitalist ideology, and so on.

Ask yourself: Why does the document not favor the formation of Christian parties? Is it because such parties will not be able to attain power and bring about the needed change? Is it because such parties, were they to attain power, would pose a hidden threat to Christianity itself? What might that threat be?

If Christians should not create their own parties, what options does the document propose? How should Christians choose what parties and movements to join? Should they join movements that are not Christian or even some that are anti-Christian (for instance, Communist parties)? Why?

ISAL and many of its supporters were accused of promoting violence. How did they respond to such accusations? What strengths and flaws do you see in their argument? How would they have responded to believers who insisted that their faith required that they have nothing to do with violence?

A fairly common way in which Christians deal with political issues is to say that, although individual believers may and even should be involved in politics, churches should stay out of it. What would ISAL say about this? Then compare this document with others you have read. Would ISAL analyze the problems of Latin America in the same way as Speer? What are the main differences between them?

The Text*

The Christian community of Latin America today finds itself in the midst of crisis and revolution of the political structures throughout the continent, immersed in a process that conditions its way of life and forms of organization, whether or not it either wills or recognizes the fact. But on finding itself thus within the process, the church cannot therefore hope to give a specifically "Christian" impulse to this change or revolution. Such an attempt would mean sacralizing the revolution, a temptation against which God continually warns us by reminding his church in every historical situation: "I am the Lord your God. . . ."

With this end, "to present every man mature in Christ" (Col. 1:28), that is, in order for Jesus Christ to become incarnate in the new interdependent society, the Christian must vitally integrate himself into the situations and communities that constitute his historic context. This integration implies no alternative or challenge to the lordship of Jesus Christ but rather a real, full, and loyal involvement in secular concerns and in the imperative decisions necessitated by the contemporary crisis. In these terms there are no grounds for the church to project a form of change or revolution which it considers distinctly "Christian" or to try to impose that same stamp on a particular social order or specific political movement. On the contrary, participation in political life and social change impels the church to assume the role of the suffering servant, to act in self-renunciation and humility for the well-being of man. On the basis of this concept we may note certain lines of action and possible responses to various anxieties of Christian individuals and churches in Latin America.

Political participation leads the Christian to responsible and creative action within the existing political parties and civic and social movements. If these do not satisfy the expressed need for social changes, he many consider joining other men similarly concerned and dissatisfied with the status quo in seeking new structures or political movements through which to direct themselves in responsible action. But he should avoid the temptation to think in terms of "Christian" political parties, which misconstrues the true foundations of the unity of the church and leads to sanctioning a particular political program with a presumed system of Christian values. . . . On the other hand he should not be afraid to participate in groups or movements whose politico-social concepts seem implicitly or explicitly incompatible with the "Christian" concept of the social system. In the first place it is doubtful whether there exists a static and definitive biblical concept of society, so all the systems which have been called "Christian" over the years have been in fact historical and therefore transitory expressions of social order, no matter how biblically inspired they may have been. Second, it is precisely within the groups and movements questioning the place of the Christian faith that the believer in Jesus Christ can attain his truly prophetic dimension and embody the presence of his Lord in the midst of the crucial decisions of contemporary society. One must recognize the danger inherent in such involvements, but at the same time, one must not fail to recognize also that the Word of God urges such a stand and that in such a way the Christian's faith and his calling to witness and service acquire concrete content.

Can the Christian participate directly in the struggle against the established legal structures when there is no prospect that these will be transformed through the actions of existing political movements and parties or social pressure groups? In other words, is it lawful for the Christian actively to participate in revolutionary movements that may resort to violence in cases where the goal of social transformation does not appear viable by any other means but which is indispensable from the viewpoint of social justice and human well-being?

A realistic consideration of this problem should bring one to realize that it is not a matter of introducing violence into a society without violence. There exists the so-called "invisible violence," or "white violence," and also moral violence, daily latent and ineradicable from our society at the present moment. This already-existent violence results at every moment in hundreds of deaths from hunger, poverty and disease in Latin America and deprives the man of our continent of the basic necessities for living under "human" conditions. This is to say that the legal social order prevents a man from fulfilling the purpose for which he was created, that of reaching human fullness, the true measure of Jesus Christ.

On the other hand it is necessary to underscore the ambiguous character of all action, violent or nonviolent; whether we choose the way of violence for the sake of effectiveness or whether we choose nonviolence in order to preserve our principles, we are equally under the judgment of God. Neither violence nor nonviolence, therefore can be settled in advance in virtue of *a priori* principles without consideration of the given situations. In the face of this ambivalence, the unequivocal responsibility of the Christian is to point out and unmask all forms of visible or invisible violence, to seek its causes and possible remedies, and to put into practice the solutions which he believes to have found in the light of the Word of God—knowing that the very realism of the Bible leads him to channel his actions through existing political and social means and social pressure groups and therefore that his action can be neither perfect nor ideal.

Finally one must realize that the Christian cannot expect absolute, definitive certainty concerning the character of his decisions. This will lead him to seek the fellowship of the Christian congregation to adopt an attitude of humility and dialogue with his brothers who have made different decisions. This will reveal to him the profound depth in which human encounter takes place in Jesus Christ, deeper even than the level of concrete decisions which of necessity we make in social living. In the same fashion as Luther, he will submit himself to the judgment of God and rely on his pardon with the words, "Here I stand . . . So help me God."

At this point one may note that there is no sure criterion for distinguishing between the action of individual Christians and the action of the church as a formal institution. Nevertheless, in certain instances the action of the institutional church must be considered as such. When the politico-social situation comes to express the demonical character of institutions and the ambition and egotism of man and when violence, direct and indirect, is unleashed in apocalyptical form, the church can and should speak out prophetically, pronouncing the judgment of God on the political parties, the economic systems, the ideologies and the governments responsible for that situation. It should indeed remember at all times that it is passing judgment in the name of the Lord also on those Christians who are actively involved in the process and that that judgment falls accordingly on the church itself. As an integral and inseparable part of the social order, the church bears the burden of collective guilt, and its judgment is always, at the same time, a confession of sin. In any case the prophetic stance implies a risk and a sacrifice on the part of the church, and nothing could be more foreign to the spirit of Jesus Christ than the assumption of a comfortable neutrality or otherworldliness indifferent to the social conflict erupting round about.

Source Six
A Poet's Fear and Faith

Introduction

The twentieth century was not kind to Guatemala, a land rocked by dictatorships, revolutions, and civil war. In the 1980s, the situation worsened as much of Central America became the stage for a proxy war between the United States and the Soviet Union. Those whom the government did not like for whatever reason were dubbed Communists. Some took advantage of the situation to massacre and take the lands of native peoples, particularly the Quiché. Poet Julia Esquivel Velásquez, a Presbyterian born in that torn land in 1930, had studied first at the local university of San Carlos and then at the Seminario Bíblico Latinoamericano in San José, Costa Rica. Returning to her land, she was profoundly pained by the violence she witnessed. Death squads—unofficial agents of the government—acted with impunity, killing any who dared speak out in defense of the poor. Esquivel felt that the words of the poor were "like knives" tearing into her flesh and therefore combined her poetry with relentless activism on behalf of peace with justice. For this reason she was repeatedly threatened and targeted by death squads. Finally, after a failed attempt to kidnap her, she went into self-imposed exile.

The poem you are about to read is part of a collection published under the title *Florecerás Guatemala* (You will bloom again, Guatemala). It was written while Esquivel was in exile in Switzerland, where she took the opportunity for further studies and for establishing contacts with church leaders from around the world. After the violence abated, she returned to Guatemala, where she now lives.

As you read this poem, note her use of the story of the crucifixion to interpret her own story and that of Guatemala. Why did she refer to Annas and Caiaphas, the high priests at the time of the death of Jesus? Why did she refer to Herod and Pontius Pilate, representatives of Roman imperial authority? What counterparts did she see in Guatemala? The unnamed friend of Jesus who allowed himself to be seduced into betraying Jesus is Judas. Where did she see Judas's counterpart in Guatemala? Who might be offended by this poem, and why? What might she have meant by a temple empty of God?

Note that the poem moves from fear to joy. Certainly, the joy has little to do with the outward circumstances having changed. What had changed? What did she mean by the Lord's wound, and hers?

The Text[+]

Tremor

I am afraid, Lord!
I am afraid
    of the fear of the powerful,
    of the insecurity of bureaucrats,
    of the egolatry of the machos,
    of those who proudly and in your name
      use money and prestige at whim.

135

They, like Annas and Caiaphas,
  or like Herod or Pilate
  are always ready
  to hang you again from a cross.

They, the important ones,
  put their prestige ahead
  of naked, shameful truth.

They are afraid of risk, Lord.
   They are in love with their position.
   They would rather dig a grave
    and make us disappear.
They, you well know,
  they speak of justice.
  They are honorable and clean . . .
  But in their deeds
   they plan to undo the just,
   and more so if it is a woman!

Lord, free me from the snares
  of the powerful.
Open before my eyes
  a path of peace.

With you I will tread
  the ancient path.
I entreat you:
  hold my hand in yours.
Hold it tightly,
  so I may take in mine
  the wound of the nail
  that held yours to the cross.

Oh, that wound of yours!
Endless like your love!
A wound brought about
  by one of your friends
    who was seduced by the priestly plan
    and gladly followed
    the fake glitter
    of institutional welfare.

136

Oh foolish friend!
What good did it do,
    having lost his soul,
    to cast away the glittering idol
    into a temple without God?

Now, oh wonderful gift!
I am no longer afraid, Lord.
I feel your wounded hand
    closely holding
    my small one!

Your wound is now mine,
    endless . . .

7
PROTESTANTS
AND CATHOLICS

Introduction

The nineteenth century brought serious difficulties to the Roman Catholic Church, not only in Latin America, but throughout the world. These arose from modern liberal ideas such as freedom of worship, separation of church and state, and public education under the control of secular governments. These challenges had taken political form in the French Revolution, which proved costly to the Catholic Church, and then in the independence of the Latin American nations. In general, the official reaction of the Church was one of resistance to change and insistence on its authority. In 1864, Pope Pius IX (1846–1878) issued *Syllabus of Errors*, a list of eighty propositions that the pope considered errors of modernity. Among these were freedom of religion, that the Catholic Church should not be treated as the only religion of a state, that science should be free from ecclesiastical authority, that public education should be available to all social classes and be placed under the jurisdiction of the state, and many others along similar lines. In 1870, in what may have been an effort to bolster the waning authority of the papacy, the First Vatican Council, attended by some six hundred prelates from all over the world, proclaimed the infallibility of the pope. But even so, that year the waning power of the pope was manifested as he lost Rome and most of the traditional papal states to the emerging Kingdom of Italy, retaining only the Vatican.

Meanwhile, many Protestant leaders and theologians were taking the opposite tack, declaring Protestantism to be fully compatible with modernity and sometimes almost equating the two. Protestantism, they said, held to many of the "errors" that the pope decried, being fully supportive of freedom of thought, worship, assembly, and scientific inquiry.

As a result, the differences between Roman Catholicism and Protestantism became quite pronounced, repeatedly leading to profound distrust, political clashes, and virulent mutual attacks.

Things were also difficult for the Catholic Church in Latin America, where the birth of new nations and the growth of Protestantism threatened the traditional authority of the Catholic Church and its hierarchy. In 1899, in response to these challenges in Latin America, Pope Leo XIII (1878–1903) convoked the First Latin American Plenary Council, which met in Rome, with the purpose of coordinating the Church's response to the difficulties looming in the region as the twentieth century approached—particularly those of modernity with its accompanying liberalism and of the growing presence of Protestantism.

Catholic strategy in response to the Protestant challenge moved in several directions. In countries such as Colombia, where the Catholic Church had the power to influence legislation in its favor, laws were passed limiting the rights and activities of Protestants. Throughout Latin America, the claims were often made that Latin culture was essentially Catholic, that Protestantism was the arm of North American imperialism, and therefore to become a Protestant was to capitulate to foreign influence. When addressing the wider world, particularly the United States and Europe, Catholic apologists often asserted that since Latin America was already Christian, foreign missions to it were unnecessary and disruptive—perhaps even opening the way for Communism.

In response to such policies and claims, Protestants both in Latin America and abroad would argue that Latin American Catholicism was far from true Christianity and that it was at least partly to be blamed for the ills of the region. Also, when laws were enacted against Protestants or where they were victims of violence, part of the Protestant response was to spread the news far and wide, hoping this would bring pressure on the governments involved. These conditions and tensions persisted through the first half of the twentieth century, until the Second Vatican Council (1962–1965) began changing the atmosphere of hostility and distrust between Catholics and Protestants.

The documents you will read in this chapter were written before the changes brought about by Vatican II. Therefore, you will find in them a strong enmity between Protestants and Catholics. Note, however, that some documents are self-critiques.

Source One, "The Archbishop Complains," is an example of the attitude of the Roman Catholic hierarchy in the face of an increasing Protestant presence in Latin America. It is a letter from the archbishop of Lima to the Peruvian minister of justice and worship objecting to the opening of a Protestant church and school. Although the letter was dated 1864, it was published three years later in a Protestant magazine in England, accompanied by a report on the events surrounding it.

Source Two, "A Catholic Woman's Plan for Action," comes from the Congreso Católico Argentino-Uruguayo, held in Montevideo in 1906. A sign of change was that, for the first time in such gatherings, women were invited as speakers. One of these was Celia LaPalma de Emery, a fairly well-to-do Argentine philanthropist whose concern was focused on street children. Part of her speech was devoted to that particular issue as well as to the plight of working mothers. She criticized the government for not providing sufficient funding for the care of orphans and abandoned children. But she was also concerned with the bigger picture, which she saw as a conflict between religion and secular governments. She blamed liberalism and socialism for the loss of influence of the Catholic Church. Her response was the proposal to create an army of *cristianos sin miedo* (fearless Christians) who would undertake a "crusade of love" and whose works of charity would give them authority to oppose the liberal and socialist leanings of governments.

Source Three, "A Call to Change from a Nobel Laureate," was written by Lucila Godoy Alcayaga, a schoolteacher best known under her pseudonym, Gabriela Mistral (1889–1957). Abandoned by her father when she was still young, Mistral constantly struggled with the consequences of poverty and prejudice against women. While still quite young, she was attracted to liberal ideas, so much so that when she applied for her first teaching position at age eighteen, she was turned down because the chaplain of the school considered her too liberal. When she wrote our document in 1924, she was beginning to emerge as a poet and social and political activist. Although a Catholic, she criticized the authorities of the Church for not responding adequately to the needs of her time. In 1945, more than twenty years after she wrote the article quoted here, she became the first Latin American to receive the Nobel Prize in Literature. Eventually she joined the Chilean diplomatic corps, representing her nation in Italy, Portugal, and the United States.

Source Four, "Justifying a Presence," comes from the pen of John A. Mackay (1889–1983), who, after long years of residence in Latin America as a Presbyterian missionary, became president of Princeton Theological Seminary in New Jersey. An important part of his career took place in Lima, where he established links with the Peruvian intelligentsia, eventually becoming Professor of Modern Philosophy at the prestigious Universidad de San Marcos. Thus, his understanding of Latin American culture was more profound than Speer's—in chapter 6, "Race and Mission."

Mackay's writing quoted here was published by the Committee of Cooperation in Latin America. This committee was formed in 1916, partly as a response to the decision to exclude Protestant missions in Latin America from the great International Missionary Conference that gathered in Edinburgh in 1910—an exclusion grounded on the argument that Latin America was already Christian and therefore was not a proper land for missions.

Source Five, "We Are Not All Catholic," was written by Gonzalo Báez Camargo (1899–1983), a nationally acclaimed Mexican poet and journalist. A Methodist, much of his writing had to do with his experience of faith in relation to his culture and particularly with the place of Protestantism in Mexico. Like the other Protestant sources in this chapter, it reflects a radical rejection of Roman Catholicism—or at least of Catholicism as it was practiced and experienced in Latin America.

Source Six, *"La Violencia,"* is one of dozens of articles and reports written by James Goff, a North American Presbyterian missionary in Colombia. As he stated in the source itself, he was appointed to investigate and document religious persecution and violence in that country. The result was a vast number of reports about murder, dynamiting of churches, and even massacres—all apparently with the connivance of both the government and the Catholic hierarchy. His reports, widely circulated in Latin America as well as in the United States and elsewhere, caused great embarrassment to the Colombian government and to the Church, which flatly denied them or declared them to be gross exaggerations. Eventually, after the Second Vatican Council and a political change in Colombia, both the government and the Church have generally admitted that Goff's reports were true. The document quoted here was written after persecution had ended, or at least abated. Although it summarizes much of Goff's other reports, its purpose was to call for changes that would prevent the recurrence of violence and persecution.

As you read these sources, consider how they are responses to the circumstances and challenges of the times as well as to one another. What would LaPalma say to Báez Camargo? How might Mistral respond to Mackay? What differences do you note between sources written by Latinos and those written by North Americans? What commonalities do you see?

Consider also how the views expressed in some of these documents relate to what you read earlier. For instance, how would Báez Carmargo react to Speer's and Bauman's explanations of what they saw as the region's social and economic underdevelopment ("Race and Mission" and "A Woman's View," both in chapter 6)?

Source One
The Archbishop Complains

Introduction

What follows is an 1864 letter from the archbishop of Lima to the Peruvian cabinet member in charge of religious matters. It was prompted by news from Callao, the port city serving Lima, five miles away, that Protestant missionaries were building a church and a school. The archbishop wrote to the government, demanding that the Protestant projects be stopped and that Protestant churches and schools not be allowed in the nation. How this letter came to be in the hands of a Protestant missionary and his supporters is not known. Somehow, it was "leaked" to them—which is not surprising, for at this time the head of the Peruvian government was Colonel Mariano Prado, known for his liberal policies. It was published in English three years later by the South American Missionary Society as part of a report from its first missionary in Callao. According to this Protestant missionary, tensions had not subsided. In Callao itself a parish priest repeatedly rallied the people against the Protestants. In Lima the debate over freedom of worship became so acrimonious that a mob of Catholic women sitting in the balcony while Congress was in session pelted the representatives of the liberal persuasion and had to be expelled by force of arms.

As you read this letter, try to understand why the archbishop felt as he did and what were the undeclared premises of his arguments. What strong points or flaws do you see in his reasoning? What did he expect Protestants to do that was so offensive? How did he view foreigners and their motives? What justification did he find for freedom of worship in other countries? Why would he not accept the same in Peru? What links did he try to establish between the good of the country and not allowing Protestant worship? What did he suspect might be the reasons for some Peruvians becoming Protestant?

Look then at what he said about Peruvians whose Catholicism was not as good as it should be. List the reasons he gave for such faulty Catholicism. Whom did he blame? On the basis of your previous readings, what other reasons should he have listed and whom else should he have faulted?

Now consider the means by which the letter itself has come to us, in English translation in a Protestant missionary magazine. Why would this magazine have published a letter by a Roman Catholic archbishop? Note that the archbishop had used the policies of Elizabethan England to bolster his argument. If you were an English Protestant reader, how would you respond to that argument?

The Text[*]

Archiepiscopal Palace
Lima, 29th September, 1864
To Mr. Minister of Justice and Worship

Mr. Minister,

I transmit to you the letter (of the 12th inst.) which the vicar of Callao has addressed to me informing me of the building of a Protestant temple and School which are soon to be opened in that city.

The work appears sufficiently advanced, and its originators doubtless pretend to ridicule our worship and show the want of respect which they have to our Constitution and the laws of our country.

I will not stop to offer any remarks on the fundamental principles of which the 4th Article of our Constitution is a corollary. God alone can prescribe the worship with which He seeks to be adored, to Him alone it is directed, and He alone can command it. Since we recognize the Catholic faith as the only true one, it is deduced by legitimate consequences that the exercise of the Catholic worship is that alone which can be offered to the Divinity. Our legislators had considered these principles well, and established in all our political institutions, that the religion of the Peruvian nation was the Catholic, Apostolic, Roman, without permitting the public exercise of any other.

But, laying aside reasons so palpable, it is sufficient to consider that the diversity of worship destroys in a nation the unity of thought, of traditions, and of customs, in which national power principally consists. The toleration of different forms of worship is not an advantage in politics, but an inconvenience, or rather an infirmity, which affects nations whose religious opinions are divided.

Religious toleration is only granted in nations where the dissidents from the established religion are numerous, and form a considerable part of that great family called a nation. Then the evil, which divides the worship and the religious opinions, is tolerated, to avoid a greater one. viz. that a great number of individuals be in want of worship and of rules of morality which may guide their conduct. In that case, it is better that a people should have some worship, however mutilated, which may preserve some notions of revelation, and of morality purified by the Gospel.

But the Peruvian nation is not in this condition. The people, without an exception, is Catholic. There does not exist the lamentable germ of religious discord. Perhaps all are not members of the Church, as they ought to be; perhaps there are men who have scarcely the smallest tincture of religion; there may be others in whom the corruption of manners has blotted out the religious feeling which is innate in man, which grows and becomes strengthened by education. But the existence of such persons is not a sufficient reason why our laws should be infringed, or our Constitution changed. Those persons, if not good Catholics, will not be Protestants. Their tendency is to have no religion, to renounce all forms of worship, and in short to forget the Divinity. For those toleration is an absurdity, and any worship whatever is an act of fanaticism. With their manners and theories they undermine the fundamental laws of society, of the family, and of the individual, and consequently, for such as these we should not infringe the laws which we obey in this matter.

Unity, Mr. Minister, in matters of doctrine, religious or political, is a great blessing to nations; all try to obtain it by means of laws, more or less repressive, each one according to the special circumstances and conditions in which it is found. When there is unity in a nation, its thoughts are noble, its force compact, and its action vigorous.

Religious unity produces great effects. It is the germ of charity; it is the principle of love, pure and disinterested, towards our country and our fellow-beings. The religious man works conscientiously, and not for individual interest or base designs.

To permit, then, that the public exercise of a new religion be established in a land which has preserved the benefit of its unity, is to sow the seed of discord in our country, and reap, at a future period, too bitter fruits.

Even in countries in which toleration is necessity in consequence of the great number of those who profess different religions, the Government, always striving at unity, protects one religion, and enacts laws which repress the action of others. In England, after the reign of Elizabeth, permission would not be given to erect a Catholic church, unless the English Catholic subjects were several millions in number. Never would the Catholic worship be tolerated, because a hundred foreigners had gone to the country for the purpose of carrying on business. Notwithstanding there being an immense number of Catholics in that country, the exercise of their religion is subject to innumerable obstacles. It is sufficient to say, that even now the English Catholic, who, by his poverty, is unable to contribute to the maintenance of his worship and the support of his religion, pays tithes, by the law of the State, to the English Church Establishment, the errors of which he deplores. This being the case, why should the public exercise of a religion, new and unknown in the country, be tolerated in Peru, where there is not a single Peruvian Protestant?

It is no answer to say that there is a considerable number of Protestant residents in Callao. These persons have come to our country to make a fortune, and that once acquired they bring their wealth to their own country. This resolution does not arise from the want of religious toleration; it proceeds from the innate love which everyone bears to the land of his birth, acquired in early years, and which is never forgotten; also from a regard to the higher grade of civilization which the European nations have reached, and the greater means of enjoyment which the man of fortune can obtain there. Those, then, who come to Peru to acquire wealth, ought, in compensation, to subject themselves to our laws, and treat them with respect.

Governments are obliged to satisfy the requirements of their subjects; but not to agree to the capricious wishes of anyone whose country is situated in another hemisphere. However great and inviolable the rights of hospitality may be, a foreigner has no right to demand that a people should deny its faith, habits and traditions, violate its own laws, and alter its national character. Neither England, nor any other nation, knowing their true interests, would permit that.

Peru is tolerant to excess, as far as true charity, religious feeling, and national honour demand. She persecutes no one because he may hold a different belief, and in return for that toleration, demands, with right and justice, that her religion be publicly respected and honoured.

But now they do not desire to observe this just measure. They seek to dogmatize in public, to place in open contest the faith and religion of the Peruvians with the beliefs of other nations. They ask for the public exercise of the Protestant worship, in order that Protestantism may be propagated, its errors preached, published and communicated to the ignorant, to the curious, to the friends of novelties, to the weak in the faith, and to the poor who may be under the protection or influence of dissidents. Protestantism seeks public exercise of its worship, in order, with that pretext, to propagate its doctrines, and diffuse its erroneous instruction among the masses, not only by means of preaching, but also by education in Schools and Colleges.

Since a Protestant temple is established in Callao, there is no plausible reason to hinder the establishment of houses and Colleges of the same kind. What difference can there be between teaching in a temple, and teaching in a room with a few benches? The difference consists only in the number and in the class of hearers. In the temple are taught small and great, the ignorant and the instructed; in schools and colleges only weak and ignorant children.

So lamentable are the consequences of an ill-understood toleration.

The reasons which I have adduced, Mr. Minister, impose on me as a Peruvian, and as Bishop, the painful but most severe duty to call the attention of the supreme Government to this question begging that fit measures be taken that our Constitution be not trodden under foot, nor our laws infringed in our own country, by persons who are not members of our nation, and were they so, are not numerous enough that their wishes should be complied with; and are neither in such conditions, as that sound reason and true policy demand that their advances be tolerated.

As Catholic Bishop, I am obliged to preserve from irreligious and heretical contagion the souls redeemed with the blood of the Saviour, and forming part of the flock of our Lord Jesus Christ, which have been confided to my charge. It is my duty, then, to give the cry of alarm against those attacks which are so imprudently made against the purity of the holy religion which we possess; and to demand the fulfilment of the laws of our Fatherland.

I have confidence in the piety of His Excellency the President of the Republic, and in the rectitude of those who, at present, form the Council of Ministers, who will consider the grave and transcendental nature of the question, and will not permit our fundamental charter to be rent asunder, thus accustoming both natives and foreigners to despise and act in defiance of the laws under which we live.

May it please your Lordship to bring this reclamation under the notice of His Excellency, &c., &c., &c.

Signed José Sebastian
Archbishop of Lima

Source Two
A Catholic Woman's Plan for Action

Introduction

Although delivered in 1906, this speech by Celia LaPalma de Emery was published in 1910 as part of a collection of her speeches and lectures—a publication that in itself was a further call for action on the part of committed

Catholics. While the selection quoted here does not include them, in this particular speech she did list many of the actions that Catholics were taking for the defense of the Church and the well-being of society.

In this document, she repeatedly referred to the need for "Catholic action." In the 1920s, with the support of Pope Pius XI, a worldwide organization was created under the name of Catholic Action. Much of the program of this new organization was what LaPalma had proposed—the creation of a cadre of militant Catholic laity to revitalize faith and commitment and to defend the rights of the Church. In Argentina, there was not an official organization under the name of *Acción Católica* (Catholic Action) until 1931, a quarter of a century after LaPalma delivered this speech and long after Catholic Action existed elsewhere. Thus, she may be considered one of the many forerunners of this organization. Her speech and activities are a clear indication of a new involvement of Latin American laity in the life of the Church—particularly in the defense of its rights and its faith in the face of what was seen as an increasingly hostile environment.

As you read this document, try to discern the manner in which LaPalma understood the situation at the time, particularly with reference to the attitude of governments. Did she see government as her ally or as an enemy needing to be subdued? How did she propose to deal with government? In the conflict between liberals and conservatives, which side would she take, and why? Whom would she blame for the threats and dangers she saw? As she enumerated the goals of the actions she proposed, how did she rank the defense of the rights of the Church and its worship in comparison to the social needs of the people? Why her sense of urgency? How was the fact that she was addressing men reflected in what she said and how she said it? Did she say anything about the role of the clergy, or was she speaking only of lay action? Why would that be, and what does that tell you about the state of the Church at the time?

The Text[†]

Now, as to how Catholics are to employ their rights as citizens, that is, how Catholic civil action is to operate, we have to be persuaded that this must be done publicly to the fullest extent, and that lay Catholics must take it from the homes to the streets, to the courthouse, to Congress, and to the other powers. This may be done by means of their talent, their prudence, their authority, and influence. It can also be done by means of their personal help, moral support, and pecuniary protection, perhaps even by merely consoling and, to speak even of the lowest possible level of support, by not discouraging those who do work.

As to the importance of what is needed, this Catholic action may refer, first, to the defense of all that pertains to worship; second, to the propagation of Catholic faith and doctrine; third, to works of charity; and, fourth, to all that is related to the rights of the church and to social welfare.

I will not list the details of what this action may entail at each point. But in short, I declare that there can hardly be a single Catholic with so little ability as not to be able to do something for the good cause, and that all must do all that is within their means.

I have already declared that Catholic action exists, and this is proven by the fact that our Church is still defended and respected, thanks to the action of good Catholics everywhere, even though in almost all nations the official institutions or parties of government are more or less hostile to the Church. And there are many among sovereigns, presidents, and ministers who clearly support this attitude.

Having established these principles [on the responsibility of Catholics], we now turn to the main point that I propose to clarify at this time and with reference to our nation: the existence of an unforgivable apathy in a good many Catholics. They do accept private pious practices but believe that they cannot commit in such a way as to draw attention to themselves. [They fear] having people talk about them. They do not take the trouble of using their influence. [They do not wish] to create a bad opinion among liberals. These indolent Catholics act thus because they do not know what their duties are nor the dangers that threaten us. They have to be reminded that in the biblical parable God did away with the useless servant, who did not invest his talent, and that a strict account will be demanded of what they were able to do through religion in defense of society and yet did not. In short, let us all know that our duty is not to be silent when it is time to speak; not to shrug our shoulders when the good cause must be defended; not to abandon Catholics who work for the cause and who are unable to conquer because they lack our help. It is necessary to enroll in the active army of Catholic action; for in these times apathy is a violation of a great duty.

The main reason why there are such Catholics is that they do not wish to know how far the evil extends and thus do not understand the need to oppose it. Their heart is asleep because they are not illumined by reason. The unforgivable apathy of these Catholics is the reason why so much of the official advantage of our cause is being lost in education. So much influence is being lost in the attitudes of most of those who, being unfavorably predisposed against the clergy and religion, shut their eyes to the good ideas being proclaimed by the word both spoken and written. It is because of them that our Catholic press, the main bulwark to support the ideas of social order, does not have the success of the impious newspapers working for evil. It is because of their indolence that we are threatened by partial defeats.

Source Three
A Call to Change from a Nobel Laureate

Introduction

This article was published in a Protestant journal, *La Nueva Democracia*, which was produced in New York with the support of the Committee on Cooperation in Latin America, and was noted as a vehicle of expression for the Latin American intelligentsia—both Protestant and Catholic. Actually, the authors of our next two sources, John A. Mackay and Gonzalo Báez Camargo, both wrote for it.

Thus, the first item to think about as you read this is what it says about Catholic-Protestant relations. In some of the readings in this chapter, you will note a decided mutual hostility and distrust. Yet Mistral published this article in a Protestant journal thousands of miles away. This indicates that, despite the general atmosphere, there was a measure of openness and contact between Catholic and Protestant intellectuals.

What did Mistral understand to be the "problem" of Latin America and its Catholicism? What would she have said about Speer's views that we saw in chapter 6, "Race and Mission," published just a few years earlier? What parallels do you see between her evaluation of the Russian Slavs and Speer's evaluation of Latin Americans? On what points would she have agreed with Celia LaPalma? What differences do you see? How would conservative Catholics react to her phrase, "Catholicism and Christianity in general"? What signs of classism can you discover in her article? What indications do you see here of a rift between liberal Catholics and the hierarchy and policies of the Catholic Church?

This was written during the rise of Communist Russia. What appeal would Communism have in Latin America, as Mistral saw it? If she were writing today, after the collapse of the Soviet Union, which of her assertions would still be valid and which not? How does Mistral's notion of "reconquest" differ from that of fifteenth-century Spain (see chapter 1, "A God-Given Destiny")?

An added point to reflect on is the following: The next Chilean to receive the Nobel Prize in Literature, Pablo Neruda, whose mentor she had been, became a Communist. To what extent could this be seen as a fulfillment of the fears that Mistral expressed?

The Text[‡]

A painful reality of Latin America at this time is the developing radical divorce between the masses of the people and religion, or rather between democracy and Christianity. Since the pattern for the most radical reformations come from the terrifying Russian dictatorship, those who follow the doctrines coming from the steppes believe that part of their program must no longer be mere lack of religiosity, but even open impiety, in solidarity with that Russian shame. During Christmas of last year there was a ridiculous procession in which the founders of religions, including Christ, were grotesquely personified.

It is well known that the Russian people were, until recently, among the most religious on earth. Upon changing their institutions, their leaders should not have rudely torn from it the religious sense of life, but rather purified it, leaving aside all superstition, elevating the Christianity of the peasants.

But in political matters these leaders have guided their people to a suicidal jump into the abyss, exchanging the brutal tsarist regime for the equally brutal Bolshevik dictatorship. The Slavic race, not prone to nuances, also made the tragic leap from the sharpest mysticism to the most cynical impiety. Thus, the contagion comes from the steppes, and since ours also are a people not given to nuances—which would come from a refined culture—what took place there can be reproduced here in very likely fashion.

Conservatism and Jacobinism

It is pleasing to read in a book by such a distinguished North American educator as is the President of Columbia University a praise for religion as an integral part of education and as a propitious contribution for the soundness of a people. I have read this with a measure of surprise, for in our South America being liberal is almost always the same as being a Jacobin.

A Jacobin could be defined as follows: He is a man of a mediocre or even inferior culture, with no fine eye for matters of the spirit. He is "thick." He does not realize that religion is one of the aspects of culture and that it has contributed to the purification of the soul of the people. Thus, he rejects religious matters as having a role in individual education and equally as having a role in society. He coarsely confuses religion with superstition, which is similar to confusing a puppet show with a Greek tragedy.

The Errors of Latin American Christianity

But if the Russian people, and like them our people, be it Mexican or Chilean, have so easily abandoned the faith of their elders, allowing themselves to be led by violent "leaders," one would imagine even with very simple logic that they must have been given enormously convincing reasons. It is not so easy to uproot an old faith that has nourished so many generations, nor to have an institution of powerful excellence fade so quickly.

In such a case, the duty of a Christian is not to respond with wrathful and desperate pejorative epithets, but rather to make a sharp analysis, as one does after a defeat, in order to see where was the fragility of a feeling that we thought was eternal.

I, who have cast my anchor on Catholicism after many years of doubt, have determined to do this analysis with a pained heart because of what my faith loses, but also with a clear mind, seeking not to condemn but rather to understand the process.

What I have seen is that our Christianity, in contrast with Anglo-Saxon Christianity, broke away from social concerns, or at least undervalued them. This Christianity has developed a paralyzed or even dead sense of justice, and now that sense has been born in others and has pulled them away from Christianity.

A faith that was born miraculously among the common people, that slowly was able to conquer the powerful, was destined not to forget that birth. While cherishing its humble origins, Christianity should have recognized that, even apart from its own origins, the so-called populace (which I would rather call the marvelous people) is, by its own size, the only grounding which would keep Christianity powerful, reigning over thousands of souls. Other social classes, no matter how select, are a poor source of support, for every religion has always sought numbers of followers, just as politics seeks them. And yet, neither by reason of its own tradition nor by calculation has our Christianity found a way to be faithful to the lower classes.

Aspects of Religion

I am well aware that service to society is not the highest level of religion. I know that St. Teresa, the mystic, is a higher religious expression than a Catholic welfare society, and that St. Augustine is greater than St. Vincent de Paul, because the saint [Teresa] and the great theologian [Augustine] received the highest gift: the message made flesh in them. But, as is the case of the Himalayas in geography, in religion only a handful can reach the highest peaks.

For the Roman plebs, the faith of Christ was a doctrine of human equality, that is, a principle of collective life, a form of politics (let us recover the nobility of that word that has become so stained). The same is the case for the people of today. That aspect of religion which was the most important for the masses did not become a reality in our lands. There is intense Catholic social action in Argentine, and in Chile it is doing important things, but it is not enough. And in other lands that will go unmentioned, it does not even exist.

The working people have been abandoned to their own lot, to a servitude that is simply medieval, and thus have divorced religion from human justice. Agitators have gone to tell them that Christianity is a siren song that seeks to quiet their quest for vindication. These "leaders" have told them that the quest after the kingdom of heaven is incompatible with the creation of a kingdom on earth, namely, one of economic well-being.

The people are not heroic. They do not possess the sacrificial character of those who have been sublime heroes. Thus, given the choice, it is not surprising that they have gone in the other direction. . . . The bad shepherds have told them that there is no possible alliance between the two [religion and social justice], and the people have gone with those who promised bread and a roof for their children.

Reconquest Is Still Possible

We cannot afford to lose so many souls, for no matter how much our own are worth, God will never forgive us for abandoning the multitudes who amount to practically the entire world. Catholicism has to conquer once again what, either for inertia or for self-interest, it has abandoned. This would be possible if we Catholics would show that we are truly capable of giving up things—basically, capable of following the very essence of our doctrine.

The small concessions that have been made to this day are not enough. What Belgian Catholicism is doing in favoring their workers and peasants is an enormous program, and those of us who know it are ashamed. What German Catholics are doing right now is also heroic, and in our lands would be considered an alarming radicalism.[§]

We have to prepare for similar action, being ready to lose many of those privileges that we slyly call rights. . . .

The hunger after justice that has awakened in the people will not be assuaged by serving them from a small table with a few concessions. Furthermore, the people know that they will manage to get essential reforms without us, and therefore their attitude is no longer one of timorous begging. We have to get used to the new accent of the masses. This accent will wound our old, effeminate and delicate ears. But our ears must listen.

Esthetic Christianity or Religious Dilettantism

The good that can be done today in favor of Catholicism and Christianity in general is to sacrifice material interests. Either that is done or one clearly declares that we take the doctrine of Christ only as a beautiful word in the Gospels or as a transcendental philosophy that elevates human dignity, but for us it is not really a religion, that is, a conduct for life.

If we are dilettantes with Scripture, esthetic repeaters of a parable by reasons of its Greek flavor or its pure beauty, we have to confess that we are epicureans. We are no more than literary or philosophic commentators on religion.

If we are otherwise, true full gospel Christians, we must go to the people. We will seek to order their confused desire of reformation in our economic system and, joined with them, we shall begin by discussing and then conceding.

And those who are staunch egotists must be told that, either with us or without us, the people will produce their reforms. What will happen in that case is what we are already seeing: a Jacobin democracy, horrible as a world catastrophe and brutal like a Tartar horde. Let us choose the right path.

Source Four
Justifying a Presence

Introduction

John A. Mackay, a Presbyterian, was one of the most respected church leaders of his time both in the United States and in Latin America. In the United States, at the time of this writing he was president of Princeton Theological Seminary, one of the most prestigious schools in the nation. In Latin America, he was respected as a missionary who really took to heart the task of understanding and appreciating the culture of the lands where he worked. In Lima, he surrounded himself with a circle that included some of the most outstanding intellectuals of the nation. He befriended and corresponded with Miguel de Unamuno, rector of the Universidad de Salamanca, who was widely viewed as the leading philosopher and literary figure of Spain. Mackay's book, *The Other Spanish Christ*, was hailed by many in Latin America as a perceptive analysis of Latin American religiosity. In the field of missions in general, he presided over the Presbyterian Board of Foreign Missions from 1944 to 1951—that is, he became president of the board five years after Speer's retirement (see chapter 6, "Race and Mission"). He was one of the leading figures in the quest for unity among Christians. As such, he attended several of the worldwide conferences that led to the founding of both the World Council of Churches and the International Missionary Council.

It is important to keep all this in mind as you read Source Four, for here you will find judgments on Latin American Roman Catholicism and views of what he calls the "Iberian spirit" that might otherwise lead to the conclusion that Mackay was narrow-minded and unjustifiably anti-Catholic. This source also helps us understand the mentalities of both Protestants and Catholics in Latin America around the middle of the twentieth century. Here you will find an example of what was considered forward thinking at the time. And, as we have seen in the source from Gabriela Mistral, there were Catholics who agreed with much of Mackay's evaluation of their church and its influence.

As you read this document, consider first of all who could have been its intended readers. If they were Protestants in Latin America, how might they view Mackay's assessment of their land and culture? If they were North American Protestants, what did he feel they needed to understand? If they were the leaders of the United States, particularly those determining North American policies vis-à-vis Latin America, what information did he seek to convey and why?

Like Speer, Mackay was pointing to a problem, but not exactly to the same problem. What was Mackay's specific concern? Whom did he blame for the problem he decried?

What did Mackay fear Catholics were doing to influence the international policies of the United States? How did he respond to such activities? What did he expect from those who read his words?

What does this tell you about the relations between Catholics and Protestants during the Second World War, both in Latin America and in the United States?

Compare this writing with Speer's document. Were their attitudes toward Latin America similar or different? How so? If you were a Latin American, how would your reactions to these two documents differ?

The Text*

It is in no sectarian or acrimonious spirit that I say there is a native intolerance of the Roman Catholic Church. The Roman Catholics perhaps would not be loathe to admit that fact. They dispute our right to be worthy representatives of the Christian religion and commit themselves whenever it is possible to put curbs and trammels in the way of the expression of Protestantism in the world.

In ordinary times nobody would pay much attention to this intolerance, nor would it be in the interests of the Roman Catholic Church to manifest it. But war-time conditions change the whole situation. Taking advantage of the fact that one of the primary plans in the present policy of the United States at the present time is closer and better understanding as well as more practical relationships with the sister republics to the south of us, the Roman Catholic Church is interested in perpetrating what can only be called a lie. The lie is that inter-American relations are being prejudiced by the presence of Protestant missionaries in Latin America. Moreover there is abundant evidence indicating that no stone is being left unturned either to convince the American public that this is so or to gain the ear of Washington that they may do their best to bring Protestant missions in Latin America to an end.

This whole question has a new status so that it is both timely and appropriate for us to consider it here. I take it that our aim in discussing this topic here is not to convince ourselves that Protestant mission work in Latin America is valid. We are convinced on that point, I think. Every open-minded Christian person who visits the field will be convinced. We are not trying to convince the Roman Catholic Church that Protestant missions in Latin America are valid. . . . What we are doing is simply this: first, to clarify our own thinking, to crystalize for ourselves what the grounds of our conviction are in being committed to this great work and secondly clarifying our own thoughts, to find means for bringing valid reasons to open-minded persons, Christian and otherwise, in the United States. I am outlining what I regard to be the foundation or the pillars which constitute the validity of Protestant work in the southern continent as I analyze the situation. These foundations are six in number:

1. *The Christian Imperative.* That imperative inspires us whether we apply it to Latin America or to any other part of the world. What is a missionary imperative? It is one in which a person feels bound to promote an idea or to represent a cause, in a word to be a crusader because he believes that what he has is of the utmost significance for others. He feels moved by what Professor Hocking[+] calls a "cosmic urge." Without this cosmic urge and unless he believes that what he presents and promotes has cosmic bearing a person cannot really be a missionary.

What does it mean to be moved by an evangelical missionary imperative? An imperative springs from the belief that the evangel or gospel is of cosmic significance and that there is good news for mankind which is cosmically important. This good news is that any human being is privileged, if he follows the divinely appointed way, to relate himself to the living God through Jesus Christ and by becoming a new man through Christ Jesus many pass through an utter transformation of character to become a soul and fulfill God's idea of man. In the Gospel there is more than that; Protestants have been too individualistic. The fact of the community, the church, the fellowship, the community of Christ, and the body of Christ, as a member of which this transformed individual can be oriented and nourished and grow up and fulfil his God-given function, this is also of utmost importance. In the Gospel properly understood there is a Christ-like personality but there is also a Christ-like society fulfilling its destiny in history. As Protestant Christians, we are moved by a cosmic urge in the great commission to promulgate the Gospel to save man and build the church of Christ in Latin America or anywhere else.

2. *The Inadequacy of the Roman Catholic Church in its approach to Hispanic America.* This is the second foundation or pillar. While I personally believe that the Roman Catholic Church is inadequate as such, I am not intolerant of that church, nor do I feel that I am sectarian. We glory in the sainthood of today and of the past in the Roman Catholic Church; I know saints within it today. Neither yesterday nor today has the Roman Catholic Church worthily represented the full Christian Gospel and that has to be told. While the Roman Church has succeeded through the ages in doing many wonderful things and given birth to a great many saints, yet she has not succeeded and does not succeed in bringing her people into personal living relationship with Jesus Christ. The Roman Church is interested in the spiritual nurture of certain individuals and quite content if the mass of the people give conventional assent to Roman Catholic doctrine and are willing to be guided by the mandates of the church. . . .

Recently an outstanding Roman Catholic philosopher, a real saint, when asked about Latin American Catholicism said: "That is not Catholicism." Some of us have been saying this for many years and some eminent Latin American authors have been outspoken on the subject. In Spain and in Latin American history not only Christianity but Catholicism as such became de-Christianized due to the tremendous self-assertiveness natural to the Iberian spirit. The Hispanic manifestation of Christianity has been a denaturalized manifestation. In no part of the world has there been such an inadequate view of Jesus Christ. That is crucial. You can judge the truth of any expression of Christianity by the place Jesus Christ has in it. Those of us who know Latin

America know that Jesus Christ as the risen Lord is not at the heart of Christianity there.

3. *The Unique Character of the Hispanic Spiritual Problem.* What is the so-called Hispanic soul in its nature and expression? I believe it is true both ethnically and anthropologically that the most potent expression of unburnished primitive human nature in all history has been the Iberian spirit. There is nothing so self-assertive in its nakedness in any anthropological study that has been made. It is so potent that it has never been tamed, so strong that it has never been subdued by any ethic or any ethos or spiritual force.

4. *The Attitude of Hispanic America toward Evangelical Christianity.* Is it true that they want us all out down there? Are we a menace to Hispanic relations? Go through the types of work that have been carried on by missionaries of the Protestant Church. Is it true that they have cursed us out and would like to see the last of us? You can conjure up all kinds of examples to show that the missionaries have become the best loved people in their communities. . . . What did Juarez mean when he said in Spanish "Oh, that Protestantism would become Mexicanized"?

5. *The Juridical Rights of Protestant Christianity.* We have a status in organized society; the Protestant Church has certain juridical rights. If our juridical right is to be disputed we are going to affirm what we do not have to affirm often. We have a right under the laws of the United States to propagate what we believe to be of great importance, of cosmic importance. . . . The government of the United States cannot deprive us of that right.

6. *The Presence of Protestant Churches in Latin America.* Evangelical work down the years has been so successful that there are now large evangelical groups in various parts which are our brethren. We must be interested in those people because they are our brethren. Who is to allow them to be separated from us? We are united with them in the bonds of Christ; the ecumenical family of God. We must stand by them. . . .

We must see to it that nothing is slipped over on the American people at this time of crisis.

Source Five
We Are Not All Catholic

Introduction

As stated in the introduction to this chapter, Gonzalo Báez Camargo was a leading figure in the Mexican intellectual elite whose work did much for the prestige and acceptance of Protestantism—or at least of some of its basic tenets—among that elite. For years his unashamedly Protestant editorials in the newspaper *El Excélsior* were widely read and discussed by Protestants and Catholics alike. Many liberal Catholics found his words refreshing and even employed them in their call to reform their church. He represented an emerging Protestant intelligentsia that was in constant dialogue with liberal Catholics as well as with the leading literary and philosophical figures of Latin America—among them, Nobel laureate Gabriela Mistral, author of an earlier source in this chapter. Thus, when he described Latin American Catholicism and distinguished its variants, much of what he said would have been confirmed by such Catholic liberals.

For these reasons, it would be well as you read this document to keep in mind the piece from Gabriela Mistral that you have already read. Try to see where the two agree and where they differ. Compare it also with Speer's views in chapter 6, "Race and Mission," and with Mackay's "Justifying a Presence."

How did Báez Camargo describe Latin American Christianity? How did he relate social class with different forms of Catholicism? What preference did he show for any of these forms? What did he feel were the greatest flaws of Catholicism in Latin America? How did this writing go beyond Protestant propaganda, if at all? Why would liberal Roman Catholics have found an ally in him?

How did Báez Camargo evaluate what he called Catholic dogmatism? How did he connect this with the Mexican Revolution and with the growing disaffection of the masses from the Catholic Church? Would Gabriela Mistral have agreed? In other words, to what degree is this a piece of Protestant propaganda and to what degree is it a fair description of what was taking place?

Imagine that you were the Catholic archbishop of Mexico at the time of this publication. How would you respond?

The Text[9]

To those who do not look at it, or who do not pay close attention, Hispanic America would seem to be profoundly and totally Catholic. Those who are professional users of the cliché and the common place, and the lyric proclaimers of a retrograde Latin America, would seek to prove that we Hispanic Americans are inevitably Catholic by birth, by tradition, and by geography. Or they would say that at least we ought to be, using no better reasons than the affinity of Catholicism with our blood, our routines, and our environment. However, a more attentive examination, without having to go too deep, shows the complexity of the religious phenomenon in Hispanic America. . . .

The masses practice a strange religion that claims to be Catholic in the traditional sense but which really includes foggy Christian ideas, pagan concepts, and fetishism. As to the aristocracy and the "enlightened Catholics," they profess their religion for reasons of social convention, as a sign of distinction, as something indispensable to provide more pomp and luster to their great occasions of life: baptism, first communion, marriage, death. . . . Thanks to their influence and money, their religion is for them rather flexible and adaptable, does not impose duties or renunciations that cannot be smoothed and adorned with a seal of elegance. Even though not confessing it, their attitude is essentially that of the elegant philosopher Seneca when he wrote about the worship of the gods: "One should never forget that the worship that we render the gods is a matter of good manners rather than of their own worth." And if we now turn to the middle class, we will find an intermediate and colorless point between the crudity of popular worship and the discreet and elegant idolatry of high society.

Everywhere one sees a tragic stupor of conscience, a cadaveric quietude in the minds, a total paralysis in the will. Catholic multitudes constantly turn their religious enthusiasm towards the practical hedonism of festivities and the exaggerations of fantasies. In order to increase their fervor, they need to lay hold of the subconscious remainders of hatred towards those who do not think like they. Their religious revivals are tiresome and are usually reduced to explosions of intolerance or sterile sentimentality. . . .

As to morality, we have lived and still live in a pagan divorce between rite and culture. Religion is approved and practiced as a system of external forms but does not invade the spheres of life as an inspiration for individual and social conduct. One of the most painful realities of our milieu is the easy fellowship between fidelity to the ritual, which to the people is true religiousness, with blasphemy and impiety. Even charity is prostituted, becoming a calculated and unfeeling gesture which is a form of publicity and a fleeting perfume of holiness over a proud egotism. . . .

And if such is the case in the domains of the traditional church, is it any better in the masses, for by now they are masses who either openly or surreptitiously have separated their consciences from the Roman flock? . . .

Although it is quite difficult to penetrate deeply into the causes of this state of affairs, one can immediately point to the most prominent: the dogmatism that leaves no room for the exercise of individual thought; a dogmatism with canned and frequently rotting answers that seek to assuage every spiritual hunger; a dogmatism which sees freedom of thought and the function of one's conscience as something less than useful, and even dangerous.

Such dogmatism could only weaken and fossilize the spiritual constitution of our people. Ecclesiasticism, which insists in placing itself between the soul and God, ended up by turning this god into a remote entity, and by extinguishing in the souls any desire for a direct communion with the divine. . . .

Another of the causes is the withdrawal of the church from the social and spiritual needs of our peoples. Little by little in human evolution, these needs have become overwhelming and urgent. By means of its preaching, the church seeks to silence and assuage the worker who hankers after a more just social order. This preaching is about a better world after death. It is about the need to have the patience to accept, without protest and without any quest for improvement, the injustices and suffering that the church itself considers part of this ephemeral and deceitful life. But in truth these injustices and this suffering are merely the result of the cruel and egotistic action of people. The church interpreted the kingdom of heaven as a state of pleasantness in the beyond and not as the reign of charity, fraternity, and justice in this very earthly world in which we live. And while it preached resignation and hope to the wretched and oppressed, it forgot to preach justice and love to the cruel masters and the capitalist slave holders. It did nothing effective in order to improve the social situation or to direct a wise evolution towards the liberation of the enslaved masses.

Then the inevitable took place: There came the revolution, with its flashing lights of vindication, to awaken the oppressed and to reform the established order, almost always in a violent fashion. The church then took fright. Since it had remained unmoved by the social needs of the peoples entrusted to its care and direction, it feared that, as the outdated structure of the ancient feudal society collapsed, it would lead the church to its ruin, for the church had very close ties with that society. Hence arose a second mistake: The church became an ally of the old order. It sought to prop it up with its preaching and its influence; it brought to its support all ecclesiastical resources. It has all proven useless. Social transformation, first ignored and then rejected by the church, has continued to take place, obeying the inalterable law of great historical needs. As a natural result, the vast masses of laborers increasingly tend to break away from the church. . . .

A culture with an appropriate religion, less dogmatism, less ecclesiasticism, more opportunity for individual thought and initiative, more understanding of social needs, would have made our America an unfertile ground for irreligiosity and fanaticism.

Source Six
La Violencia

Introduction

The political conflict between liberals and conservatives, present in most Latin American countries from their very birth, was particularly virulent and prolonged in Colombia. A series of riots in Bogotá in 1948 led to a period of fifteen years known by Colombians as "la Violencia." During that time conservatives ruled with an iron fist, and the suppression of liberalism took a violent turn—often at the hands of the police and the military, who were generally given free rein in dealing with real or presumed liberals. Since the Roman Catholic hierarchy had long sided with the conservatives, it generally supported, or at least ignored, such violence and also had a hand in directing it against Protestants—who in any case were mostly liberals.

As Goff stated in this document, this alarmed missionary agencies abroad—particularly the Presbyterian Board of Foreign Missions in the United States. They took steps to have the aggression against Protestants investigated and the results publicized. Goff devoted much travel and many years to this task.

The document you will be reading was written in 1961, after the violence had abated. During the course of that decade, in part due to the new spirit of the Second Vatican Council and in part due to the conviction of the Colombians themselves that they had already had enough violence, the situation continued improving.

As you read this document, consider: What connection do you see between political and religious differences and conflicts? What connections would there be between the Catholic hierarchy and the Conservative Party? What would each of these two parties gain from such connections? Why would the Colombian government and the Vatican agree to the policies that Goff cited? What threat would Protestantism pose to the government, to the Catholic Church, or to the nation itself and its culture? What were the charges against Protestantism? How does the Catholicism described in this document reflect attitudes similar to those expressed much earlier by the archbishop of Lima (see "The Archbishop Complains")?

Why would it take a foreign board of missions to move Protestants in Colombia to document and publicize what was going on? What might be the purpose and the results of such documentation and divulgation? Why would the Roman Catholic hierarchy claim that these documents and reports were not circulated in Colombia itself?

Compare this article with the one by Gabriela Mistral. How are the attitudes of the Catholic leadership to which she referred similar to what you find in this document, a third of a century later? Look again at the writings by Speer ("Race and Mission") and Mackay ("Justifying a Presence"). How does what Goff reported confirm or contradict what they said about Latin American Catholicism?

The Text*

Historians are no doubt ready to say that violent religious persecution against Colombian Protestants ended with the change in government in 1958. But the fact is that persecution in diminished intensity continues, and there is great danger that it may erupt in violent form again, because its underlying causes have never been removed. Under the surface, awaiting a change in the political climate, are pressures and hatred of Protestants—and a series of pseudo-legal acts of the Colombian government—that could produce another bloodbath for the Lord's people.

Thirteen years of religious persecution in Colombia have resulted in an appalling total of 116 Protestant Christians martyred because of their religious faith, 66 Protestant churches and chapels destroyed by fire or dynamite, and over 200 Protestant day schools closed. Will Christendom soon forget these atrocities—and will Colombia herself now take measures to guarantee religious freedom for her citizens? A new attitude on the part of the Roman Catholic hierarchy, plus positive action in defense of freedom by the Colombian government, could change the picture almost overnight.

Over and over we are asked in the United States, "Are these stories of persecution coming out of Colombia really true? Can it be that medieval religious persecution is going on, in a civilized Western nation, in the 20th Century?"

The answer is simply, "Yes." Let's review what has actually taken place in Colombia in the last 13 years.

Political terrorism and violence broke out in Colombia in 1947. The Roman Catholic hierarchy, seizing its opportunity, began a simultaneous campaign to suppress Protestant Christianity and to annihilate it where possible.

Bewildered Protestants, believing that the national government would protect them, made repeated official complaints and requests for help, but without avail. It soon became shockingly clear that the National Police had been indoctrinated against Protestantism, and that police themselves were the main persecuting agents.

In 1951, at the suggestion of the Presbyterian Mission, the Evangelical Confederation of Colombia (CEDEC) ordered a documentary study of the persecution. Mr. Lorentz Emery and I, both of the Presbyterian Mission, were released for part-time work with the Confederation, and an appropriation of $1000 was made by the Presbyterian Board of Foreign Missions to help finance the investigation.

We traveled throughout the country, from the northernmost Guajira Peninsula south to Popayán, interviewing victims and eyewitnesses of the persecution and visiting the scenes of violence. As the investigation proceeded, an indescribably shocking array of atrocities committed against Protestant Christians began to unfold before our eyes, taking the form of crimes against personal, religious, political and educational rights of Colombian citizens. A list of the 24 main forms of persecution we discovered is included as part of this article.

Christians in Colombia, upon seeing the mounting gravity of our investigation reports, felt they could no longer keep quiet. In 1952 the Evangelical Confederation authorized the publication of news releases on acts of persecution as they occurred. Since then, 67 bulletins have been published, plus a number of special news releases. These have been sent to editors, correspondents and news agencies, as well as to the Vatican, the Colombian Government, the United States Government, the United Nations, the Organization of American States, the Panamerican Union, and the principal religious denominations.

As investigations continued, several questions kept demanding answers: "What are the real roots of the anti-Protestant persecution? Why does Colombia seem to be worse in this regard than any other nation in the world?" And soon our research began to yield the answers.

The roots of the persecution are found deep in Colombian history. Space doesn't permit a full exposition of many of these factors, but we will elaborate on the major ones. Causes of the persecution included the following:

- Clerical domination of the Conservative Government which ruled Colombia from 1946 to 1958

- The Roman Catholic hierarchy's determination to extirpate Protestant Christianity

- The peculiar nature of Colombian Catholicism, which is the purest projection of Medieval Spanish Catholicism into the 20th Century

- Dangerous accusations against Protestants by the Roman Catholic clergy, especially the grave charges that "they are destroying national unity," and "they are introducing Communism"

- Indoctrination of the National Police Force by the Roman clergy to halt the advance of Protestantism and drive it out of Colombia
- A basic hate-Protestantism campaign by the Catholic clergy, which aroused popular suspicion and hatred and eventually erupted into acts of violence and vicious discrimination

But significant as the above causes were, and sad as the results they succeeded in producing, there remain three even more serious official and semi-official acts of the Colombian Government which provide a "legal" basis and sanction to the persecution. They are:

- The Concordat—a long-standing treaty negotiated by the government with the Vatican which gave official status and powers to the Roman Church
- The Treaty on Missions, which granted exclusive rights for the propagation of religious beliefs in the vast majority of Colombian territory to Roman Catholicism
- The "Circular Orders," an executive action which severely restricts freedom of assembly of Protestants.

These last three causes——the Concordat, the Missions Treaty, and the Circular Orders—are so fundamental to the basis of persecution that it will be worth our while to describe them in further detail. If violent persecution comes again to Colombia—and this is an ever-present possibility—it will be because these government acts will give them "legality."

The Concordat. In 1887 President Rafael Núñez and Pope Leo XIII negotiated a concordat which gives the Roman Catholic Church far-reaching privileges. The first article of the concordat, which was actually a part of the country's constitution from 1886 to 1936, shows what kind of document it is:

> "The Apostolic Roman Catholic Religion is the Religion of Colombia. The public powers recognize it as an essential element of the social order, and they are bound to protect it and make it respected, likewise its ministers, at the same time leaving it in the complete enjoyment of its rights and privileges."

With this *carte blanche* of authority for the Church as an opener, the Concordat goes on to say that public education, from primary grades through university, must be organized and directed in conformity with Catholic dogmas and morality. Religious instruction in the Catholic faith is obligatory in all grades, and the pious practices of the Catholic Church must be observed in the schools. The Archbishop of Bogotá is given the power of censorship over all textbooks, and he may remove any teacher or professor who is not in accord with Catholic dogma.

By terms of a supplemental agreement (1892) the administration of public cemeteries is turned over to the Catholic Church. The Concordat also provides that the government and the Vatican may enter into agreements for the evangelization of barbarian tribes. This has given rise to the Mission Treaties of 1902, 1928, and 1953.

The Mission Treaty. In 1953, Acting President Roberto Urdaneta and Pope Pius XII negotiated a Treaty on Missions which set up 19 Roman Catholic Mission Territories (officially called Vicariates and Apostolic Prefectures). The combined area of the 19 Territories is three-fourths the area of the country. Each of the 19 Territories is under the direction of a Catholic religious order. No education of any kind is permitted for the Colombians living in the Territories except under the supervision of the Catholic Mission Chiefs, over half of whom are foreigners.

Protestantism is effectively outlawed in the Mission Territories; dozens of Protestant schools and churches have been closed there. The government promises to: contribute annual sums of money for each Mission; make gifts of land for buildings; subsidize the construction of Catholic schools, seminaries, orphanages and hospitals; and help the work of the Catholic missionaries in every possible way.

The Treaty, which was never submitted to Congress for approval as the Constitution requires, is to continue for 25 years.

The Circular Orders. Dr. Lucio Pabón Núñez, Minister of Government under the military dictatorship of 1953–1957, issued a series of "circular orders" restricting Protestant Christianity in the following ways: (1) In the Mission Territories Protestants are prohibited from having religious services or schools; (2) in no part of the nation may they make any public manifestations of their faith; and (3) they must notify the civil authorities in writing of the time and place of their meetings. Although Protestants consider the orders to be unconstitutional and thus null and void, priests are still able to force the civil authorities to observe them in certain places. The present National Front Government has thus far hesitated to declare the Circular Orders inoperative.

Thus we see that where violence fails, pseudo-legal means may be sought to suppress Protestantism, such as the Circular Orders and the Missions Treaty. And further, that it is during times of political strife and turmoil that such efforts have taken place and are likely to succeed. And always the alleged justification for the anti-Protestant attacks is that Protestants serve as agents of communism, or that they destroy national unity, both of which charges are patently false.

During the first four years of the persecution Protestants did little to publicize it. In 1952, the Evangelical Confederation became convinced not only that the conservative government would not remedy the situation, but that it was in fact a partner to the persecution. The Confederation authorized its Office of Information to publish releases for the press. The 67 bulletins which have been issued have covered hundreds of acts of persecution. Reporting is done in a detailed, documentary manner to facilitate investigation by any government agency which might want to check the reports.

The Roman Catholic spokesmen charge that the Confederation severely restricts the circulation of the reports within Colombia, while giving them wide distribution abroad. They say that CEDEC has thus acted deceitfully, knowing that Colombians, who are presumed well-informed of what is happening in their own country, would promptly denounce the bulletins as false and calumnious.

This charge is false. If the Colombian public is ignorant of persecution within their country, it is because the Catholic hierarchy has successfully suppressed the news, for the Confederation bulletins are sent widely to the Colombian press, diplomatic corps—and to members of the Roman hierarchy itself! Twenty-one Colombian newspaper editors and the editors of the weekly news magazines *Semana* and *Cromos* are on the mailing list, as are 11 news correspondents in Bogotá and four radio newscasters. During the State of Siege (1945 to 1958), government censors prohibited the publication of news about the persecution on the insistence of the hierarchy. Editors who slipped in notices of the persecution felt the wrath of the bishop and the diocesan Catholic Action Committee. Colombians who receive the bulletins include the president of the Republic, the 13 cabinet members, governors of the 16 Departments and nine Territories, the Attorney-General, the President of the Senate and the Speaker of the House of Representatives.

The Roman Catholic officials who receive the bulletins are the Archbishop of Bogotá (who is the Primate of the Catholic Church in Colombia), the Apostolic Nuncio (Papal Ambassador), and the Secretariat of the Colombia Episcopacy.

Has the publicity achieved its desired effect? The Evangelical Confederation of Colombia believes that it has, and has continued the publicity with several purposes in mind. First, to inform the world about the treatment of Colombian Protestants. Second, to document the persecution for the sake of Church history. Finally, it has been continued with the hope of alerting Protestants abroad to the danger of political Catholicism carried to its logical extreme.

Although the Colombian government and the Catholic Church in Colombia have consistently denied the existence of persecution, the Catholic church abroad, particularly in the United States, has cautiously admitted that Protestants may have suffered. The attitude of Protestant churches abroad has been a deep concern and sympathy, with the sole exception of the Canadian Council of Churches, which in 1958 chided Colombian Protestants for being "overly aggressive" in "proselytizing" in a predominantly Catholic country.

Persecution in Colombia has been accompanied by astounding growth in the Church, so closely following the New Testament pattern of dispersion and intensified witness. In the seven-year period from 1953 to 1960, Church membership increased over 2½ times, from 11,958 to 33,156. Think of an average growth rate of 16 per cent per year, compounded! The total Protestant constituency is estimated at five times the baptized membership, or some 165,500 persons. How does this compare with the total population of the country? Based on the government's 1959 population estimate of just over 14 million inhabitants, Protestants comprise 1.17 per cent of Colombia's population.

Under Colombia's liberal President, Dr. Alberto Lleras-Camargo, who took office in 1958, Colombia is making a return to democracy and constitutional government. The orientation of Dr. Lleras-Camargo has reached down through the levels of government, and violence, both political and religious, is on the decline.

But although religious persecution, especially in its violent form, has diminished, its basic causes have not been removed. Until the Colombian Congress abrogates the Concordat and the Treaty on Missions, the position of Protestant Christianity is precarious. The present government, not being dominated by the Roman clergy, is willing to overlook the restrictive provisions of these two documents, but the return of a conservative government will mean that they will be applied with renewed vigor.

8
THE CATHOLIC CHURCH
FACES NEW SITUATIONS

Introduction

The second half of the twentieth century was a period of political turmoil and social unrest in Latin America. During the Second World War, conflicts thwarted trade across the Atlantic and Pacific Oceans, forcing the United States to increase its trade with Latin America and leading many countries there to a brief period of unprecedented prosperity. In contrast, the postwar years were often marked by economic stagnation and even recession. Even in the most prosperous countries, economic growth lagged behind population growth. These factors came together to create a volatile situation. The resulting unrest was exacerbated by two other factors: the increasing concentration of wealth in a few hands and the allure of Communism. In 1959, the Cuban Revolution gave Communism a firm foothold and a possible beachhead in Latin America, and soon its leaders Fidel Castro and Ernesto "Che" Guevara became iconic figures for many from the Rio Grande to Tierra del Fuego.

In reaction to such unrest, governments of "national security" arose, particularly during the 1970s and 1980s. These were usually military dictatorships that used their power ruthlessly in order to respond to what they claimed was the menace of Communism. Thousands suspected of opposing their rule disappeared, and many were imprisoned and tortured. Since these governments collaborated among themselves, for the first time in Latin

American history, it was seldom possible for those fleeing persecution to find political asylum in a neighboring country. With the notable exception of Jimmy Carter, most North American presidents either openly supported such governments of national security or simply let them be. All of this led to a growing polarization between radical and conservative groups both in the Catholic Church and in society at large.

In previous chapters we have seen that there was always within Latin American Catholicism a tension between those whose main concern was supporting ecclesiastical order and the existing institutions and those who felt that Christians should take more radical action in support of the poor and exploited. Now this tension came to the foreground. Everywhere, Catholic groups arose that not only opposed the policies of military dictatorships but also promoted a radical change in the social and economic order. In 1965, sixty Argentinean priests founded Sacerdotes para el Tercer Mundo (Priests for the Third World). They immediately clashed with the hierarchy of the church, which failed in its efforts to suppress this and other radical organizations. Three years later a similar movement arose in Colombia, and one of its priests, Camilo Torres, joined the guerrillas fighting against the existing order.

It was in the context of this turmoil that the Consejo Episcopal Latinoamericano (Latin American Council of Bishops, also known as CELAM) gathered first in Bogotá and then in Medellín, also in Colombia, in 1968, for its Second General Conference. Although CELAM had traditionally been rather conservative, there were now among its membership those who felt that the Church must take a stand in the face of the existing political and social repression. A visit by Pope Paul VI, who arrived in a military helicopter and thus seemed to support military repression, was not well received by many of those present at Medellín. Therefore, the documents of Medellín, represented in Source One, "The Bishops Look Forward," sought to respond to the existing social unrest by acknowledging its roots in ways that the Catholic Church had never done.

Source Two, "Liberation and Change," comes from the pen of Latin America's most famous theologian, the Dominican Gustavo Gutiérrez. Born in 1928, Gutiérrez devoted most of his life to work among the poor in his native Peru. But he was also trained theologically at some of the most prestigious Catholic institutions both in Peru and in Europe—including the Universidad de San Marcos in Lima, where John A. Mackay, whom we read in our previous chapter, taught. Gutiérrez's work with the poor, combined with his theological studies, led him to a vision of the central message of Christianity as one of liberation—liberation not only from what has traditionally been called "sin" but also from the social and economic dimensions of sin, poverty, oppression, and exploitation. Although not yet as famous as he would later become, Gutiérrez was one of the theological advisers to CELAM at its Medellín meeting, and his influence may be seen in the emphasis on social issues of Source One. His most famous book, *Teología de la liberación*, was published in 1971 and is generally considered the beginning of Latin American liberation theology—a theology that emphasized the social and political dimensions of the gospel, relating them to all the central doctrines of the Christian faith.

Source Three, "An Official Reprimand," represents the response of the Vatican to liberation theology, seeking to put a stop to it or at least to make it more moderate. Its lead author, Cardinal Joseph Ratzinger, would later become Pope Benedict XVI. At the time when he issued this statement, he headed the Congregation for the Doctrine of the Faith, which is the continuation of the Supreme Sacred Congregation of the Holy Office—better known as the Inquisition. The response of the leading liberation theologians—Gutiérrez among them—was that, since this document did not describe their position accurately, it did not really refer to them, and therefore it did not ban their teachings and opinions.

Upon reading Ratzinger's condemnation of liberation theology, many thought that his primary concern, perhaps even more important than a Marxist influence, was that liberation theology promoted such participation by the laity in the life of the church that it undermined the authority of the hierarchy. This was particularly true of the Base Ecclesial Communities (*comunidades eclesiales de base*, commonly known as CEBs), whose gatherings, often without the guidance of priests, included discussions about the Bible and its significance for current social struggles.

In a way, Source Four, "The Magi," represents one such CEB, although in this case there is a priest present. The participants are mostly poor people, with an occasional student, in the small settlement of Solentiname, on an island near Managua, Nicaragua. Shortly after the discussion recorded here, the Solentiname community was practically wiped out by government forces. Father Ernesto Cardenal, who is reporting the conversation, would later become part of the Sandinista government.

This source is also a stepping-stone between the previous three sources and the ones that follow. While the first three sources are more theological in nature and come from the pens of highly educated persons, this fourth source consists of conversations that include a learned priest as well as everyday people, many of them with little formal education. It is an indication of how common folk reacted to liberation theology and how they interpreted it.

The next two sources—Sources Five and Six—are two *retablos*. "Retablos" give us a deeper insight into the faith of the common people, for they are far removed from the world of theologians and of bishops' conferences. They are paintings commissioned by believers, usually to thank God or one of the saints for a miraculous intervention, such as a healing or deliverance from danger, or to ask for such an intervention. The pictures depict the event and include a written explanation of what the retablo celebrates or asks for. Normally fairly small (no larger than eight by ten inches), they are valued both as religious objects and as folk art providing insight into the faith of the people.

Source One
The Bishops Look Forward

Introduction

The following is a segment of one of the documents resulting from CELAM's meeting in Medellín. Read it, keeping in mind the conditions outlined in the introduction to this chapter. Then ask yourself: How did the Latin American bishops gathered in Medellín view what was taking place in Latin America? Did their analysis coincide with what was said in our introduction? How did it differ? What new elements were added? What might this document mean by the "lack of socio-cultural integration"?

The document also speaks of "an erroneous conception concerning the right of ownership." What was its critique of the common understanding of ownership? How does that reflect what you know of the history of Latin America? What would they have proposed instead of the "erroneous conception"? What did the bishops dislike about liberal capitalism? (Note that here "liberal" is not what we often understand by that term. By "liberal capitalism" the bishops understood a capitalism with little or no restraints from government—in other words, what today in the United States is called "conservatism.") What did the bishops dislike about Marxism? What would be the marks of "a truly human economy"? What relationship do you see between what is proposed here and Gabriela Mistral's suggestions (chapter 7, "A Call to Change from a Nobel Laureate")?

The document then turns to what should be the attitude of the Church and particularly of its bishops. What changes did they envision?

The Text*

Pertinent Facts

1. There are in existence many studies of the Latin American people. The misery that besets large masses of human beings in all of our countries is described in all of these studies. That misery, as a collective fact, expresses itself as injustice which cries to the heavens.

But what perhaps has not been sufficiently said is that in general the efforts which have been made have not been capable of assuring that justice be honored and realized in every sector of the respective national communities. Often families do not find concrete possibilities for the education of their children. The young demand their right to enter universities or centers of higher learning for both intellectual and technical training; the women, their right to a legitimate equality with men; the peasants, better conditions of life; or if they are workers, better prices and security in buying and selling; the growing middle class feels frustrated by the lack of expectations. There has begun an exodus of professionals and technicians to more developed countries; the small businessmen and industrialists are pressed by greater interests and not a few large Latin American industrialists are gradually coming to be dependent on the international business enterprises. We cannot ignore the phenomenon of this almost universal frustration of legitimate aspirations which creates the climate of collective anguish in which we are already living.

2. The lack of socio-cultural integration, in the majority of our countries, has given rise to the superimposition of cultures. In the economic sphere systems flourished which consider solely the potential of groups with great earning power. This lack of adaptation to the characteristics and to the potentials of all our people, in turn, gives rise to frequent political instability and the consolidation of purely formal institutions. To all of this must be added the lack of solidarity which, on the individual and social levels, leads to the committing of serious sins, evident in the unjust structures which characterize the Latin American situation. . . .

Projections for Social Pastoral Planning

. . . 10. In today's world, production finds its concrete expression in business enterprises, the industrial as well as the rural; they constitute the dynamic and fundamental base of the integral economic process. The system of Latin American business enterprises, and through it the current economy, responds to an erroneous conception concerning the right of ownership of the means of production and the very goals of the economy. A business, in an authentically human economy, does not identify itself with the owner of capital, because it is fundamentally a community of persons and a unit of work, which is in need of capital to produce goods. A person or a group of persons cannot be the property of an individual, of a society, or of the state.

The system of liberal capitalism and the temptation of the Marxist system would appear to exhaust the possibilities of transforming the economic structures of our continent. Both systems militate against the dignity of the human person. One takes for granted the primacy of capital, its power and its discriminatory utilization in the function of profit-making. The other, although it ideologically supports a kind of humanism, is more concerned with collective man, and in practice becomes a totalitarian concentration of state power. We must denounce the fact that Latin America sees itself caught between these two options and remains dependent on one or the other of the centers of power which control its economy.

Therefore, on behalf of Latin America, we make an urgent appeal to the businessmen, to their organizations and to the political authorities, so that they might radically modify the evaluation, the attitudes and the means regarding the goal, organization and functioning of business. All those financiers deserve encouragement who, individually or through their organizations, make an effort to conduct their business according to the guidelines supplied by the social teaching of the Church. That the social and economic change in Latin America be channeled towards a truly human economy will depend fundamentally on this. . . .

Within the context of the poverty and even of the wretchedness in which the great majority of the Latin American people live, we, bishops, priests and religious, have the necessities of life and a certain security, while the poor lack that which is indispensable and struggle between **anguish** and **uncertainty**. And incidents are not lacking in which the poor feel that their bishops, or pastors and religious, do not really identify themselves with them, with their problems and afflictions, that they do not always support those that work with them or plead their cause. . . .

Pastoral Orientations

. . . 8. Because of the foregoing we wish the Latin American Church to be the evangelizer of the poor and one with them, a witness to the value of the riches of the Kingdom, and the humble servant of all our people. Its pastors and the other members of the People of God have to correlate their life and words, their attitudes and actions to the demands of the Gospel and the necessities of the men of Latin America. . . .

Pre-eminence and Solidarity

. . . 9. The Lord's distinct commandment to "evangelize the poor" ought to bring us to a distribution of resources and apostolic personnel that effectively gives preference to the poorest and most needy sectors and to those segregated for any cause whatsoever, animating and accelerating the initiatives and studies that are already being made with that goal in mind.

We, the bishops, wish to come closer to the poor in sincerity and brotherhood, making ourselves accessible to them. . . .

We want our Latin American Church to be free from temporal ties, from intrigues and from a doubtful reputation; to be "free in spirit as regards the chains of wealth," so that her mission of service will be stronger and clearer. We want her to be present in life and in secular works, reflecting the light of Christ, present in the construction of the world.

Source Two
Liberation and Change

Introduction

This document appears in a book containing writings by Gustavo Gutiér-rez and Richard Shaull, a Presbyterian missionary of long experience in Latin America well known for his support of radical social transformation and of Christian participation in that process. It was published in English, for its audience was not so much Latin Americans as North Americans seeking a fundamental understanding of liberation theology. At the time of the document's publication, that theology was usually presented in the North American media as little more than Marxism disguised as Christianity. What Gutiérrez and Shaull sought to do with this book was to show readers in the United States that liberation theology was not only Christian but also the proper understanding of the gospel in the Latin American context. Thus, a general question as you read this source is: To what extent did they succeed? At what points did they seem to fail?

More specifically, consider first of all what Gutiérrez said about the problem in Latin America not being the presence of non-believers but rather the challenge of non-persons and how this relates to the Christian view of God as loving. What did he mean by this? How did he understand the situation in Latin America and its causes? If the church has traditionally thought of its main audience as non-believers and now decides that its proper audience is non-persons, how might that affect what the church says and does?

What did Gutiérrez mean by "a liberating praxis"? (Although our word *practice* derives from the Greek *praxis*, when contemporary theologians speak of *praxis* they mean the way in which life is lived as a whole.) How would he relate praxis to faith and to action? Why would Gutiérrez propose starting with such praxis rather than with philosophical or theoretical positions? What would be the implications of this procedure, and how would it differ from traditional theology? Why would traditional theologians reject it and perhaps even feel threatened by it? Gutiérrez himself rejected "such theologies as those of development, revolution, and violence." Why did he object to each of these?

The "hermeneutical circle"—the circle of interpretation—is a common theme in liberation theology. Try drawing such a circle and then placing themes such as commitment, solidarity, faith, reflection, etc., where Gutiérrez might place each in the circle.

The Text[†]

Gustavo Gutiérrez on Liberation and Change

In a continent like Latin America, the challenge does not come to us primarily from the non-believer, but from the *non-person*, that is to say, from the individual who is not recognized as such by the existing social order: the poor, the exploited, who are systematically deprived of being persons, they who scarcely know that they are persons. The non-person questions before anything else, not our religious world, but our *economic, social, political and cultural world*; and thus, a call is made for the revolutionary transformation of the very bases of a dehumanizing society. Our question, therefore, is not how to announce God in an adult world; but rather, how to announce him as *Father* in a non-human world. What are the implications when we tell a non-person that he or she is a child of God? . . .

Theology, in this context, will be a critical reflection on the historical praxis when confronted with the Word of the Lord lived and accepted in faith; this faith comes to us through multiple, and at times ambiguous, historical meditations which we make and discover everyday. Theology will be a reflection in and on faith as a liberating praxis. The understanding of the faith will proceed from an option and a commitment. This understanding will start with a real and effective solidarity with discriminated races, despised cultures and exploited classes and from their very world and atmosphere. This reflection starts from a commitment to create a just fraternal society, and must contribute to make it more meaningful, radical, and universal. This theological process becomes truth when it is embodied into the process of liberation.

Theology, thus, will be liberated from a socio-cultural context which prevents it from establishing its presence where the oppressed and the discriminated in the world are struggling to be accepted as human persons. Theology becomes a liberating and prophetic force which tends to contribute to the total understanding of the Word which takes place in the actions of real life. This fact, and not simple affirmation or "models of analysis," will free theology from all forms of idealism.

The theology of liberation differs from such theologies as those of development, revolution, and violence not only in a different analysis of reality based on more universal and radical political options, but above all, in the very concept of the task of theology. The theology of liberation does not intend to provide Christian justification for positions already taken and does not aim to be a revolutionary Christian ideology. It is a reflection which makes a start with the historical praxis of people. It seeks to rethink the faith from the perspective of that historical praxis, and it is based on the experience of the faith derived from the liberating commitment. For this reason, this theology comes only after that involvement, the theology is always a *second act*. Its themes are, therefore, the great themes of all true theology, but the perspective and the way of giving them life is different. Its relation to historical praxis is of a different kind. . . .

That is then the fundamental hermeneutic circle: from people to God and from God to people; from history to faith and from faith to history; from the human word to the word of the Lord and from the word of the Lord to the human word; from fraternal love to the love of the Father and from the love of the Father to fraternal love; from human justice to the holiness of God and from the holiness of God to human justice; from poor to God and from God to poor.

Source Three
An Official Reprimand

Introduction

When this document was published by the Congregation for the Doctrine of the Faith, under the direction of Cardinal Ratzinger, it was generally seen as a rejection of liberation theology or at least as a caution against it. Even so, at various points the document seems to grant that some of the claims of liberation theology are true. Therefore, as you read this document, consider not only how and where it rejects liberation theology, but also how it affirms some of the concerns of that theology. Note that, while the document seems to ignore the words of the bishops at Medellín, it does endorse the subsequent conference of bishops, which took place in Puebla, Mexico, in 1979, and which sought to soften the declarations of Medellín.

Look then at some of the specifics, and try to discern the points at which Ratzinger felt compelled to reject liberation theology. Look, for instance, at his understanding of sin. On the basis of Sources One and Two ("The Bishops Look Forward" and "Liberation and Change") and of any other knowledge you may have of liberation theology, how do you think the bishops gathered at Medellín and Gutiérrez would have responded to this document's view of sin? Imagine a discussion between Ratzinger and the Medellín bishops on the subjects of sin and salvation. On what would they have agreed? What would each side have stressed? What would each side have seen as lacking or deficient on the part of the other? On what points would they have found it misguided? How did the document relate economic oppression and exploitation to the spiritual slavery of sin?

Then, what about the very concept of "liberation"? Look at the words *fundamental* and *by-product*. What would Gutiérrez have said in response to this ordering of priorities? What would have been the practical consequences of the differences between Gutiérrez and Ratzinger?

Note, however, that much of the document deals more specifically with the manner in which liberation theology and its support for CEBs undercut the authority of priests and of the hierarchy. As you compare this document with Source Two ("Liberation and Change"), how does it differ in its evaluation of the laity's ability for independent thinking and on the wisdom of the unlettered?

When Gutiérrez read this document, his response was that what it called "liberation theology" was not what he was proposing, and therefore he need not take it as a rejection of his theology. On the basis of what you have read here and in the previous source, imagine yourself as Gutiérrez and explain why the document did not really refer to you.

The Text[‡]

The Gospel of Jesus Christ is a message of freedom and a force for liberation. In recent years, this essential truth has become the object of reflection for theologians, with a new kind of attention which is itself full of promise.

Liberation is first and foremost liberation from the radical slavery of sin. Its end and its goal is the freedom of the children of God, which is the gift of grace. As a logical consequence, it calls for freedom from many different kinds of slavery in the cultural, economic, social, and political spheres, all of which derive ultimately from sin, and so often prevent people from living in a manner befitting their dignity. To discern clearly what is fundamental to this issue and what is a by-product of it, is an indispensable condition for any theological reflection on liberation.

Faced with the urgency of certain problems, some are tempted to emphasize, unilaterally, the liberation from servitude of an earthly and temporal kind. They do so in such a way that they seem to put liberation from sin in second place, and so fail to give it the primary importance it is due. Thus, their very presentation of the problems is confused and ambiguous. Others, in an effort to learn more precisely what are the causes of the slavery which they want to end, make use of different concepts without sufficient critical caution. It is difficult, and perhaps impossible, to purify these borrowed concepts of an ideological inspiration which is [in]compatible$ with Christian faith and the ethical requirements which flow from it.

The present Instruction has a much more limited and precise purpose: to draw the attention of pastors, theologians, and all the faithful to the deviations, and risks of deviation, damaging to the faith and to Christian living, that are brought about by certain forms of liberation theology which use, in an insufficiently critical manner, concepts borrowed from various currents of Marxist thought.

This warning should in no way be interpreted as a disavowal of all those who want to respond generously and with an authentic evangelical spirit to the "preferential option for the poor." It should not at all serve as an excuse for those who maintain the attitude of neutrality and indifference in the face of the tragic and pressing problems of human misery and injustice. It is, on the contrary, dictated by the certitude that the serious ideological deviations which it points out tends inevitably to betray the cause of the poor. More than ever, it is important that numerous Christians, whose faith is clear and who are committed to live the Christian life in its fullness, become involved in the struggle for justice, freedom, and human dignity because of their love for their disinherited, oppressed, and persecuted brothers and sisters. More than ever, the Church intends to condemn abuses, injustices, and attacks against freedom, wherever they occur and whoever commits them. She intends to struggle, by her own means, for the defense and advancement of the rights of mankind, especially of the poor.

. . . In this present document, we will only be discussing developments of that current of thought which, under the name "theology of liberation," proposes a novel interpretation of both the content of faith and of Christian existence which seriously departs from the faith of the Church and, in fact, actually constitutes a practical negation. . . .

But the "theologies of liberation" of which we are speaking, mean by 'Church of the People' a Church of the class, a Church of the oppressed people whom it is necessary to "conscientize" in the light of the organized struggle for freedom. For some, the people, thus understood, even become the object of faith.

Building on such a conception of the Church of the People, a critique of the very structures of the Church is developed. It is not simply the case of fraternal correction of pastors of the Church whose behavior does not reflect the evangelical spirit of service and is linked to old-fashioned signs of authority which scandalize the poor. It has to do with a challenge to the 'sacramental and hierarchical structure' of the Church, which was willed by the Lord Himself. There is a denunciation of members of the hierarchy and the magisterium as objective representatives of the ruling class which has to be opposed. Theologically, this position means that ministers take their origin from the people who therefore designate ministers of their own choice in accord with the needs of their historic revolutionary mission. . . .

The warning against the serious deviations of some "theologies of liberation" must not be taken as some kind of approval, even indirect, of those who keep the poor in misery, who profit from that misery, who notice it while doing nothing about it, or who remain indifferent to it. The Church, guided by the Gospel of mercy and by the love for mankind, hears the cry for justice and intends to respond to it with all her might.

Thus a great call goes out to all the Church: with boldness and courage, with far-sightedness and prudence, with zeal and strength of spirit, with a love for the poor which demands sacrifice, pastors will consider the response to this call a matter of the highest priority, as many already do.

All priests, religious, and lay people who hear this call for justice and who want to work for evangelization and the advancement of mankind, will do so in communion with their bishop and with the Church, each in accord with his or her own specific ecclesial vocation.

Aware of the ecclesial character of their vocation, theologians will collaborate loyally and with a spirit of dialogue with the Magisterium of the Church. They will be able to recognize in the Magisterium a gift of Christ to His Church and will welcome its word and its directives with filial respect. . . .

The acute need for radical reforms of the structures which conceal poverty and which are themselves forms of violence, should not let us lose sight of the fact that the source of injustice is in the hearts of men. Therefore it is only by making an appeal to the 'moral potential' of the person and to the constant need for interior conversion, that social change will be brought about which will be truly in the service of man. . . .

The theses of the "theologies of liberation" are widely popularized under a simplified form, in formation sessions or in what are called "base groups" which lack the necessary catechetical and theological preparation as well as the capacity for discernment. Thus these theses are accepted by generous men and women without any critical judgment being made.

That is why pastors must look after the quality and the content of catechesis and formation which should always present the 'whole message of salvation' and the imperatives of true liberation within the framework of this whole message.

In this full presentation of Christianity, it is proper to emphasize those essential aspects which the "theologies of liberation" especially tend to misunderstand or to eliminate, namely: God and true man; the sovereignty of grace; and the true nature of the means of salvation, especially of the Church and the sacraments. One should also keep in mind the true meaning of ethics in which the distinction between good and evil is not relativized, the real meaning of sin, the necessity for conversion, and the universality of the law of fraternal love. One needs to be on guard against the politicization of existence which, misunderstanding the entire meaning of the Kingdom of God and the transcendence of the person, begins to sacralize politics and betray the religion of the people in favor of the projects of the revolution.

The defenders of orthodoxy are sometimes accused of passivity, indulgence, or culpable complicity regarding the intolerable situations of injustice and the political regimes which prolong them. Spiritual conversion, the intensity of the love of God and neighbor, zeal for justice and peace, the Gospel meaning of the poor and of poverty, are required of everyone, and especially of pastors and those in positions of responsibility. The concern for the purity of the faith demands giving the answer of effective witness in the service of one's neighbor, the poor and the oppressed in particular, in an integral theological fashion. By the witness of their dynamic and constructive power to love, Christians will thus lay the foundations of this "civilization of love" of which the Conference of Puebla spoke, following Paul VI. Moreover there are already many priests, religious, and lay people who are consecrated in a truly evangelical way for the creation of a just society.

181

Source Four
The Magi

Introduction

This source comes from Nicaragua at a time when the country was under the Somoza dictatorship. In his introduction to the book *The Gospel in Solentiname*, from which this conversation is taken, Father Ernesto Cardenal explained that he began these discussions with his flock and that they were so interesting he decided to record them. Those participating were mostly peasants, fisherfolk, and their families, with an occasional student returning home from Managua for a short vacation. Cardenal gave little information about most of the participants. But he did say that Laureano was born on the island and that he interpreted everything in terms of revolution. Apparently, Felipe was of like mind, for he was always concerned for the "proletarian struggle." In contrast, Oscar constantly called for unity. "Old Tomás Peña," the father of Tomás Peña, was illiterate but frequently spoke words of profound wisdom. About the rest, we know only their names.

The narrator is Cardenal himself, who was clearly committed to revolution. After the downfall of the Somozas and the triumph of the Sandinista revolution, he became Secretary of Culture for the new government. You may have seen a famous photograph of him kneeling at the Managua airport before Pope John Paul II, who is wagging a finger at him for his participation in politics.

As you read this source, ask yourself: What was the role of Cardenal in the conversation? Was he telling people what to think or to say? How did he contribute to the conversation? How did he use his authority as a priest? On the basis of what people say, try to explain why this sort of conversation would provoke the response of a man like Ratzinger in Source Three ("An Official Reprimand"). Would Ratzinger see in this conversation a sign of the ability of lay people to think for themselves and of the wisdom of the unlettered? Or would he see in it proof of their need for guidance? Explain your response.

You will note the excitement of participants as they read the Bible and uncovered various things in it. They certainly would have heard the story of the Wise Men, which is quite popular in Latin America. In fact, in most of Latin America it is the Wise Men—and not Santa—who bring gifts to children on Epiphany. Yet, the believers in Solentiname were eager to read the story and looked into every detail, and they read it in their own fashion. What connection do you see between this eagerness to read the Bible and what you read in chapter 6, Source Two ("Unwelcomed Peddlers")?

The Text*

"The Visit of the Wise Men" (Matt. 2:1-12)

> Jesus was born in Bethlehem of Judea in the days of Herod the King. Then to Jerusalem came wise men from the East saying: "Where is the King of the Jews that has been born? For we saw his star in the East and we have come here to worship him."

We were in the church. I said by way of introduction that these words of Matthew, "in the days of Herod the King," are telling us that Jesus was born under a tyranny. There were three Herods, as we might say in Nicaragua three Somozas: Herod the elder, Herod his son, and a grandson Herod. Herod the elder, the one at the time of Jesus' birth, had ordered two of his sons to be strangled on suspicion of conspiracy, and he also killed one of his wives. At the time of Jesus' birth he killed more than three hundred public servants on other suspicions of conspiracy. So Jesus was born in an atmosphere of repression and terror. . . .

Laureano said: "I think these wise men sh** things up when they went to Herod asking about a liberator. It would be like someone going to Somoza now to ask him where's the man who's going to liberate Nicaragua."

Another of the young men: "The way I figure it, these wise men were afraid of Herod and didn't want to do anything without consent."

Tomas Peña: "They went to ask him for a pass . . ."

The same young man: "They probably went first to consult Herod because they were afraid of him, and all those people of Jerusalem were filled with fear when they heard talk of a Messiah just like Nicaraguan people are afraid when they hear talk of liberation. The minute they hear that young people want to liberate those of us who are being exploited, they begin to shake and be afraid. When they hear people say that this government must be overthrown, they shake and are afraid."

Adán: "It seems to me that when those wise men arrived they knew that the Messiah had been born and they thought Herod knew about it and that the Messiah was going to be a member of his family. If he was a king, it was natural that they should go to look for him in Herod's palace. But in that palace there was nothing but corruption and evil, and the Messiah couldn't be born there. He had to be born among the people, poor, in a stable. They learned a lesson there when they saw that the Messiah had not been born in a palace or in the home of some rich person, and that's why they had to go on looking for him somewhere else. The Gospel says later that when they left

183

there they saw the star again. That means that when they reached Jerusalem the star wasn't guiding them. They'd lost it.

Félix: "They were confused. And it seems to me that since they were foreigners they did not know the country very well, and they went to the capital, where the authorities were, to ask about the new leader."

> When Herod the king heard this he was very troubled, and all the people of Jerusalem also.

Oscar: "I figure that when Herod found out that that king had been born he was furious because he didn't want to stop being the ruler. He was as mad as hell. And he was already figuring out how to get rid of this one like he had got rid of so many already."

Pablo: "He must have felt hatred and envy. Because dictators always think they are gods. They think they're the only ones and they can't let anyone be above them."

Gloria: "And he was probably afraid, too. He had killed a lot of people not long before, and then some gentlemen arrive asking where's the new king, the liberator."

Félix: "He surely must have put all his police on the alert. I think that's what the Gospel means here: 'He was very troubled.'"

One of the young people: "And the Gospel says that the other people of Jerusalem were also troubled. That means his followers, the big shots, like the Somoza crowd. Because for them it was very bad news that the liberator was arriving. But for poor people it was great news. And the powerful people knew that the Messiah had to be against them."

Old Tomas Peña: "That king who ruled that republic with a firm hand— he ruled a million people or however many there were then—he didn't allow anyone to say anything he didn't like. You could only think the way the government wanted, and they surely didn't allow any talk about messiahs. And they must have been annoyed when outsiders came talking about that, as if they were talking about a new government."

Manuel: "The people had been waiting for that Messiah or liberator for some time. And it's interesting to see that even out of the country the news had got around that he had been born, and these wise men found out, it seems to me, from the people. But in Jerusalem the powerful were entirely ignorant of his birth."

> Then the king called all the chiefs of the priests and those who taught the law to the people, and he asked them where Christ was going to be born.

Felipe: "The clergy are summoned by a tyrant who has killed a lot of people. And the clergy answer the call. It seems to me that if they went to his palace it's because they were his supporters, they approved of his murders. Just like today the monsignors who are supporters of the regime that we have. It means that those people were like the people we have today in Nicaragua."

> They told him: "In Bethlehem of Judea: for thus it is written by the prophet."

I said that they [the priests and teachers of the law] knew the Bible well and that they knew that the Messiah was to be born in the little town called Bethlehem.

Don Jose: "They knew he was going to be born in a little town, among the common people. But they were in Jerusalem, visiting with the powerful and the rich in their palaces. Just like today there are a lot of Church leaders who know that Jesus was born in Bethlehem, and every year they preach about this at Christmas, that Jesus was born poor in a manger, but the places they go to all the time are rich people's houses and palaces."

Source Five
A Retablo

Introduction

The first retablo comes from Rincón de Ramos, a fairly small town in the state of Aguascalientes, in central Mexico. It is dedicated to the "Lord of Mercy," or "Divine Mercy," a devotion that began spreading out of Poland in the late 1930s. His feast day is May 14. Note that this retablo is dated just a few days before that, on May 5. Although some of the writing is illegible, enough can be read to give us a glimpse at the story behind it and at the religiosity of the woman commissioning it. The grammar and spelling in the Spanish text clearly show that it is written by a person of little formal education. That text is reproduced below so that, if you know Spanish, you may see this for yourself. Although it is not altogether clear, apparently Meregildo Macías is the writer of the text, and José Hernández is the painter.

As you look at this picture and read its caption, ask yourself: How does the piety reflected here mirror or contrast with what you have found in the previous sources in this chapter? How would the woman commissioning it relate to the debates about liberation theology? Note that she is probably one of the oppressed whose liberation that theology sought. How does this retablo illumine or illustrate what you already know about Mexican migration to the United States?

Note that this retablo is dated 1945 and that therefore it took less than a decade for the devotion to the Divine Mercy to travel from Poland to a small town in Mexico. What does this tell you about popular piety, and how it is communicated?

The Image[+]

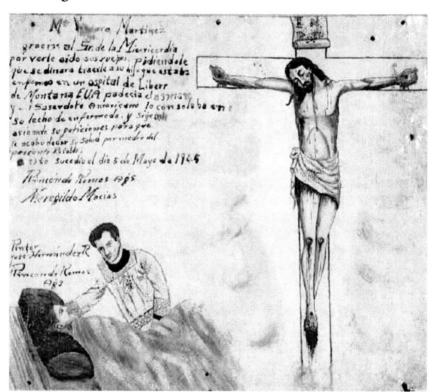

Figure 8.1

The Spanish text reads:

> Ma. [?????]ra Martinez
> gracias el Sr. de la Misericordia
> por verle oido sus ruegos, pidiendole
> que se dinara traerle a su hijo que estaba

enfermo en un ospital de Liberr
de Montana E.U.A. padecia de astma
y el sacerdote americano lo consolaba en
su lecho de enfermeda y sige
asiendo su peticiones para que
le acabe de dar su salud por medio del
presente Retablo.
Esto sucedio el dia 5 de Mayo de 1945
Rincón de Ramos Ags
Meregildo Macias
Pintor
José Hernández R
Rincon de Ramos
Ags

The English translation of the text is:

Maria [?]ra Martínez thanks the Lord of Mercy for having heard her
petitions, asking that he would deign to bring back [home] her son
who was ill in a hospital in Liberr [Laurel?] in Montana U.S.A. He
suffered from asthma and the American priest comforted him in his
bed of illness and [she] continues making her petitions so that he [the
Lord of Mercy] will completely give him back his health by means of
the present retablo. This happened on May 5, 1945.
Rincón de Ramos, Aguascalientes
Meregildo Macias
Painter
José Hernández R
Rincón de Ramos, Aguascalientes

Source Six
Another Retablo

Introduction
The narrative for this retablo, which comes from Mexico, is completely
illegible. Whether it was erased on purpose is unclear. Thus, it is impossible
to tell its date, context, or the story behind it. Apparently, it was presented by
one or both of the couple in the foreground with three pigs. On the left is a
crucifix arising from a bed of flames. And, to make matters more interesting,
one of the four people amid the flames wears a papal tiara and another has an
imperial or royal crown.

Look at the attitudes of the various characters. On the basis of what you know of the religious history of Mexico, what could possibly be the story behind such a retablo? Try writing a caption for it. Have fun letting your imagination run!

The Image⁵

Figure 8.2

9
A COMPLEX REALITY

Introduction

The earlier chapters of this book (chapters 1 to 5) centered on the Roman Catholic Church and its history, particularly during colonial times and in the first decades after independence. In chapter 6 we have seen the arrival and development of traditional Protestantism. Then, in chapter 7, we explored the interplay between Roman Catholicism and Protestantism, and in chapter 8 we looked into the history of Roman Catholicism and Roman Catholic theology in the twentieth century.

We would be wrong, however, to think that the total picture is that simple. In the first two chapters, you had a glimpse into the manner in which the original inhabitants of what we now know as Latin America coped with the religious changes they had to face with the coming of the Europeans. Later, in cases such as Guiomar d'Oliveira ("Magic and Love"), you have seen that religious dissent and forbidden practices continued, often in secret, despite all the efforts of the Church to root them out. And the case of Manuel Bautista Pérez ("The Inquisition at Work") shows that the Church always feared the continued presence of Jewish practices and traditions. With independence, dissent came to the foreground in the form of liberal and radical ideas and in Protestantism. The former led to constant tension that erupted into outright violence in places such as Mexico (in the Mexican Revolution) and Colombia (in la Violencia). The latter gave birth to relatively small but growing churches throughout the region.

The latter half of the twentieth century and the first years of the twenty-first brought about even more variety and complexity. Although there are a number of other developments that could be considered, we have chosen to center our attention on the three that may well be the most influential in the religious future of Latin America.

The first is the rise of the Pentecostal movement. Although the origins of Latin American Pentecostalism are connected with similar movements elsewhere, much of it was homegrown. Beginning in 1909 with what at first was a local disagreement among Methodists in Chile, Pentecostalism soon spread throughout the region. Then it was further encouraged by Pentecostal missionaries, primarily from the United States. Today Pentecostalism in its various forms is by far the second largest religious group in Latin America, surpassed only by Roman Catholicism—and in some countries approaching it in the number of followers. Pentecostals and others with similar emphasis on the extraordinary gifts of the Spirit—speaking in tongues, visions, healings, ecstasies, and so on—are also called "Charismatics," from the Greek word *charisma*, which means "gifts." Here we use the term *Pentecostal* for the denominations that arose from the Pentecostal revival and *Charismatic* for those in other denominations with similar experiences and emphases. Sources One, "The Holy Spirit in Chile," and Two, "Quichua Pentecostals," will offer you a glimpse into the Pentecostal movement that is drastically changing the religious landscape in Latin America. Furthermore, Source Three, "A Charismatic Priest," will show that renewed emphasis on the Holy Spirit has also made an impact on the Catholic Church, resulting in a strong charismatic movement within that church.

The second development is the resurgence of ancient Indian and African religious practices that had been submerged or suppressed since the colonial era but are now showing surprising vitality. The instructions of Pachacama to his followers (chapter 2, "A God Compromises"), instructing his people to worship both him and the god of Christians, are an indication of how the ancient religion managed to survive. Today, sites that had long seemed to be only ruins visited by tourists and studied by archaeologists have once again become places of worship for the Mayans, the Aymaras, and many others. Something similar has happened with African religious traditions brought by the slaves and long pushed underground. A number of circumstances in several Caribbean countries—particularly in Cuba—and in Brazil have once again brought these into the open. In this chapter, we will focus our attention on the subsistence and revival of ancient African religion, of which Sources Four, "Shangó," and Five, "Reyita's Faith," are two expressions.

There is a third development that must be taken into account, particularly by readers in the United States and Canada. Until 1910, the flow of migration between the United States and Latin America was mostly southward. Then the Mexican Revolution and other events reversed that trend, which grew in the second half of the twentieth century to such a point that the United States now has the third largest Spanish-speaking population in the hemisphere—after Mexico and Argentina. In other words, Latin America has come to North America. The result is that at the beginning of the twenty-first century, more than half of all Roman Catholics in the United States are Latinos or Latinas. In any major city in the United States, there are hundreds of Latino Pentecostal churches and probably dozens of more traditional Protestant Latino churches. Source Six, "An Immigrant's Tale," will show one of the many ways in which the religiosity of these immigrants and their descendants has been affected by conditions in the United States. Sources Seven ("The Catholic Response") and Eight ("A Protestant Response") show how the Roman Catholic Church and a major Protestant denomination in the United States are seeking to respond to the growing presence and influence of Hispanics in the nation.

The first of these two is part of an official statement issued in 1987 by the Roman Catholic bishops in the United States, approving and establishing the "National Pastoral Plan for Hispanic Ministry." For several decades Roman Catholic leaders had expressed concern that their church had not developed a concerted response to the growing number of Hispanics among its flock, and therefore there was a tendency of recent immigrants to lose contact with the church of their ancestors. Under the auspices of the United States Conference of Catholic Bishops (USCCB), and under the direction of Hispanic leadership, there was a series of three *encuentros* (meetings or gatherings) of Hispanic and other Catholic leaders and their parishioners. These began in 1972 and gained impetus as they progressed, as seen in the number of participants in each encuentro, rising from 250 in 1972 to 1,200 in 1977, and finally to 2,000 in 1985. After this process of extensive consultation, the bishops endorsed the "National Pastoral Plan for Hispanic Ministries." This 1987 plan, after a series of corrections and adjustments, still serves as the blueprint for Catholic ministry among Hispanics.

The second of these two denominational plans, the United Methodist Plan for Hispanic Ministry, was also the result of a prolonged process. For a number of years Hispanics in The United Methodist Church had called for a concerted denominational plan for Methodist work among Hispanics. Finally, in 1992 The United Methodist Church approved the "National

191

Plan for Hispanic Ministry," making it the first major Protestant denomination to develop a comprehensive plan for Hispanic ministries and to allot significant funding for it. With a number of adjustments, this plan is still in force.

Finally, Source Nine, "Graffiti Theology," is a puzzling combination of two graffiti. It is included in this final chapter as an invitation for further reflection, imagination, and intellectual curiosity.

Source One
The Holy Spirit in Chile

Introduction

Willis C. Hoover had been serving as a Methodist pastor in Chile for twenty years when unexpected occurrences began taking place in his church in Valparaíso on New Year's Eve, 1909. A few years earlier Hoover's parish had been through a number of difficulties, including an outbreak of smallpox and an earthquake that destroyed the church building. It had been greatly strengthened by these difficulties, particularly in terms of lay leadership. Finally, in 1908, it had inaugurated the largest Methodist church building in Chile. Suddenly, as they awaited the New Year, many felt impelled to pray together out loud, and all fell to their knees in prayer. Hoover said that both he and the congregation were greatly surprised by this, but all were convinced that it was the work of the Holy Spirit. Sometime later, people began having other experiences, including speaking in tongues.

The Methodist Church of Chile did not favor these happenings in Valparaíso and tried to put a stop to them. But similar events then began occurring in Santiago. The new movement, and its conflict with the authorities of the Methodist Church, became a *cause celèbre* discussed in the local newspapers, much to the chagrin of both sides. After much debate and mutual recrimination, a large portion of the Methodists in Valparaíso withdrew from the denomination and called Hoover to be their pastor. This was the beginning of the Methodist Pentecostal Church, which soon outgrew the Methodist Church, and out of which emerged many of the other major Pentecostal denominations in Chile.

Hoover wrote *History of the Pentecostal Revival in Chile* in order to set the record straight about the entire process that led to severing ties with the Methodist Church. Thus, much of his book is devoted to a step-by-step narrative of measures taken by one side or the other, actions against him on the part of the Methodist Church, his responses, and so on. But the vast majority of the book deals with events such as the ones described in the selection below—sudden conversions, people coming to the church unexpectedly, visions, healings, and so on.

As you read this selection, ask yourself why other Methodists might dislike what was taking place in Valparaíso. Why would they speak of "order" and "dignity"? How might Methodists—and perhaps other Protestants—feel their social prestige threatened by these occurrences? Imagine, or even try to construct, a dialogue between Hoover and his Methodist detractors. What would each side say?

What might Hoover have meant by "carnal" actions, attitudes, or manifestations? Did he mean things related to physical inclinations and desires; did he mean something emerging not from the spirit of God but rather from oneself; or did he mean both? What criteria did he offer to distinguish between the work of the Spirit and the work of demonic powers? Why would he have felt compelled to write this history, essentially a defense of his own actions?

What connections do you see between this form of religion and those you have found in earlier documents? What social and political views and what understanding of sin are manifested in the list of evil things confessed by the man who came to Hoover's door?

What does the explosive growth of Pentecostalism throughout the region tell you about the relevance of Roman Catholicism for people's lives? What about the relevance of more traditional Protestantism?

The Text*

I believe that the true secret of the entire matter is that we really and truly believe in the Holy Spirit—we truly trust him—we truly acknowledge him—we truly obey him—we truly allow him his freedom—we truly believe that the promise made in Acts 1:4, 5 [sic]† and in Joel 2:28, 29‡ is for us, even though some have ceased to speak of it, to believe in it, as we calmly go on, without any hope, in our mutual routine.

Thus we believe, hope and pray, and HE HAS DONE THESE THINGS BEFORE OUR EYES. MAY HIS NAME BE PRAISED! . . .

From the very beginning, the awakening was marked by extraordinary manifestations of various sorts: laughter, weeping, shouting, singing, strange tongues, visions, ecstasies in which people fell to the ground and felt translated elsewhere, to heaven, to paradise, to beautiful fields, and with various experiences in which they spoke with the Lord, with angels, or with the devil.

Those who went through these experiences were very joyful and usually were also very transformed and full of praise, the spirit of prayer, and love.

Obviously, these things seemed strange to us. But they appeared gradually and normally were accompanied by good fruits, which proved to us that they came from God. Sometimes there was evidence of the work of other spirits, but this did not frighten us, nor did it lead us to unbelief (although we were tempted in that direction), but rather led us to test the spirits and reminded us of what is said in the book of Job: "when the children of God came before the Lord, among them Satan also came." And when Moses appeared before Pharaoh performing the miracle that God commanded, the magicians did the same with their incantations. We are then satisfied remembering that the rod of Moses swallowed the rods of the magicians. . . .

One Sunday afternoon, a young man who was a servant in a private home in Viña del Mar was at our meeting, perhaps for the second or third time. He was praying with many others at the altar when he suddenly arose and with a countenance alight with fervor screamed, as by an irresistible impulse, "God is love! God is love!" He repeated it several times, then said, "I have to proclaim it in the street." He ran through the entire aisle of the church, pushed aside the wooden screen by the door, and went out. Kneeling in the middle of the street, he repeatedly shouted, "God is love!" and immediately he said, "God is love in the kitchen, and God is love in the cantina!" In saying "cantina," he got up and ran to a nearby cantina, and when he went in he once again cried out in a loud voice, "God is love!"

The bartender did not like the message, and even less the messenger, so he called a guard and sent the young man to the police station. Someone who had followed the young man from church picked up his hat and as he was leaving, the young man told him, "It doesn't matter, the message has been delivered."

In the evening after the service several brothers were talking near the altar when suddenly the wooden screen by the door was opened and the young man who had been taken away by the guard came running in, just like he had run out. He rushed to the altar, and kneeling, he praised God for his mercy.

This young man was so new to our community that no one knew either his name or anything else about him until after this incident.

One afternoon, when the pastor [Hoover] went to answer a knock at the door, he found an unknown man, hat in hand, shaking from head to toe, who said to him, "Are you the pastor?" "Yes." With a voice that showed either surprise or fright the man said, "I am a very bad man, and I come to have you pray for me." The pastor invited him to come in and sit, but upon entering, the man immediately fell to his knees weeping violently. The pastor had no alternative but to kneel by him and pray, even though the man was paying no attention to anything. But amid his weeping, in as much as he was able, he spoke thus to God, "I have been a very bad man. I have been a blasphemer. I have denied you, Lord," and so on for quite a while.

When the violence of the storm finally abated and there was some quiet, he was heard to say, with a voice that was both surprised and joyful, "Lord I had always imagined that you were so far away, and you are here with me!" The pastor had no need to pray (although he did), because the man was dealing directly and by himself with God. Upon sitting after the prayer, that man said, with an expression that reminded one of the sun shining after a rain, "How am I going to be able to join my brothers?"

What would this man know about brothers? He was a blasphemer, an atheist, the head of a socialist group in the bakers' guild (as he told us while he sat there), a famous speaker, who was much applauded when he denied the existence of God.

He said that a day or two earlier, while he was sleeping during the daytime, he woke up weeping without knowing why, and greatly surprised he shook himself asking, "What is this? Am I mad? No, I am sane. What, then, can this be? Could it be that the demons are departing from me?" Then he said, "I dealt with God as with a friend, and I said to him, 'Lord, be with me in my vow never again to drink'." From that moment he had no peace until he had found the pastor. . . .

Those who do not know the power of God can easily stand aside and speak of "order," "dignity," and so on. But when we ask God to lay his power on us and this is the result, things are otherwise. And in this case it is usually more beneficial than many of the best sermons I might preach. People say, "Who can doubt such an experience?" And I repeat, "Who can doubt such an experience?"

There are times when we do not have any such manifestations. During those times no one has been baptized with the Holy Spirit. Even though there has been much profit from instruction on the Word and from personal testimonies, etc., almost nothing with definitive results has been derived from all this.

I now expect to be accused of allowing myself to be carried away by carnal manifestations. But those who know me and have heard me preach for the last two years know well that no one can be more opposed than I to all that is carnal. And they know that I have constantly taught that it is a sin for one to do something moved by the flesh or self-driven. . . . I simply call every child of God to begin by completely subjecting himself to God, trusting in the purifying blood of Christ, asking God to give him the gift of the Holy Spirit, and then letting him work in his own fashion. . . .

Allow me to insist that I am against all fanaticism. And it would be futile to deny that there have been within this movement some manifestations that come from the flesh. There is no doubt that some have gone to extremes, and this simply shows that they are still in the flesh—that is, they try to do something on their own, and the result is always bad. But the purpose of this writing is not to say what we should do but rather what God does through the Holy Spirit.

Source Two
Quichua Pentecostals

Introduction

The Gospel Missionary Union, an outgrowth of the YMCA, headquartered in Kansas City, Missouri, was the first evangelical body to establish permanent missionary work in Ecuador. This work began in 1896, after the liberal government of Eloy Alfaro lifted the long-standing prohibition against foreign missionaries originally imposed by the conservatives at the behest of the Catholic hierarchy.

In the 1970s, one of the churches belonging to the Union, Misión Evangélica Ríos de Agua Viva, in the Quichua village of Pulucate, began having contacts with non-Quichua Pentecostal churches nearby. (The Quichua are Native Americans who still speak the language of the Incas.) Eventually, Pentecostalism took hold of the church in Pulucate, alienating it from the Gospel Missionary Union and leading to its independence. During this process, Ríos de Agua Viva also founded other churches, thus resulting in the first Pentecostal denomination among Quichua speakers in Ecuador. After some time, this denomination became affiliated with the Church of God, a Pentecostal body originating in the United States. Even so, Ríos de Agua Viva retained its autonomy, which allows it to benefit from the wider contacts of the Church of God while administering its own affairs.

You will be reading two interviews conducted in Ecuador by Eloy H. Nolivos, as part of his PhD dissertation research on the origins and early development of Pentecostalism among the Quichua people in Ecuador. In the first interview, Nolivos spoke with the Administrative Bishop for Native Territories of the Church of God, Guillermo Vasconez, who reported what he was told about these events. In the second, Nolivos interviewed two of the Quichuas who participated in the early revival: Rosendo Guaman, the president of Ríos de Agua Viva, and Francisco Pilataxi, pastor of the main church. Thus, these two interviews provide us with different perspectives: one from the outside and the other from the inside.

As you read these interviews, ask yourself: What would lead these members of the Gospel Missionary Union to look elsewhere in order to learn more about the Bible? How did this relate to their complaint that the Quichua-language Bible institutes of the Gospel Missionary Union were too basic and superficial? What does this indicate about the way the Gospel Missionary Union saw the Quichua people and the way they thought of themselves? Why would Pilataxi and others seek studies beyond the confines of the Gospel Missionary Union? Why would the latter frown on such efforts? What similarities or differences do you see between the reaction of the Gospel Missionary Union to this Pentecostal movement and the reaction of the Methodist Church in Chile to Hoover and his revival, in our previous source? Why would the Misión Evangélica Ríos de Agua Viva seek contact with Pentecostals outside of their indigenous community, and why would the Church of God provide such support? What does the affiliated yet autonomous status of the Misión Evangélica Ríos de Agua Viva vis-à-vis the Church of God tell you about Pentecostal openness to new and varied structures and institutional arrangements?

Vasconez spoke of "carnality," of things being "of the flesh," as does Hoover in "The Holy Spirit in Chile." What differences or similarities do you see between these two sources as to what they mean by "flesh," or by "carnal"?

Compare the two interviews. What differences do you see between them? How well informed was Vasconez about the events in Pulucate? How did he evaluate them?

The Text

First Interview[§]

Nolivos: What was the date of the Quichua Pentecost?

Vasconez: I don't know the exact date but it was in the beginning of the '80s. They had a revival, but what they discovered was that they had the baptism of the Holy Spirit.

Nolivos: Who were the main leaders?

Vasconez: Rosendo Guaman, Manuel Aucancela, Francisco Tenemasa, and other leaders of the congregation who were surprised with this situation.

They had never been taught about being Pentecostal nor heard about Pentecostalism.

Nolivos: What were some of the antecedents of this event?

Vasconez: Basically this congregation was from the Gospel Missionary Union. What began to occur was that they began to sense that they wanted something more, something special from God. The church had fallen into a routine, and they wanted something more from their Christian experience. From here emerged the desire to pray and fast, and the result of this search was the Pentecostal revival.

Nolivos: What happened in the Pentecost?

Vasconez: The story I have heard is that they decided to pray and fast for three days, calling all the congregation, especially the leaders. They shut themselves in to pray in their church. On the third day, they began to sense a manifestation that was different and strange. All of a sudden, they felt a great joy and a great divine heat that they had never experienced. On the third day, some of them began to speak in different tongues and did not know what was happening. At first this caused some confusion because they did not know how to react. Some reacted negatively and said this does not come from God because it is too strange. But others began to reflect that they had been fasting and praying to God for three days. How can it be that God would not respond and respond with something strange? They began to search in the Bible to understand how to interpret the occurrence. And the Holy Spirit guided them to understand that what they were receiving at the moment was coming from the Spirit of God.

Nolivos: What have been some of the results, the impact even today, both positive and negative?

Vasconez: The negative and positive results were various. Once they came to the conclusion that this was something that came from the Holy Spirit, they began to experiment other things that at some point went to a negative extreme. Some began to do things that were out of order. They would let their physical joy, their carnality, be manifested, and they were criticized by other surrounding congregations, because at this time there existed no Pentecostals among indigenous Quichuas in Chimborazo. The manifestations that they began to receive were so strange that they began to be seriously criticized, taking these manifestations to the extreme. It appears that people began to reject them—the other congregations and churches that were nearby.

The positive results were that little by little they started to feel zeal to preach the word. [It was] a fervent desire to make known their faith to all those around them and to neighboring communities. They started to become a missionary church. This attitude of being a missionary church means that through the years they have established more than twenty churches. Some of these churches were somewhat large, others much smaller, but almost all of them in distant communities where before there had not been any preaching of the gospel of Jesus Christ. Therefore, I believe that the positive results have been greater [than the negative ones] and also with time they have come to mature, reflect on their faith and on their Pentecostality. A positive result of this is that among the indigenous Pentecostals, they are the most mature; they have a clear vision of their mission in the kingdom of God; and they have impacted their community in a very particular way. It is a community that has prospered not only spiritually but also has grown to the point that currently the majority is Evangelical Pentecostal. They have a school, a high school. They have a daycare. They have a process for developing their community so that one notices that God has made them prosper.

Nolivos: Regarding their recent origins, what happened after the Pentecostal revival and their relationship with the Gospel Missionary Union? And also since they are now affiliated with the Church of God, how did that come about?

Vasconez: What happened was that after the Pentecostal experience and as this grew among them, they began to identify themselves as Christians filled with the Holy Spirit. Little by little they came to realize that there were others—not *indígenas*—who were Pentecostals. It was here that they came into contact with other Pentecostal movements in other places. Therefore, they started to look for help in the area of theological education from Pentecostal people because at the same time they were being totally rejected by the Gospel Missionary Union. The Gospel Missionary Union became highly critical. They [the Pentecostals] were declared apostates as people who denied the faith, heretics. Hence, they started to look for support from other Pentecostals. We [the Church of God] were starting our work [in the indigenous area] when we heard about them, and we met Rosendo Guaman, who is one of the early leaders. We talked about working together in order to enlarge the kingdom of God. They needed help in the churches where they were working, biblical/theological formation, and even secular formation for their pastors and members. First we made an agreement to work together and later it was an affiliation. As an organization, they have their own by-laws, but these state that they are affiliated with the Church of God although they have autonomy. They work autonomously; they have their own organizational structure, but they still participate in the administrative structure of the Church of God.

Second Interview*

Nolivos: Can you tell the story of the movement of the Holy Spirit in your church?

Pilataxi: We were part of Gospel Missionary Union for many years.

Nolivos: This church is a daughter church to the Gospel Missionary Union?

Pilataxi: Yes, it is the daughter church of Emmanuel Church. We grew up in Emmanuel but then there was a split, and we built this church around 1977. We started with about 150 people. We had a Christmas service, and after the service there was a great storm that flooded the whole community. It only lasted about 15 minutes. People from the hills came down to the church, and it became a torrential rain, a deluge. It caused a tremendous disaster. People and animals were swept several miles away from their homes. Families and houses were lost. I was with about five people right over there where the little store was, and we escaped the landslide coming from the hills.

Guaman: The newspapers and the army came. People and churches came from Quito and Guayaquil. Even from Colombia people came to study and see what had taken place. There were seven families that died, and their relatives went to San Martin to recover the bodies. Everything was a disaster.

Pilataxi: We asked the *cabildos* [the local government] if we could build a small church on our own property [after losing the other with the storm]. They allowed us to do it. The founding pastor was José María. We began to worship here at this church. The institutes of the Association [the Gospel Missionary Union] where they taught in Quichua were basic and superficial. So we found deeper teachings with Spanish seminaries that would come and teach us pastoral theology, and we brought the materials. I attended that study with my nephew and others, a total of four of us from here. There were students from all parts here in our community studying. At this time, . . . [the Gospel Missionary Union and its leaders] were saying we were studying another doctrine, other religions. We were not supposed to be doing this. That was when we discovered fasting, prayer, and divine healing. . . .

Pilataxi: Let's continue. Fasting, praying, and divine healing. This was new for us. When others heard the doctrine, our very own church pastor José

María turned against us, the four of us who were learning it. We wanted to preach this new doctrine but he would say "that's another doctrine, a false one," and he went to the Association. Brother, then began a time of great criticism and we suffered greatly as they accused us of a false doctrine, saying this should not be and we should not be doing it. As we shared it with the church, some were in agreement with us while others were with Brother José María. There was a division arising in the church. We continued in our studies while the Association took a stand against those who were studying.

Nolivos: You were preaching what you learned?

Pilataxi: Yes. We would go and preach outdoors. People began to invite us here and there in other communities. . . . Some of the deacons agreed while Pastor José María and others did not. Pastor Manuel Aucancela (who was not a pastor back then) supported us and my father-in-law. . . . So the brothers began with the fast, and they asked us to help with fasting and praying, putting the youth in the hands of God. So when we returned from the revival, people told us something was happening. We didn't know what was happening to the brothers. It had been two days already that they were in there, in the church, when we arrived.

Guaman: I was in my home and when I went outside to the street I could hear sounds of screaming and squealing. I live just a little ways up from here and I could hear these sounds clearly. I drew near the street and Aaaayyyyy!!!! There were some [people] screaming with loud voices crying out to God. I asked myself, what is this?

Nolivos: Do you remember what they were saying?

Guaman: Yes, they were saying, "Father, thank you, thank you Father for this manifestation, thank you!" And the people across the street and all over came out as if there had been an accident. Everyone came to the church to see. When we came down from our house to open the door of the church, we saw people screaming, others jumping, and others sprawled out on the floor and on their backs receiving the baptism of the Holy Spirit.

Pilataxi: See, something happened here. Brother, when we arrived at the church, at the door, there was so much fire that people broke out! Then we went in and there had been a lot of people on the outside looking in through the windows. When we entered, I said, "Thank you Lord." I had been fasting.

Nolivos: How many people were inside?

Pilataxi: Approximately 15 or 20, there were not many inside. When we entered, we thanked God for what he was doing according to the Bible. Because we still did not know what the manifestation was or what the power of the Holy Spirit was. . . . We were concerned because we did not know what this was, what was happening. Then we noticed a sister, Rosa Guaman, speaking in tongues. And there was another sister who grabbed the Bible. She was illiterate, yet she began to read it. Other brothers were prophesying, "This is going to happen . . . ; this is what the Lord is saying . . . ; to these young people, God is going to speak to them." Some were singing and jumping and saying, "Glory to God." We did not know this phrase "glory to God" until that moment, or Hallelujah.

Nolivos: You had not heard this before?

Pilataxi: No, it was prohibited by the Association, and the pastors would not allow it or clapping because the *mestizos* do this and that is different doctrine. They would tell us we couldn't do this; it was prohibited. So then back in the church people were singing, clapping, and saying, "glory to God." We only had instruments, and they began to play them and people began to worship, to sing, to dance and they spoke in tongues. These things took place, Brother. At this point Brother Rosendo seriously doubted everything that was taking place. He entered and saw the people and said, "You should not be doing this." But how could he stop it? Because no one can stop the power of God. He was afraid of what had never taken place among us before: the praising, the glorifying and the kneeling. . . .

Guaman: Not only was the manifestation taking place at the church but in various homes. Those who were afraid and doubting at home would be saying, "Dear God, how is this possible? I have never seen anything like this before." And the Spirit started to move in their homes, so they realized the manifestation was true. A few days later they went to the church and shared the experiences that God had given dreams, visions demonstrating it. . . .

Pilataxi: We didn't know anything about tongues. How were we supposed to know about this? So we decided to visit the homes of people who had doubts and pray with them. So we went here and there visiting. We already knew about the imposition of hands from our earlier theological studies. We said, "Help us understand in what language they are speaking. Speak to us Lord." We put it in his hands, and this gave the brothers and sisters a little bit of peace. They would come to the church, to the worship services that were very long. Prayer meetings ended up lasting two to three hours. There were many commentaries that had arrived at the Association of Churches. They became our enemies on the radio saying, "Those in Pulucate Centro are crazy, they are fanatics, and they have false doctrine. We need to prevent, ask, and see what is happening."

Source Three
A Charismatic Priest

Introduction

The Pentecostal movement in Latin America has made a significant impact in almost all denominations. Methodists, Presbyterians, Disciples, Baptists, and many others have adopted several of the traits of the movement, and in many denominations a charismatic movement has developed—including more emotional worship, speaking in tongues, prophesying, healing, and so on. In the Roman Catholic Church, the number of those who have been influenced by charismatism is rapidly growing. One of the earliest manifestations among Latin American Catholics took place in Santo Domingo, under the leadership of Father Emiliano Tardif (1926–1999).

Tardif, a Canadian, was sent to the Dominican Republic as a missionary by the Missionaries of the Sacred Heart. From the very beginning, he devoted most of his efforts to work among the poor. Then, in 1973, he regained his health after a serious illness and came to the conviction that his return to health was the result of the fervent prayers of a group of charismatic believers. He joined the movement, and soon both they and he decided that God worked marvelous healings through Tardif's prayers and that he had uncommon gifts of discernment. Father Emiliano then founded the Comunidad Siervos de Cristo Vivo (Servants of the Living Christ). This is a charismatic community originally centered in Santo Domingo but whose influence soon spread throughout Latin America and further. As the fame of this community spread, Tardif began spending eight months of the year traveling and only four in Santo Domingo. Soon after his death many of his followers called for his beatification and eventual canonization as a saint, and as part of that process thousands of testimonials of healings and other miracles performed by him have been collected.

The letter you are about to read is Tardif's report of some of his activities as he traveled in Paraguay. Note that within Catholicism the charismatic movement is often known as "charismatic renewal" or simply "renewal."

As you read this source, you will see that once again the theme of faith healing comes to the foreground. Try to connect this with previous readings. In what ways have the ideas of faith healing evolved?

Next, connect this source more specifically with the previous two in this chapter. What common emphases are there? What differences? Consider in particular the relationship of the charismatic groups in each of these documents to its denominational connections. You will notice that in every instance there is opposition from above. How does Tardif's response differ from the others? What might have been the practical result of his response as opposed to the response of the Protestant groups in the other texts?

The Text⁺
December 1993

I am just returning from Paraguay. We are really living in a beautiful time: Saturday, November 27, there were about 17,000 people in the sports center in Asunción, Paraguay. When communion was being celebrated the Lord healed a man who had been blinded for 25 years. He had not been able to see a thing! It was a stunning moment when this man, who is 51 years old, came weeping after communion. He wanted to offer his testimony. He said that during communion he felt a great heat in his eyes, and he began to see a fog. Then the fog disappeared and he began seeing people. He offered his testimony immediately that evening.

The next day on television, people were talking about "the healing of the blind man" (just like the "blind man of Jericho,"⁹ isn't it?). This is a sign that Jesus lives today. The same Jesus who healed the "blind man of Jericho" has healed the "blind man of Asunción."

The Lord has blessed us greatly. But the people did not let us rest for even half a day. Fifteen days full of activities, traveling from one place to another!

In one diocese, the bishop there does not accept Renewal, and I did not go there. The leaders of Renewal knew that the bishop didn't accept it. Then they prepared a healing mass with an "afternoon of evangelization" at the border with Brazil, and they told us, "They cannot bother us there. We're going to celebrate in Brazil." But it turns out that the bishop learned about this the evening before, and he sent word to us that he would not allow Renewal in his diocese.

I didn't go, but the people did. There were more than 6,000 people. They came in buses from Brazil and from all the nearby cities in Paraguay. It was a shame! The story came out in the newspaper, and I found myself on the front page. Jokingly, I told the president of Paraguay, Juan Carlos Wasmosy, "I took your place," because every day usually the president is on the front page of the paper. But now, on that page it said, "Tardif is not given permission to celebrate a healing mass in the diocese of Concepción." I did not go. The truth is that I didn't mind much, but the people were greatly distressed.

Eventually there was a lot of talk about this over the radio, as well as in the newspapers and on television. That bishop has publicized the Charismatic Renewal as no one else has! Because there were many people who did not know the name of Charismatic Renewal, and now everybody wanted to know what it was!

Two days later I was to preach at the National Sanctuary of Our Lady of Caacupé, and there were 40,000 people there. On December 8, they were preparing to celebrate the feast day of Our Lady of Caacupé, who is the patron saint of Paraguay. I lectured on "the Virgin Mary as a model of charismatic life." I spoke of the spiritual gifts of the Virgin, who is a model of life in the spirit. The gifts of the Most Holy Mary are those of miracles, healing, and prophecy. And I said that the Most Holy Mary is the mother of all believers. She is the model for charismatic life, and her faith is not alienating. The newspaper reporters got hold of this and in great headlines they said, "Tardif says, 'The faith of the Virgin Mary is not alienating.'"

The bishop is already 76 years old. I think he lost the battle. I didn't go to the battlefield.

I simply obeyed the bishop. I would never preach in a diocese where the bishop does not invite me or at least does not accept Renewal. But I tell you that there are very few bishops in the world who reject Charismatic Renewal.

Those whom I have met in the 59 countries where I have preached up to now are so few that one could count them with the fingers of one hand. Since the pope encourages us to continue along the lines of Charismatic Renewal, in general, bishops encourage or at least accept this Renewal.

From all of this I arrive at the conclusion that obedience is first and foremost. If we obey, we will have no difficulties. After the cancellation of our meeting, a journalist came to me with a recorder in hand in order to try to tape some commentary of mine on what had taken place. He asked me, "What do you want to say to our people who listen to this radio station throughout the nation? What do you say about the rejection of Charismatic Renewal by the bishop of Concepción?" I answered, "NOTHING. I have nothing to say. If the bishop does not accept Renewal, I will not preach in his diocese. Period! I have nothing else to add. I will go preach in other dioceses, but we are constantly receiving requests for retreats from everywhere. And we will continue preaching in those dioceses of bishops who invite us or who at least are not opposed to our charismatic ministry." Such is the nature of obedience in the Church.

Source Four
Shangó

Introduction

This source will introduce you to some of the dominant elements in Afro-Caribbean religion by means of a narrative and a photograph. The first is a brief introduction to that religious tradition by Miguel Ramos, Ilarií Obá, a scholar who has also attained the high ranks of an *olorisha* ordained to Shangó and an *Obá Oriaté*, master of ceremonies for Lucumí ordination rites and other ceremonies. The second is a photo with an explanation, also provided by Ramos, of an altar or throne of Shangó—one of the principal *orishas* (divinities), and the most widely venerated by Afro-Caribbean devotees. These two will serve as an introduction to some of the elements of the religion commonly—and mistakenly, as Ramos explains—called "Santería." This religious tradition has shown great resilience and persistence, for after being long suppressed first by the Inquisition and then by social and cultural pressure, it reemerged with doubtless vigor in the latter half of the twentieth century.

As you read Ramos's account and examine the picture of a throne of Shangó, ask yourself: What does this say about the power of a religion to preserve and affirm a group's identity? Conversely, what does it say about how such an identity strengthens a religion? How could these beliefs and practices continue despite the watchful eye of the Inquisition? Consider Ramos's assertion that the presence of Catholicism itself, particularly as practiced by the masses, helped preserve the Yoruba religious tradition. What points of contact do you see between the two? Why would orisha priests insist that their followers be baptized? What does this tell you about their view of baptism? What does it tell you about the attitude of these priests toward Catholicism? On this point of baptism, you may wish to go back to the source in chapter 4, "Travels in Brazil," in which there are also references to the baptism of slaves. What would be the connection between that source and what Ramos says about baptismal practices in Cuba?

Ramos speaks of offerings of an okra and cornmeal porridge. Okra comes from Africa, and corn (maize) from America. How does this illustrate the influence of one culture on another? Can you find other similar connections?

How does the picture help you understand what Ramos says about his religious tradition? Note that he relates the sharing of fruit to Christian communion. How does this reflect the influence of one tradition on the other? How may this relate to what he says about baptism?

Part A*

A very large portion of the slaves brought from Africa across the Atlantic to the Caribbean were Yoruba [people from Nigeria and Benin]. Even in the midst of their physical captivity and institutionalized dehumanization, the Yoruba found ways to preserve much of their identity and religion. The culture they brought with them left its mark on the culture of Cuba and the other lands where they were enslaved—a mark that may be seen to this day. This was particularly so because the Yoruba, supposedly friendlier and more docile than other slaves, frequently served as house slaves, so that the involvement of Yoruba women in the rearing of their masters' children was an early contributor to the unique Cuban culture that was emerging—a culture that inherited important elements from both Spain and Africa. Today it is easy to find vestiges of Yoruba culture in the music, art, folklore, and cuisine not only of Cuba, but also of much of the Caribbean as well as of Brazil.

In the field of religion, the Yoruba found ways to insure the survival of much of their ancient traditions, although with a number of adaptations to the new environment. One of these adaptations was connecting the traits and attributes of some of the ancient minor African deities known as *orishas* with similar traits and attributes of Catholic saints. For instance, Shangó, the most widely recognized of the ancient *orishas* in the Western Hemisphere, whose domain included thunder, was connected with Saint Barbara, the patron saint of artillery and explosions. For this reason, outside observers have often dubbed this religion "santería"—which means the "cult of the saints"—when in fact this is only one of several elements in Afro-Caribbean religion. More exactly it should be seen as "Afro-Cuban Orisha tradition," or "Lucumí religion"—after the older name for the people today known as Yoruba.

For as long as Cuba was a colony of Spain, Catholicism held a religious monopoly on the island. When it came to African slaves, while the Church required that they be converted and baptized, the slaves themselves found points of contact between their own religious tradition and what the Church taught. Most particularly, it was easy to find such points of contact with the popular expressions of Catholicism that the slaves saw in the lives of their masters. In Yoruba religion, as in the Catholic faith, there was a single supreme God, Olodumare, the creator of heaven and earth. Olodumare also created the *orishas* as bridges or intermediaries between heaven and earth. Each of these *orishas* is related to one or more elements of nature and of human existence on earth. They are divine, for they not only represent Olodumare, but

207

also manifest his omnipresence and omnipotence. Devotees then often seek the aid and support of specific *orishas*, particularly in times of duress, decision, illness, or other such need.

All of this could easily be connected with what the Church taught and individual Catholics practiced, for in Catholicism too there was a supreme God, creator of heaven and earth, and in the popular Catholic piety that had developed during the Middle Ages, and was still dominant in Cuba, the saints were seen as intermediaries between petitioners and God—each saint having, like the *orishas*, particular attributes, concerns, and fields of responsibility.

Like the Catholic saints, the *orishas* are not distant powers. On the contrary, they are humanlike. For this reason, they can relate directly with their devotees. And, like the saints, they too have particular spheres of influence, places of habitation, ritual emblems and paraphernalia, distinctive colors, etc. For instance, Shangó, the powerful *orisha* of lightning and thunder, often receives his offerings at the foot of royal palms or ceibas—silk cotton trees, which popular Catholicism also holds to be sacred, on the basis that lightning does not strike them. While he is ready to come to the aid of his devotees, he rejects all deception or lies. More specifically, he is served with sacrifices of roosters, rams, and turtles, and he also likes bananas, *mamey* (a tropical fruit), and a porridge of okra and corn meal. His colors are red and white, which he wears on his clothing as well as on beads. In his dances he carries a two-bladed ax.

Scholars and other students and practitioners of Afro-Cuban religion differ widely on the degree to which the two religious traditions merged and also on the reasons for any such merger. Some tend to interpret what took place as a mixture or syncretism between the two religious traditions. Others believe that the Yorubas and those who embraced their religious traditions hid their beliefs and rites under a camouflage of Catholic popular piety, thus avoiding the harsh measures that would otherwise have been taken against them. Normally, Afro-Cuban devotees try to make a clear distinction between their religion and Catholicism, but it is clear that popular Catholicism and the *orisha* tradition have influenced one another. This may be seen in the interplay between the Afro-Cuban *orishas* and the Catholic saints, to the point that for nearly every *orisha* there is a corresponding saint. Certainly, this encounter has left its mark on both, and the Yoruba religion as practiced in Cuba shows that a number of its original African elements have been modified or diluted by Catholic influence. No matter how one interprets or evaluates the influence of these two religious traditions on each other, there is no doubt that there are profound similarities between the two. These similarities made it possible for

Yoruba religion both to survive and to be understood and adopted by people of European descent.

As a rule, followers of Yoruba religion distinguish between an *orisha* and its corresponding saint. Saint and *orisha* are not fused nor confused. Even so, some aspects of Yoruba theology have been modified or obscured by Catholic doctrine and piety, especially in the case of Catholics who have converted and embrace the tradition of the *orishas* without fully detaching themselves from Catholicism.

In times of slavery, *orisha* priests insisted that their followers be baptized as Catholics, and this is still the common practice in Cuba—although it is disappearing in the Cuban diaspora. Since a number of the traditional rituals were not possible within the context of slavery and under the eye of the Church, they were replaced by parallel Catholic rites and ceremonies with similar aims. Thus the traditional ceremonies connected with times of passage such as birth, marriage, and becoming an adult were displaced by those generally practiced in Catholicism.

Nevertheless, the vast majority of Yoruba customs and traditions still survive. They are transmitted from one generation to the next by means of oracles and *patakis*, which are myths (akin to biblical passages) told by diviners in contact with the *orishas*. These *patakis* are also influenced by the surrounding society and context, and therefore have often been adapted and reinterpreted. But still, a careful examination of the body of *patakis* shows that they reflect the richness and variety of Yoruba culture.

Again, one must emphasize that the *orishas* are not distant beings, alienated from the worshiper. They are not deities to which a devotee prays on a weekly basis. On the contrary, they are a palpable constant presence that is active in all the dimensions of daily life. When the devotee has reasons for joy or sorrow, the *orisha* rejoices or mourns. This creates a constant bond between the *orisha* and the devotee—a bond of mutuality, in which the devotee is committed to the *orisha*, and the *orisha* to the devotee.

While all believers may feel this bond with the *orishas*, some are called to serve them more directly, eventually undergoing the ordination rituals to become an *olorisha* (ordained priest). It is these few who, knowing that their lifetime is but a short period, or a grain of sand in the vast ocean of human experience, continue to pass on their knowledge and the traditions of the ancients to new generations. As an ancient ritual chant says, *alagba-lagba ofe n'soro*—the ancients have seen, and they have spoken.

Part B

Figure 9.1

Shangó is the *orisha* of thunder and lightning, and he takes special responsibility for assuring that divine justice is carried out on earth. In Cuban devotion, he is also identified with masculinity, joy, and the good life in general. His feminine counterpart is Oshún, often called "the Yoruba Venus."

In this throne, Shangó is dressed in red and white, depicting lightning and power. The leopard skin symbolizes his ability as a hunter—although Shangó most often hunts those who disobey the principles and rulings of the Supreme Being, executing justice on them. The two-edged ax is also a symbol of Shangó as lord both of thunder and of justice, which he is able to mete out with lightning speed.

The breasts on the central image symbolize the maternal loving and nurturing care of the orisha, much like a mother's love for her children.

The bowl atop the image's head is called the *batea*, or trough. It contains the implements related to the orisha. It, too, is covered with a cloth or fur in imitation of a leopard's markings.

The fruit at the foot of the altar are offerings that will be shared later among those attending the rite, in a common meal, a sort of communion.

Source Five
Reyita's Faith

Introduction

Source Five comes from the memoirs of an Afro-Cuban woman of the twentieth century. María de los Reyes Castillo Bueno (1902–1997) was commonly known by the feminine diminutive "Reyita," derived from part of her name—de los Reyes. Born in the same year in which Cuba attained independence, Reyita was well aware of the poverty and discrimination that the descendants of slaves still suffered in Cuba and therefore became an activist. In her forties she joined the Partido Socialista Popular, which later became the Communist Party. Her daughter, Daisy Rubiera Castillo, collected and published Reyita's oral memoirs in 1997.

Reyita's memoirs speak of her life in every dimension. She tells us, for instance, that she decided to marry a white man, not because she thought less of her own race, but rather because she did not want to see her children suffer the same discrimination and lack of opportunity she and her friends suffered. She speaks quite openly of her frustrations, her sexuality, and her hopes. And she speaks of how conditions changed after the Cuban Revolution.

However, what interests us here is her religious beliefs and practices and the manner in which they combine Catholicism with other beliefs. In her case, we see a merging of popular Catholic religiosity with elements of African origin, particularly with spiritism. The latter, which some European writers in the nineteenth century had dressed up as a science, held to reincarnation and emphasized communication with the spirits of the dead through particularly gifted persons called *mediums*.

The "Rubiera" mentioned at the beginning is Reyita's husband. The St. Lazarus to whom she makes a promise is the poor man by that name in Jesus' parable in the Gospel of Luke.[††] In that parable, Lazarus was a man so poor and so afflicted that dogs licked his sores. He is usually depicted in rags and surrounded by dogs. It should be no surprise, therefore, that popular piety has turned him into the patron of the poor and the ill. His counterpart in Afro-Caribbean religion is Babaluaye, the orisha whose domain is disease and epidemics. The "Virgencita" or Virgen de la Caridad de El Cobre (Virgin of the Charity of El Cobre) is an apparition of the Virgin Mary that has become the patron saint of Cuba.

The two sorts of "spiritism" that Reyita mentions are quite different. The *espiritismo de cordón* (chain spiritism), which she did not follow, is closer to the European form of spiritism, in which believers hold hands in a circle, much as in a traditional séance. *Espiritismo cruza'o* (literally "crossed spiritism") has strong African influences. Here the emphasis is not so much on communicating with the dead as it is on securing their rest, so that they will bless and not disturb one's earthly life.

As you read Reyita's words, note the nature of her dealings with St. Lazarus by making him a promise and her faithfulness in keeping her side of the bargain. How does this relate to the religiosity of the retablos in chapter 8? How does it relate to the orisha tradition discussed in the previous source? Note also that neither her husband nor her children agreed with her actions on behalf of St. Lazarus. But her husband's reasons for this were different from her children's. Consider her children's opposition. What did this have to do with their being raised Catholic?

Look also at the roles of St. Lazarus and the Virgin in the entire selection. Did Reyita see them as rivals or as collaborators? What was her role in the events of December 16? What would people mean by saying that Reyita had "good vision"?

Compare Reyita's story with what Ramos says about his religious tradition. What points of contact do you see? What differences? What would Reyita find in her religion that she did not find in Catholicism? Why would she raise her children as Catholics and not in her own belief? What connections do you see (or suspect) between religion and social mobility? Between religion and race? Between race and social mobility?

The Text[‡‡]

The Promise to Saint Lazarus

In 1952 Rubiera had a duodenal ulcer which burst, despite the treatment he'd received. When I saw him with that huge haemorrhage, I went crazy. And before taking him to the hospital, I knelt down and begged for his life and his health, but not to my *Virgencita*, but rather to Saint Lazarus, a saint who frightens me with his sores and flies. I promised him if he saved my old man I'd put him in the front hall of my house facing the street sharing the position with the Virgin of Charity of El Cobre. An awesome pledge, if you take into consideration that he wasn't the saint of my devotion! That's why I had faith he would help me. Your dad was saved and I fulfilled my promise when I moved to Bayamo a little while after the old man's illness.

I set up a very large altar, almost reaching the ceiling; we made a fine cape for the saint and I always had lots of flowers and candles for him. You kids didn't like it—you hadn't been raised with these beliefs, but with the holy fear of God, you practised Catholicism, were baptized, took communion, and were married in the church—but you respected my decision. Also for this reason I made sure it was pretty, as if it were a decoration. Then came his saint's day. The 16th of December, the eve of the celebrations, besides flowers and candles, we gave him fruits, candies, rum, tobacco, a platter with basil leaves and an empty glass into which I threw a few coins.

The ceremony held on the eve of the saint's day fiesta is called the wake; I held one for Saint Lazarus. At midnight on that day not one more soul would fit in my house. Your dad was furious, he didn't believe in anything, my promise didn't matter to him; and since he couldn't get me to get all those people out of the house, he went to sleep at the transport company, but not before hurling a string of foolish remarks at me.

At exactly midnight I asked my *Virgencita* for strength and clarity to attend to all those people and do what needed to be done in the circumstances, to which I was neither accustomed nor, therefore, prepared. We began with the orations I thought we should say and then sang a few prayers I knew. Then I began to *despojar* [to cleanse, clear] everybody, and I started to feel some radiations that ran all through my body, something like shivers. I told each person what came into my head and recommended some cure. I finished very late and completely exhausted but I went to bed satisfied at having fulfilled my obligation contracted to the saint when I'd made the promise.

In the morning your sister Moña, joking around with me, said:

—Hey, mama! If you keep fulfilling that promise you're going to get rich.

She said that because the money vessel had about a hundred pesos in it from what people had given to do their duty by the saint. That didn't matter to me, I couldn't charge for charity, but why deny it was very helpful. After that day news began to spread: 'What good vision that María has, the fat black woman with white hair'; I became the spiritualist of the day. Many people knocked on my door, I never said no to anybody. I still do it today

213

although I'm old, with almost a hundred years behind me.

They call the spiritualism I practise *espiritismo cruza'o*. People from Bayamo prefer *espiritismo de cordón*; these believers, when they meet, join hands in a ring and sing and pray, while circling around the person they're going to consult or from whom they're going to remove a spirit. In this way they create a magnetic current which makes the faithful fall into trances. There were many of those places in Bayamo.

Source Six
An Immigrant's Tale

Introduction

This is a transcript of an interview with Presbyterian pastor Trinidad Salazar, conducted in 1987 by historian Jane Atkins-Vásquez in preparation for a volume celebrating the hundredth anniversary of Presbyterian work among Hispanics in California. Although he does not say this in his interview, Salazar was a respected leader among Hispanic Presbyterians. For more than fifty years he wrote and edited influential church publications in Spanish. He served as the pastor of churches in Los Angeles, Redlands, San Francisco, Phoenix, and Gardena. His prestige and influence were such that he was a commissioner to the General Assembly—the highest governing body of the Presbyterian Church—not once, but five times. He died shortly after this interview, before the book—which is dedicated to his memory—was published.

Remember this as you read this material. Note his humble origins, his early struggles, and his eventual success and influence. You may have difficulty finding his hometown, Cusihuilatchi—also called Cusihuiriachi—on a map. When Salazar was born, it was a small silver mining town of less than two thousand inhabitants. Now the silver mines are closed, and the population has fallen to fewer than one hundred. The "Tayamaras" to whom he refers, his mother's people, are probably the Tarahumara, who live mostly in the state of Chihuahua, and who number some sixty to seventy thousand. Chihuahua is a large state in central northern Mexico, bordering Texas. Its largest city is Ciudad Juárez, across the Rio Grande from El Paso.

Consider first of all what he says about the Mexican Revolution and how it affected his family. The year he crossed into the United States, 1924, was also the beginning of the tense relations between church and state that would soon lead to the rebellion of the Cristeros. As a reminder of the tense conditions of the time, look back at the confrontation between the president of Mexico and the leaders of the church in chapter 5, "A Last-Ditch Effort." Try to imagine living in a family divided by civil war, as his was. What would you say was Salazar's view of the Mexican Revolution? What would be the connection between this and his being fired when he worked in a theater in El Paso? Why would he be considered a Bolshevik, even though he did not know the meaning of the word? Try tracing his nonconventional streak through his entire story.

Note that his first crossing into the United States was temporary. But eventually he returned, this time to stay—although he says that only by implication. What would have prompted his wife's family—and apparently he with them—to move to El Paso, Texas?

Pay special attention to what he says about his religion. What was the role of his wife's family in his conversion to Protestantism and in his eventually joining the Presbyterian Church? Why would Salazar's going to the cantina bother the pastor? Note his reference to his first learning "something about Christianity" and then to having been raised as "a very conservative Roman Catholic." What does this tell you about his view of Roman Catholicism? How can this be reconciled with his father's believing "in God, but not in the priests, nor the church"?

What is the connection between Salazar's conversion to Protestantism and active participation in the Presbyterian Church and his educational achievements? What does this tell you about the church as an agent for social and economic improvement among immigrants to the United States? Note the role of Pastor Warnhuis in Salazar's life and career development. What patterns of authority within the Presbyterian Church of the time does this reveal? Would Salazar have been able to achieve what he did had he not submitted to Warnhuis's authority? Note also that Salazar was ordained before he had the requisite education and that this was done because the growth of El Siloé Church required it. What does this tell you about the willingness of the Presbyterian Church to bend the rules before a perceived need? How might this have helped the early growth of Presbyterianism among Hispanics in the Southwest?

The Text[§§]

I was born in Cusihuilatchi, in the Sierra Madre, the land of the Tayamaras, in the state of Chihuahua. My mother had some Tayamara background, and I claim it. My father was a school teacher.

When the revolution came the schools were closed and my education was delayed for a while. For a few years I lived in Chihuahua, with my oldest sister who had been widowed because her husband was a soldier with the government. On the other side my mother's brother, Uncle Gabino, was with

Pancho Villa. *El Bandillo Cano* [the White-Haired Bandit], we called him; he was a colonel. His regiment was called the *Cazadores De La Sierra* [Hunters of the Sierra]. That is how I got to know Pancho Villa, because he came to the house.

I went to the United States with my sister in 1924. I crossed illegally, a wet-back, at El Paso. I had worked as an electrician at a movie house in Chihuahua, and then as a manager for two theaters in Hidalgo del Parral. I went to work at a theater in El Paso, where they threw me out as a Communist. I didn't know what a Bolshevik was; the only thing I knew was that I was a rebel.

I came back, met Guadalupe Payán and we got married in 1926. My wife was a Presbyterian. Someone had invited her family to attend special services in Ciudad Juárez and all of them were converted. When they went to El Paso they joined the Methodist church, except my wife. She began to attend the little Presbyterian church where Abrán Fernández was the minister. She and Fernández pestered me to go. I would go from work to the cantina, just to bother Fernández.

I finally began to attend church regularly That is where I first learned something about Christianity. I had been a very conservative Roman Catholic, which is characteristic of the Mexican culture. My father took us to mass because he believed in God, but not in the priests, nor the church. I felt I knew little about religion. Brother Fernández gave me an enormous Bible and that's how I began my Christian studies, with the Bible. I was there with Guadalupe Armendáriz, who was superintendent of the Sunday school.

With the depression we moved to California in 1930 where we attended El Divino Salvador Presbyterian church in Los Angeles. Huberto Falcón was the pastor. In 1932 Paul Warnshuis was looking for someone to help at El Siloé. He went to El Divino Salvador and asked the session if some of the elders** wanted to help while a pastor was sought. I had been elected an elder in El Paso, but I still didn't feel I knew anything. I hadn't even taught Sunday school. Six men volunteered. Warnshuis took their names to El Siloé, and from those six the members of El Siloé chose the one they didn't know—me.

El Siloé was a little chapel, which had been constructed at the same time the church at La Verne was built. While I had the responsibility of the church—preaching, teaching and all that—I went to high school to learn English. I was 31 years of age. Warnshuis helped me go to Redlands, where I worked at the little church and went to college at San Bernardino and then to the university. I went there alone; they gave me $30 a month salary. My wife worked too, and she stayed in Los Angeles. I earned my bachelor's degree in sociology, with a minor in psychology. Warnshuis helped me, because he pushed me.

The church at Redlands was receiving new members, and we had to ask the pastor of the American church, Chester Green, to come over all the time. He was the reason I was ordained, because he told Riverside Presbytery that he couldn't get his work done from baptizing, marrying, assisting with communion, receiving new members at our church. So I was ordained before completing my university work.

In 1941 Warnshuis sent me to the church at San Francisco so I could attend San Francisco Theological Seminary.

Then we went to Phoenix. I didn't want to go to Arizona, but Warnshuis sent me to Phoenix, where Abrán Fernández had been. We were there seventeen years. While I was there I decided that if I were going to continue in the ministry I wanted to have more education. At Tempe I earned a master's degree in education while I was a pastor. So when they tell me they can't do something, I say it is stewardship of their time.

When I returned to California from Phoenix in 1969 a group of Hispanic ministers were organizing La Raza Churchmen here. We elected Arturo Archuleta as president. The goal was to work together. All through life we had been fighting among ourselves, and we wanted to be together. Tony Hernández, Livingston Falcón, Peter Sámano, Huberto Falcón were some of those who participated. Lay people were also there.

All my life I have been involved in controversy. If someone says something to me, I immediately see the opposite, or try to see the negative results. This is my spirit. I have to restrain myself. We should see the Biblical teaching, not to conform but to be transformed, which is the basis of Christianity.

Source Seven
The Catholic Response

Introduction

In order to understand the significance of this "National Pastoral Plan for Hispanic Ministry," one must take into account the series of *encuentros* (meetings) that led to it. These encuentros gathered Catholic leaders, lay and ordained, to discuss the mission of the Church among Hispanics. But the gatherings themselves, and the discussions that took place, helped raise the consciousness of Hispanic Catholics as to their need to have a greater

and more coordinated voice in the life of the Church. While those encuentros emphasized the importance of evangelization, they also stressed the
connection of evangelization with social justice and with "integral education." On the subject of evangelization, the third encuentro had declared
that "the Church exists in order to evangelize" and that "an evangelization
incarnated in a given culture is essential for all peoples." On social justice, all
three encuentros affirmed that it was part of evangelization and that it was
a particularly important theme for Hispanics "because of their own social
condition." Finally, integral education was defined by the third encuentro as
"a global formation in the economic, political, social, cultural, family, and
church aspects of life, which leads to maturity of faith and a sense of responsibility for history."++

The sections of the "National Pastoral Plan for Hispanic Ministry" included
here have been selected as examples of its general direction and theological perspective. It is important to note, however, that these rather general words served
as the foundation for a very comprehensive plan of action involving every level
of the church, from the national to the diocese and to the parish, as well as a
vast number of national and regional organizations, religious orders, educational
institutions, and lay organizations. The plan also established the National Advisory Committee to work in collaboration with the Secretariat for Hispanic Affairs
of the United States Conference of Catholic Bishops (USCCB), which was given
general oversight and responsibility for the implementation of the plan.

The plan refers to *novenas, pastorelas, posadas, nacimientos,* and *via crucis.*
These are various acts of devotion. A novena is a sequence of nine days of
prayer. Pastorelas are Christmas plays. Posadas are reenactments of the quest
of Mary and Joseph to find a place to stay in Bethlehem. A nacimiento is a
nativity scene. The via crucis is the stations of the cross, in which one moves
from one scene of the passion of Jesus to another.

As you read this document, keep in mind what you have read earlier.
Note, for instance, the reference to the Virgen de Guadalupe. What does this
tell you about the roots of Hispanic Catholicism as it exists in the United
States? How did the bishops look on the pre-Hispanic cultures of Latin
America and on their religiosity? What echoes do you see here of the process
of conquest and conversion five centuries earlier? Remember what Reyita said
about her religion, her devotion to St. Lazarus, and the altar at her home.
Would they see Reyita's religiosity as a starting point on which to build or
rather as an obstacle to their mission?

Then look back at the Protestant documents you read in chapters 6 and 7.
How would Speer ("Race and Mission") and Mackay ("Justifying a Presence")

respond to this document?

What reasons did the bishops give for their decision at this particular time to endorse this plan? Note what the document says about integration and assimilation. What consequences might each of these have in the actual life of the church? What problems did the bishops see in the manner in which the Church had responded to the Latino presence in the United States? What does the document tell you about the bishops' concern over Hispanics leaving the Catholic Church?

If you had to choose three words to characterize the essential mood of this document, what words would you use?

The Text[5]

Nov. 18, 1987

Preface

This pastoral plan is addressed to the entire Church in the United States. It focuses on the pastoral needs of the Hispanic Catholic, but it challenges all Catholics as members of the Body of Christ.[1] . . .

We, the Bishops of the United States, adopt the objectives of this plan and endorse the specific means of reaching them, as provided herein. We encourage dioceses and parishes to incorporate this plan with due regard for local adaptation. We do so with a sense of urgency, and in response to the enormous challenge associated with the ever-growing presence of the Hispanic people in the United States. Not only do we accept this presence in our midst as our pastoral responsibility, conscious of the mission entrusted to us by Christ,[2] we do so with joy and gratitude. For, as we stated in the pastoral letter of 1983, "at this moment of grace, we recognize the Hispanic community among us as a blessing from God."[3]

We present this plan in a spirit of faith—faith in God, that he will provide the strength and the resources to carry out his divine plan on earth; faith in all the people of God, that all will collaborate in the awesome task before us; faith in Hispanic Catholics, that they will join hands with the rest of the church to build up the entire Body of Christ. We dedicate this plan to the honor and glory of God and, in his Marian year, invoke the intercession of the Blessed Virgin Mary under the title of Our Lady of Guadalupe. . . .

Introduction

This plan is a pastoral response to the reality and needs of the Hispanic people in their efforts to achieve integration and participation in the life of our Church and in the building of the Kingdom of God.

Integration is not to be confused with assimilation. Through the policy of assimilation, new immigrants are forced to give up their language, culture, values, traditions and adopt a form of life and worship foreign to them in order to be accepted as parish members. This attitude alienates new Catholic immigrants from the church and makes them vulnerable to sects and other denominations.

By integration we mean that our Hispanic people are to be welcomed to our church institutions at all levels. They are to be served in their language when possible, and their cultural values and religious traditions are to be respected. Beyond that, we must work toward mutual enrichment through interaction among all our cultures. Our physical facilities are to be made accessible to the Hispanic community. Hispanic participation in the institutions, programs and activities of the church is to be constantly encouraged and appreciated. This plan attempts to organize and direct how best to accomplish this integration. . . .

History

The United States of America is not all America. We speak of the Americas to describe a hemisphere of many cultures and three dominant languages— two from the Iberian peninsula and one from a North Atlantic island. Since the Church is the guardian of the mission of Jesus Christ, it must forever accommodate the changing populations and shifting cultures of mankind. To the extent the Church is impregnated with cultural norms, to that extent it divides and separates; to the extent it permeates cultural norms with the primacy of love, it unites the many into the Body of Christ without dissolving differences or destroying identity.

Culture

The historical reality of the Southwest, the proximity of countries of origin and continuing immigration all contribute to the maintenance of Hispanic culture and language within the United States. This cultural presence expresses itself in a variety of ways: from the immigrant who experiences "culture shock," to the Hispanic whose roots in the United States go back several generations and who struggles with questions of identity while often being made to feel an alien in his own country.

Despite these differences, certain cultural similarities identify Hispanics as a people. Culture primarily expresses how people live and perceive the world, one another and God. Culture is the set of values by which a people judge, accept and live what is considered important within the community.

Some values that make up the Hispanic culture are "a profound respect for the dignity of each *person* . . . deep and reverential love for *family life* . . . a marvelous sense of *community* . . . a loving appreciation of God's gift of *life* . . . and an authentic and consistent *devotion* to Mary."[4]

Culture for Hispanic Catholics has become a way of living out and transmitting their faith. Many local practices of popular religiosity have become widely accepted cultural expressions. Yet the Hispanic culture, like any other, must continue to be evangelized.[5]

Social Reality

The median age among Hispanic people is 25. This plus the continuous flow of immigrants ensures a constant increase in population.

Lack of education and professional training contribute to high unemployment. Neither public nor private education has responded to the urgent needs of this young population. Only 8 percent of Hispanics graduate at the college level.[6]

Families face a variety of problems. Twenty-five percent of the families live below the poverty level and 28 percent are single-parent families.[7]

Frequent mobility, poor education, a limited economic life and racial prejudice are some of the factors that result in low participation in political activities.

As a whole, Hispanics are a religious people. Eighty-three percent consider religion important. There is an interest in knowing more about the Bible and a strong presence of popular religious practices.[8]

Despite this, 88 percent are not active in their parishes. On the other hand, the Jehovah's Witnesses, Pentecostal groups and other sects are increasing within the Hispanic community. According to recent studies, the poor, men and second generation Hispanics are those who least participate in the life of the church.[9]

Assessment

1. The Catholic heritage and cultural identity of Hispanics are threatened by the prevailing secular values of the American society. They have marginal participation in the Church and in society, they suffer the consequences of poverty and marginalization.

2. This same people, due to its great sense of religion, family and community, is a prophetic presence in the face of the materialism and individualism of society. Since the majority of Hispanics are Catholic, their presence can be a source of renewal within the Catholic Church in North America. Because of its youth and growth, this community will continue to be a significant

presence in the future.

3. The current pastoral process offers some exciting possibilities on both social and religious levels: more active participation in the Church, a critique of society from the perspective of the poor and a commitment to social justice.

4. As the year 1992 approaches, celebrating the 500th anniversary of the evangelization of the Americas, it is more important than ever that Hispanics in the United States rediscover their identity as well as their Catholicity, be re-evangelized by the word of God and forge a much-needed unity among all Hispanics who have come from the entire spectrum of the Spanish-speaking world. . . .

Evangelization: From a Place to a Home

[The] small ecclesial communities promote experiences of faith and conversion as well as concern for each person and an evangelization process of prayer, reflection, action and celebration.

The objective of the programs which follow is to continue, support and extend the evangelization process to all Hispanic people. In this way we will have a viable response by the Catholic community to the proselytism of fundamentalist groups and the attraction they exercise on our people. In addition, we will be more sensitive to our responsibility to reach out in a welcoming way to newcomers and to the inactive and unchurched. . . .

Missionary Option: From Pews to Shoes

. . . *1. Background.* Throughout the process of the III Encuentro, the Hispanic people made a preferential missionary option for the poor and marginalized, the family, women and youth. These priority groups are not only the recipients but also the subjects of the Hispanic pastoral ministry.

The *poor* and *marginalized* have limited participation in the political, social, economic and religious process. This is due to underdevelopment and isolation from both Church and societal structures through which decisions are made and services offered. . . .

2. Specific objective. To promote faith and effective participation in church and societal structures on the part of these priority groups (the poor, women, families, youth) so that they may be agents of their own destiny (self-determination) and capable of progressing and becoming organized. . . .

Spirituality and Mistica

The spirituality of the Hispanic people, a living reality throughout its journey, finds expression in numerous ways. At times it takes the form of prayer, novenas, songs and sacred gestures. It is found in personal relationships and hospitality. At still other times, if surfaces as endurance, patience, strength and hope in the midst of suffering and difficulties. Their spirituality can also inspire a struggle for freedom, justice, and peace. Frequently it is expressed as commitment and forgiveness as well as celebration, dance, sacred images, and symbols. Small altars in the home, statues, and candles are sacramentals of God's presence. The *pastorelas, posadas, nacimientos, via crucis,* pilgrimages, processions, the blessings offered by mothers, fathers, and grandparents are all expressions of this faith and profound spirituality.

At various times through the centuries these devotions have gone astray or have been impoverished due to the lack of a clear and enriching catechesis. This pastoral plan with its evangelizing, community-building and formative emphasis can be a source of evangelization for these popular devotions and an encouragement for enriching liturgical celebrations with cultural expressions of faith. It seeks to free the Spirit who is alive in the gatherings of our people. . . .

Source Eight
A Protestant Response

Introduction

The document below is a series of excerpts from the "National Plan for Hispanic Ministry" of The United Methodist Church recommended by the Committee to Develop a National Plan for Hispanic Ministry and approved in 1992 by the General Conference. As in the case of its Catholic counterpart, the Methodist plan involved every board and agency of the church, as well as every level in its system of governance. The selection below, however, stresses the fundamental vision behind the plan, leaving out its concrete recommendations and assignment of various responsibilities.

As you read this document, compare it with the Catholic plan. In what ways are they alike? How do they differ? What themes or emphases in the Catholic plan do you not find here? What themes or emphases are here that are not in the Catholic plan?

What assets does this document claim the Methodist Church has in its efforts to widen its Hispanic ministry? What liabilities? How do these compare with the Catholic document?

If you had to choose three words to describe the essential mood of this document, what words would you use? Would they be the same you would choose for the Catholic plan? If not, why not?

The Text**

Vision and Opportunity

A new reality is being born in our generation, as the Lord of history brings together peoples of various cultures and traditions. It is an exciting time; it is a time laden with opportunity.

It is within this larger context that The United Methodist Church must look at its Hispanic ministries. Such ministries are not just an attempt to serve Hispanics; they are also and above all a call to faithfulness on the part of the entire church, so that we may all join God's action in the creation and development of the new reality that is being born. If we are to "reform the continent and spread Scriptural holiness," we must first of all respond faithfully to what God is doing in the land. We must eradicate racism and cultural chauvinism from our perspectives, and rejoice in the future God is opening to us. This is the main challenge which the growing Hispanic presence poses to The United Methodist Church.

Ours is a vision of a church which, as in the first Pentecost, all can hear of the mighty works of God in their own tongue (Acts 2:8)—which is not merely a matter of language, but also of cultural identity, family traditions, etc. At Pentecost, the Holy Spirit did not destroy or ignore the cultural identity of those present, but rather made the Gospel available to them in whatever language they spoke. This led the early church to new life and new growth. Likewise, in the church today, we must find ways to affirm the various cultural identities of those among whom we witness. And they in turn must be encouraged to speak of the mighty works of God "in their own tongue." As in that first Pentecost, some will not understand; some may even accuse the church of being "filled with new wine" (Acts 2:13). In such a case, our task, like Peter's, will be to rise up and proclaim that what the world is witnessing is none other than the action of God (Acts 2:16 "this is what was spoken through the prophet. . .").

At the same time, ours is a vision of a church in which such diversity, rather than dividing, unites, joining all in a common task, in a variety of circumstances, toward a common goal (I Cor. 12:12-13).

Ours is a vision of a dynamic and growing church, joyously sharing and living the Good News of Jesus Christ in a multiplicity of places, urban and rural, in congregations large and small, and in a variety of cultural settings. In this church, groups which traditionally have been disenfranchised will be full partners in Christ's ministry, and the gifts of every Hispanic—male and female, young and old, factory worker and professional, immigrant and native—will be put to use for the upbuilding of the entire body (I Thes. 5:11).

In this vision, the church as people of God, as *laos*, is primarily a people in pilgrimage. Those from among this *laos* who are ordained to specific ministries are so ordained to enable the entire people for their various ministries, rather than to perform all the ministries of the church, or to take away the ministry of the laity.

In this vision, United Methodist congregations—both Hispanic congregations and others—will be profoundly and actively committed to an understanding of mission grounded on the connection between church growth and service to the community, between witness by word and witness by action. Or between evangelism and advocacy. In evangelizing, we invite others to follow a God whose love for the world is manifested in self-giving, and who promises us both life eternal and a reign of love, peace and justice. In standing for justice for ourselves as well as for others, we witness to the same God. We invite others to join us both in accepting life eternal through Jesus Christ, and in living as those who, through the same Jesus Christ, expect and seek to pre-enact the coming Reign of God.

Within this vision, an increased Hispanic presence and active participation would be an asset for The United Methodist Church, not only in terms of added numbers, but also in terms of the gifts Hispanics bring to our denomination—gifts born out of a long history of struggle and suffering, through which faith has been proven and revitalized. The vitality of Hispanic faith and worship, the seriousness with which Hispanics study Scripture and seek in it guidance for the present, the joy with which Hispanics experience and share their faith, the sharing which takes place within Hispanic congregations, and the eagerness with which many Hispanics seek to translate all of this into works of mercy and of justice, would be a significant contribution to the life of the entire church.

This exciting time is also a frightening time. Resistance to change provokes and stirs the forces of racism that have always plagued our society. The emergent multi-cultural society offers the opportunity for greater understanding and a brighter future. Yet, we also risk missing that opportunity if our planning, outreach and commitment are such that we fail to reach this population. In that case, we shall have written off a very large percentage of the people to whom we are called to minister and to witness (a percentage that by the year 2080 may well be as high as 28% of the total population). Our mainline church must either respond to the needs of this population, or

225

allow itself to be marginalized.

On the other hand, if the people called United Methodist, hearts aglow with a vision of the future to which God is calling us, are willing to take the necessary steps to reach this Hispanic population, the result could be an astounding new vitality and growth for the entire denomination.

Such a vision of the church and its ministry among Hispanics is the driving force behind this Committee's report and recommendations. It is not a matter of the church doing something on behalf of Hispanics, but rather of all the church, including all ethnic groups within it, responding to the challenge before us. We are convinced that God is facing us with a major challenge in which our commitment and our discipleship are being tested. Therefore, as we prayerfully urge General Conference to adopt the recommendations in this report, we even more invite the entire United Methodist church to share the vision we have glimpsed. . . .

[The] long experience also reveals to us some of the assets which The United Methodist Church has, as well as some of the difficulties it will have to face, as it engages in more intentional Hispanic ministry.

First of all, given the circumstances in which most Hispanics live, and the racism they suffer, Hispanics increasingly look askance on any supposedly Christian piety which is divorced from works of mercy and justice. United Methodism could be particularly attractive to Hispanics in that it has traditionally insisted on the need for both "works of piety" and "works of mercy." At its best, the Methodist tradition provides both of these elements in a holistic understanding of the Gospel of Jesus Christ.

Secondly, the variety of forms and expressions of worship for which United Methodism allows has traditionally proven attractive to Hispanics. Within that variety, room is available for those who wish to preserve much of their cultural and religious heritage. There is room also available for new forms of worship which incorporate and affirm Hispanic culture and traditions.

Thirdly, United Methodism proclaims itself to be ethnically and culturally pluralistic, and as such affirms a place for Hispanics and other minorities, without their having to abandon their identity. While much is yet to be done, the explicit stance of United Methodism is certainly an asset among Hispanics. . . .

Fourthly, United Methodism has nurtured and developed leadership for the Hispanic community, both in the church and beyond, well exceeding the proportion of Hispanics who are United Methodists. This has gained respect and even admiration in various Hispanic circles for The United Methodist Church.

Finally, Hispanic United Methodists represent an important asset for the global mission of the church. In the international arena, Hispanics in the United States have long had close bonds across borders and seas. At the outset, Mexican/American Methodism was organically one with Methodist work south of the border. The same was true of Cuba and Methodism in South Florida. United Methodism in the Northeast and Midwest owes much to its connection with Puerto Rico. At present, there is growing contact between MARCHA, the national Hispanic caucus and CIEMAL, the council of Methodist churches in Latin America. Such relationships are important to Hispanics, both in the church and beyond, and are a valuable resource for the global awareness and missionary outreach of the entire United Methodist Church.

On the other hand, a number of obstacles remain if we are to be faithful and effective in Hispanic ministry, and these go far beyond the obvious barriers of language and culture.

These obstacles are many, but foremost is a long history of wavering and lack of a concerted direction in Hispanic ministries. Policies fostering Hispanic identity and self-determination have often been interrupted by other policies fostering assimilation and dismantling programs and structures which encourage and express self-determination. As these cycles have succeeded each other, often without due consultation with Hispanics themselves, Hispanics have felt ignored and disenfranchised. This is one reason why we need a comprehensive National Plan for Hispanic Ministry which, while set in motion in the coming quadrennium, will hopefully engage the commitment of an entire generation of United Methodists.

Secondly for lack of a national plan, of a vision behind it, and of the resources necessary to implement it, Hispanic ministry is often undertaken in a haphazard way, with little knowledge of the issues involved or of past experiences which could prove instructive.

Thirdly, for a number of reasons we have not developed, or have even dismantled, the policies and structures necessary for ministry among the poor, supported and performed by the poor themselves. Bluntly stated, the manner in which the typical United Methodist congregation is conceived, structured and supported is such that in many poor Hispanic communities such congregations are not feasible. We must develop structures and resources adequate for a church of the poor, so Hispanic ministries will neither bypass the vast majority of the Hispanic population, nor be so dependent on outside resources as to foster dependency and a low self-image.

Finally, and partially as a result of the foregoing, the recruitment and training of Hispanic leadership, both lay and ordained, has lagged behind the needs for such leaders. In particular, there is at present a serious shortage of ordained ministers, and this shortage is expected to grow worse as the demographic shifts discussed above impact the church. . . .

In our vision, "congregational development" and "community ministries," while representing two foci of the Christian mission, are inseparable. The congregational development envisioned here seeks to create and to nurture congregations which from the very beginning see community ministry as a fundamental part of their mission. Likewise, our vision of community ministry does not withhold from the community the unparalleled blessing of gathering for worship and for the study of Scripture, and thus developing into a congregation.

Given the variety of settings and circumstances in which Hispanics live, our national plan must envision a variety of congregational models serving Hispanics, including Hispanic Congregations with most or all services in Spanish, bilingual and bi-cultural congregations, English-speaking Hispanic congregations, and English-speaking congregations in which some Hispanics will worship. Our National Plan must also envision existing congregations, as well as the development of new ones. In the case of existing congregations, the Plan will seek their revitalization—by which is meant their becoming active centers, not only for worship and community life, but also [for] mission. All of these existing models should be affirmed, strengthened and given new vitality. . . .

However, none of these patterns, or all of them together, will suffice to bring to fruition the vision of a United Methodist Church with hundreds of Hispanic congregations scattered throughout the nation, feeling the pulse of responding to the needs of the Hispanic population. That vision is closely connected with the vision of Hispanic United Methodism as a pilgrim people—a *laos*—on the move. In that *laos* those empowered for Christian ministry by virtue of their baptisms (the laity) and those commissioned for specific ministry by virtue of a specific ordination (the clergy) form a partnership for the service of all, both within and outside the church. In this *laos*, all are partners working in congregational development and community ministries.

Therefore, while affirming the value of the models described above, our national plan should focus primarily on a model of lay and clergy partnership patterned after the traditional Methodist class system and its circuit riders. This ministry will be primarily the work of a corps of lay missioners for Hispanic Ministry, . . . in partnership with the ordained ministry of the church, and normally working as missional teams. They will start new faith communities in a variety of settings, will revitalize existing congregations, and will work in the development and support of community ministries. It will be the task of pastors, congregations, annual conferences, and general agencies to present the laity with the possibility that they may be called to this task, to identify those who are indeed called, and to see that they are properly trained and equipped for their task.

From the very outset, it will be expected that each of these faith communities will gather for the worship of God and the study of Scripture, for prayer, and to seek God's will for them in their setting. They will promote full congregational development by sharing their faith, inviting others to follow the Lord, and by seeking ways to be involved in whatever forms of ministry and advocacy for justice the Lord requires in their communities. They will understand themselves as centers for evangelism, mission action, and mission training, both at the local level and globally. From the very outset, these faith communities will understand that stewardship is crucial to Christian discipleship, and will be encouraged to contribute financially to their own support as well as to the total mission of the church.

Source Nine
Graffiti Theology

Introduction

This is a photograph of a wall near the main campus of the University of Puerto Rico, in San Juan, taken late in the twentieth century.

The words in these two graffiti are easy to understand, but their meaning is subject to a variety of interpretations. The original one said, "Christ is not religion." Then someone attempted to cover or delete the word "not," so that the graffito would now read, "Christ is religion."

Obviously, it is impossible to know exactly what each of the two writers might have meant. But, as a fun exercise and as a means for reflection and discussion on what you have learned, imagine that both were militant Christians. What would the first one mean? What would he or she have understood by "religion"? On the basis of all you have read in this book, what features of "religion" would this person try to dissociate from Christ? Then think about the second writer, imagining once again that she or he was a convinced Christian. How would such a person interpret the first graffito? What would seem offensive about it? Why seek to wipe out the "not"?

Now imagine a conversation between these two people. What would each of them find objectionable in the other's position? Where would they agree, and where would they disagree?

Conversely, imagine that the first writer was attacking Christianity. What would the graffito then mean? Is it possible that the second writer harbored anti-Christian sentiments? In that case, what would be the purpose of deleting the "not"?

What connections can you see between the issues raised in your reflection on these graffiti and any of the various opinions you have encountered in the rest of this book? Which of the sources that you have read would come closer to the first writer, and which to the second?

The Image***

Figure 9.2 Graffiti on wall near main campus, University of Puerto Rico, San Juan, late twentieth century. *Cristo no es religion* means "Christ is not religion."

EPILOGUE

It is now more than five hundred years since Montesinos mounted the pulpit on that last Sunday before Christmas, 1511, a "voice crying in the wilderness" calling for justice. Our voyage of five centuries has taken us to very disparate places. We have seen abuse, exploitation, and even genocide in the name of religion, and we have also seen religion stand as a defender of the colonized, the poor, and the oppressed. We have seen bishops protest against the least infringement of what they took to be their rights and privileges, and we have seen bishops call for a church of the poor, a church that would be instrumental in bringing about a new order of peace and justice. We have learned of a church under the patronage of the crown, and we have also learned of conflicts between church and state. We have met an extraordinary genius forced to pursue her studies in the kitchen just because she was a woman, and we have also met women of privilege trying to understand and to interpret the plight of other women. We have seen the horrors of the Inquisition, and we have heard a woman who hoped to regain her husband's love through magic. We have heard a god trying to come to an entente with the Christian God, and we have seen the Christian God employed to justify theft and rapine. We have heard from poets, politicians, and preachers. We have witnessed racial and cultural prejudice at work. We have heard the distant but insistent echoes of ancient African drums. We have learned of revivals, missionary enterprises, and apparently miraculous healings.

And yet, we have barely scratched the surface of a vast region where there are more Catholics and more Pentecostals than anywhere else in the world. There is so much more to be told and to be learned! There is the story of a saintly priest who would doff his hat to an African slave, but on seeing a slaveowner approaching, he would cross to the other side of the street. There is the story of a missionary who proved his claim that the settlers' bread was kneaded in blood by squeezing blood from a tortilla. There is the plight of children raised in church-sponsored orphanages and sent out to fend for themselves as adults at the age of five. There were slave and Indian rebellions, mission stations in remote places, martyrs and charlatans, sages and dilettantes, missionaries who insisted on peaceful means, and others who proved to be able generals.

As we must now take leave of you, we do so with the hope that what you have read and learned will inspire you to further inquiry. There are in Latin America examples of moral rectitude that rise high above the Andes, stories of faith whose mystery is just as alluring as those of Machu Pichu, of Teotihuacán, or of Tiahuanaco, intellectual currents and countercurrents that flow as wide and as deep as the Amazon itself.

NOTES

Unless otherwise indicated in the notes, the editors themselves have translated non-English-language archival and published documents. In some cases paragraph formatting and other typographical matters have been modernized for ease of reading. In other instances, the original style has been retained, even though some of these may be inconsistent and differ from modern usage.

Symbols are used to indicate note references so that Arabic numerals, which are used as note references in primary material, could be retained.

Introduction

* Bartolomé de Las Casas, *Historia de las Indias*, vol. 2 (Mexico: n.p., 1951), 441–42, in *Latin American Civilization: History and Society, 1492 to the Present*, trans. and ed. Benjamin Keen (Boulder, CO: Westview Press, 1991), 71–72.

1: Foundations

* Lucio Marineo Sículo, *Vida y hechos de los Reyes Católicos*, ed. Jacinto Hidalgo (1587; repr., Madrid: Ediciones Altas, 1943), 68–74, 102–4.

† Fr. Bernardino de Sahagún, *Historia general de las cosas de Nueva España*, numbered, annotated, and ed. Angel María Garibay K. (1575–1577; repr., Mexico City: Editorial Porrúa, S.A., 1989), 191–92.

‡ Bernal Díaz del Castillo, *Historia verdadera de la conquista de Nueva España* (1601; repr., Barcelona: Editorial Ramón Sopena, 1975), capítulo XCII, 292–94.

§ Diego de Castro Titu Cusi Yupanqui, *Instrucción del Inca Don Diego de Castro Titu Cusi Yupanqui al Licenciado don Lope García de Castro*, in *Relación de la conquista del Perú y hechos del Inca Manco II*, ed. Horacio H. Urteaga (Lima: Imprenta y Libería Sanmarti y Compañía, 1916), 74, 76–77,

101–2, http://mith.umd.edu//eada/html/display.php?docs=titucusi_instruc cion.xml.

★ Felipe Guaman Poma de Ayala, "El primer nueva corónica y buen gobierno," The Guaman Poma Website, *The Royal Library of Denmark*, May 2001, http://www.kb.dk/permalink/2006/poma/info/es/frontpage.htm.

✛ Photograph provided by one of the authors.

2: Arrival

* Frances Gardiner Davenport, ed., *European Treaties Bearing on the History of the United States and its Dependencies to 1648* (Washington, DC: Carnegie Institution of Washington, 1917), 75–78, http://www.nativeweb .org/pages/legal/indig-inter-caetera.html.

† Juan López Palacios Rubios,"*Requerimiento,*" *Las clases de historia de México*, accessed October 3, 2012, http://lasclasesdehistoriademexico. blogspot.mx/2012/10/reto5.html.

‡ Bartolomé de Las Casas, *De las antiguas gentes del Perú*, ed. Marcos Ji-ménez de la Espada (Madrid: Tipografía de Manuel G. Hernández, 1892), 69–70, http://archive.org/stream/delasantiguasge00casagoog#page/n133/mode /2up, which itself is an excerpt from Las Casas's *Apologética historia sumaria*, c. 1550.

§ David K. Jordan, "Nican Mopohua: Here It Is Told," University of California, San Diego, accessed November 24, 2012, http://weber.ucsd. edu/~dkjordan/nahuatl/nican/NicanMopohua.html. Translation from Na-huatl by David K. Jordan. Used by permission.

★ Teófilo Urdanoz, ed., *Obras de Francisco de Vitoria: Relecciones teologi-cas* (1557; repr., Madrid: Biblioteca de Autores Cristianos, 1960), 676–83.

✛ Padre Antônio Vieira, *Sermões* (São Paulo: Hedra, 2003), 453, 456, 458–59, 460–61, 462–63, 465, 466.

3: Shaping

* José de Acosta, *Historia natural y moral de las Indias*, vol. 2 (Sevilla: Casa de Juan de Leon, 1590; repr., Madrid: Ramón Anglés, 1894), 141, 142, 143, 348–50, http://archive.org/stream/historianatural00acosgoog#page /n13/mode/2up.

† *Proceso de beatificación de fray Martín de Porres*, vol. 1, *Processo dio-cesano, años 1660, 1664, 1671* (Palencia: Secretariado Martín de Porres, 1960), 141, 142–43, 145, 251–53.

‡ "Sor" is the title for a nun, similar to the English "sister."

§ Sor Juana Inés de la Cruz, *A Sor Juana Anthology*, trans. Alan S. Trueblood (Cambridge, MA: Harvard University Press, 1988), 111, 113.

★ Sor Juana Inés de la Cruz, "Respuesta de la poetisa a la muy ilustre Sor Filotea de la Cruz," *Antología del Ensayo: Sor Juana Inés de la Cruz*, accessed February 2, 2012, http://www.ensayistas.org/antologia/XVII/sorjuana/sor juana1.htm.

✛ 1 Cor. 14:34.

❡ Fernando de Montesinos, *Auto de la fe celebrado en Lima a 23 de enero 1639: Al tribunal del Santo Oficio de la Inquisición de los reynos de Peru, Chile, Paraguay, y Tucuman* (Lima: Pedro Cabrera, 1639), n.p., http://archive.org /stream/autodelafecelebr00trib#page/n59/mode/2up.

♠ Heitor Furtado de Mendoça, *Primeira visitação do Santo Officio as partes do Brasil: Confissões da Bahia, 1591–92* (São Paulo: Homenagen de Paulo Prado, 1922), 76–79.

4: Reforms

* Archivo General de las Indias, Indiferente General 3041. Extraordinary Consultation of the Tribunal, of July 3, 1768, quoted in Elisa Luque Alcaide, "Reformist Currents in the Spanish-American Councils of the Eighteenth Century," *The Catholic Historical Review* 91, no. 4 (October 2005): 749–50.

† Vatican, "Concordato de 1753," liacismo.org, accessed on November 5, 2012, http://www.laicismo.org/detalle.php?pk=17709.

‡ "Instrucción de lo que deberán executar los Comisionados para el Estrañamiento y ocupación de bienes y haciendas de los Jesuitas en estos Reynos de España e Islas adjacentes, en conformidad de lo resuelto por S.M.," *Documentos para el estudio de la Historia de la Iglesia en América Latina*, April 23, 2008, http://webs.advance.com.ar/pfernando/DocsIglLA/Expulsion_jesuitas_intro .html.

§ "Real Decreto—Pragmática de Matrimonio de 23 Marzo 1776," *Nuestra genealogia*, n.d., http://asociacion-aiam.es/aiam-archivos-abierto/aiam /documentos/doc_interesantes/D_-_Real_Decreto_de_1803_-_Pragmatica _de_Matrimonio.pdf.

★ Antonine Tibesar, ed. and trans, *Writings of Junípero Serra*, vol. 3 (Washington, DC: Academy of American Franciscan History, 1956), 407, 409, 411, 413, 415. Used by permission.

✛ Henry Koster, *Travels in Brazil*, vol. 2 (London: Longman, Hurst, Rees, Orme, and Brown, 1817), 237–38, 240–41, 243–44, 262–63, 264–66.

5: Turmoil

* Vatican, "Esti longissimo terrarum," *Núcleo de la Lealtad*, October 12, 2007, http://nucleodela lealtad.blogspot.com/2007/10/enciclica-legitimista .html.

† Richard Alan White, "Colección José Doroteo Bareiro, Archivo Nacional de Asunción, Paraguay, Sección de Dr. José Gaspar de Francia, vol. 2," *Issuu.com*, April 2011, pp. 130–32, http://issuu.com/corelmania/docs /dr._jose_gaspar_de_francia_-_volumen_2__1813-1817_.

‡ Gerónimo Valdés, "Reglamiento de esclavos," in *Bando de gobernacion y policia de la Isla de Cuba* (Havana: Imprenta del Gobierno y Capitania General, 1842), 59–60, 63, 64, http://books.google.es/books?id=2WtDAAAAIA AJ&dq=ezpeleta%20cuba&pg=PA1#v=onepage&q&f=false.

§ Biographical information about Miguel Perdomo Neira can be found in David Sowell's book cited below. He also graciously provided materials from which we excerpted the selections below.

★ David Sowell, *The Tale of Healer Miguel Perdomo Neira: Medicine, Ideologies, and Power in the Nineteenth-Century Andes* (Wilmington, DE: Scholarly Resources, 2001), xi.

✣ J. Mora, *Un ultraje inmerecido* (Quito: Oficina Tipográfica de F. Bermeo, 1867), 3, 4.

¶ *El Tradiconista*, 7 May 1872.

♠ Miguel Perdomo Neira, "Al público i a la conciencia humana en su calmada luz natural," *La Ilustración*, 4 June 1872.

** *The United Methodist Hymnal: Book of United Methodist Worship* (Nashville: The United Methodist Publishing House, 1989), 7.

†† *Credo de los liberales*, quoted in Jean-Pierre Bastian, *Los disidentes: Sociedades protestantes y revolución en México, 1872–1911* (Mexico City: Fondo de Cultura Económica, 1989), 266.

‡‡ Jean Meyer, "La entrevista de la última oportunidad," *Revista Relaciones* 31, no. 8 (summer 1987): 111, 112, 113, 116–17, 118–19, 121, 135, http://www.colmich.edu.mx/files/relaciones/031/pdf/documento.pdf. We thank Matthew Butler for graciously suggesting this source.

6: Protestant Presence

* James Thomson, *Letters on the Moral and Religious State of South America* (London: James Nesbit, 1927), 34–37, 41–43, http://archive.org/details /lettersonmorala01thomgoog.

† *Eighty-First Annual Report of the American Bible Society, Presented May 13, 1897* (New York: American Bible Society, 1897), 93–95, 96–97.

‡ Robert E. Speer, *South American Problems* (New York: Student Volunteer Movement for Foreign Missions, 1912), 70–74, 128–29.

§ Mrs. E. M. Bauman, "Women's Work in Missions in Latin-America" in *Conference on Missions in Latin America* (Lebanon, PA: Sowers Printing Co., 1913), 137–40.

★ *Iglesia y Sociedad en América Latina*, "Church and Society in Latin America," in *Social Justice and the Latin Churches* (Richmond, VA: John Knox Press, 1969), 118–22.

✢ Julia Esquivel Velásquez, "Temblor," in *Florecerás Guatemala* (Mexico City: CUPSA, 1989), 25–27. Used by permission.

7: Protestants and Catholics

* *South American Missionary Magazine* 1 (July 1867): 97–100.

† Celia LaPalma de Emery, *Acción pública y privada en favor de la mujer y del niño en la República Argentina* (Buenos Aires: Alfa y Omega, 1910), 23–24.

‡ Gabriela Mistral, "Cristianismo con sentido social," *La Nueva Democracia* (June 1924), quoted in "Prosa Religiosa," *Gabriela Mistral,* accessed April 2, 2013, http://www.gabrielamistral.uchile.cl/prosa/cristsoc.html.

§ Mistral is referring to attempts by Belgian and German Catholics to organize unions and to defend the rights of the poor, generally following the guidelines set by Pope Leo XIII in his encyclical *Rerum novarum* (1891). In that encyclical, the pope called for the formation of Catholic labor unions in order to ensure that workers were treated fairly.

★ John Mackay, *The Validity of Protestant Missions in Latin America*, September 26, 1942, Annual Meeting of the Committee on Cooperation in Latin America, National Council of the Churches of Christ in the United States of America, Division of Oversees Ministries Records, 1914–1972, NCC RG 8, box 44, folder 8, Presbyterian Historical Society, Philadelphia, PA.

✢ William Ernest Hocking, Professor of Philosophy at Harvard University from 1914 to 1943.

¶ Gonzalo Báez Carmargo, *Hacia la renovación religiosa en Hispano-América* (Mexico City: Casa Unida de Publicaciones, 1930), 9-13, 14-15, 17.

♠ James E. Goff, "What's Behind the Persecution in Colombia?" *Latin American Evangelist* (May-June, 1961): 2-5. Courtesy of Yale Divinity School Library.

8: The Catholic Church Faces New Situations

* Second General Conference of Latin American Bishops, *The Church in the Present-day Transformation of Latin America in the Light of the Council,*

II *Conclusions* (Washington, DC: Division for Latin America–USCC, 1973), 40–41, 43–45, 189, 191–92, 194.

† Gustavo Gutiérrez and Richard Shaull, *Liberation and Change* (Atlanta: John Knox Press, 1977), 79, 82–83. Used by permission.

‡ Congregation for the Doctrine of the Faith, "Instructions on Certain Aspects of the 'Theology of Liberation,'" *Vatican: The Holy See*, August 6, 1984, www.vatican.va/roman_curia/congregtions/cfaith/documents/rc_con _cfaith_doc_19840806_theology-liberation_en.html.

§ The English version, apparently in an inadvertent error, says "compatible." Both the original Latin and the Spanish translation clearly state that the two are incompatible.

★ Ernesto Cardenal, *The Gospel in Solentiname* (Maryknoll, NY: Orbis Books, 2010), 31–34. Copyright 1976, 2010 by Orbis Books. All rights reserved. Reprinted by permission of the Publisher.

✛ New Mexico State University Art Gallery. Retablo 1966-5-127. Used by permission.

¶ New Mexico State University Art Gallery. Retablo 1966-5-56. Used by permission.

9: A Complex Reality

* Willis C. Hoover, *Historia del avivamiento pentecostal en Chile* (Valparaíso, Chile: Imprenta Excelsior, 1948), 39, 40–41, 47–48, 101–2.

† He means Acts 2:4: "All of them were filled with the Holy Spirit and began to speak in other languages, as the spirit gave them ability."

‡ "I will pour out my spirit on all flesh; your sons and your daughters shall prophesy, your old men shall dream dreams, and your young men shall see visions. Even on the male and female slaves, in those days, I will pour out my spirit."

§ Guillermo Vasconez, interview by Eloy H. Nolivos, Quito, Ecuador, June 30, 2006, tape recording. Translated and graciously provided by Dr. Nolivos.

★ Rosendo Guaman and Francisco Pilataxi, interview by Eloy H. Nolivos, Quito, Ecuador, June 25, 2006, tape recording. Translated and graciously provided by Dr. Nolivos.

✛ John Fleury, *El Padre Emiliano nos escribe* (Santo Domingo, DR: Editora Corripio, 2007), 68–70. Used by permission of John Fleury.

¶ Luke 18:35-43.

♠ Miguel "Willie" Ramos, "Afro-Cuban *Orisha* Worship," in *Santería Aesthetics in Contemporary Latin American Art* (Washington, DC: Smithsonian Institution Press, 1996), 51–56, 72–73. Adapted and condensed by Ramos.

** Photograph and explanation graciously provided by Miguel Ramos, Ilarií Obá.

†† This Lazarus, who appears as a fictional character in a parable, is not the Saint Lazarus of official Catholic religion—the brother of Mary and Martha whom Jesus raised from the dead according to the Gospel of John.

‡‡ María de los Reyes Castillo Bueno, *Reyita: The Life of a Black Cuban Woman in the Twentieth Century* as told to her daughter Daisy Rubiera Castillo and translated by Anne McLean (Durham, NC: Duke University Press, 2000), 87–88, 105. Used by permission.

§§ Jane Atkins-Vásquez, ed., "Trinidad Salazar: A Call to Service," in *Hispanic Presbyterians in Southern California: One Hundred Years of Ministry* (Los Angeles: Synod of Southern California and Hawaii, 1988), 160–61. Used by permission.

★★ The "session" is the governing body of a local Presbyterian church. An "elder" is a member of the session.

⁜⁜ United States Conference of Catholic Bishops, "Cultural Diversity in the Church: The III Encuentro Nacional Hispano de Pastoral," *USCCB*, http://old.usccb.org/hispanicaffairs/iii.shtml.

¶¶ United States Conference of Catholic Bishops, "National Pastoral Plan for Hispanic Ministry," in *Hispanic Ministry: Three Major Documents* (Washington, DC: United States Conference of Catholic Bishops, 1995), 65, 66, 68–70, 76–77, 79, 80, 88. Used by permission. The footnotes in this document are part of the original text.

1. 1 Cor. 12:12-13.
2. Matt 28:18-20.
3. National Conference of Catholic Bishops, "The Hispanic Presence, Challenge and Commitment," pastoral letter of the US Bishops (Washington, DC: USCC Office of Publishing and Promotion Services, 1983), No. 1.
4. "The Hispanic Presence, Challenge and Commitment," No. 3.
5. *Evangelii Nuntiandi*, No. 20.
6. Census Bureau, December 1985.
7. Ibid.
8. Northeast Catholic Pastoral Center for Hispanics, Inc. *The Hispanic Catholic in the United States: A Socio-Cultural and Religious Profile*, 1985, by Roberto González and Michael LaVelle.
9. Ibid.

♣♣ "Report of the Committee to Develop a National Plan for Hispanic Ministry," *Daily Christian Advocate Advance Edition* 1 (February 1992): 715–16, 718–19.

*** Photograph provided by one of the authors.